Betweenity

From its inception psychoanalysis has sought to effect a cure through the therapeutic relationship between analyst and analysand. *Betweenity* looks at what happens when the established framework of the psychoanalytic process is challenged by those with borderline personalities.

In this book Judy Gammelgaard looks at how we might understand the analysand who is unable to engage with therapy and how we might bring them to a point where they are able to do so.

Areas of discussion include:

- the border between psychiatry and psychoanalysis
- early mother–child relationships
- the splitting of the ego

This book will be essential reading for all psychoanalysts, psychotherapists and practitioners wishing to learn more about working with borderline personality structures and disorders.

Judy Gammelgaard is a training analyst, and a member of the Danish Psychoanalytic Society and the International Psychoanalytical Association. She is professor and head of the Centre of Psychoanalysis at the Department of Psychology, University of Copenhagen and lectures widely throughout Scandinavia.

THE NEW LIBRARY OF PSYCHOANALYSIS
General Editor Dana Birksted-Breen

The New Library of Psychoanalysis was launched in 1987 in association with the Institute of Psychoanalysis, London. It took over from the International Psychoanalytical Library, which published many of the early translations of the works of Freud and the writings of most of the leading British and Continental psychoanalysts.

The purpose of the New Library of Psychoanalysis is to facilitate a greater and more widespread appreciation of psychoanalysis and to provide a forum for increasing mutual understanding between psychoanalysts and those working in other disciplines such as the social sciences, medicine, philosophy, history, linguistics, literature and the arts. It aims to represent different trends both in British psychoanalysis and in psychoanalysis generally. The New Library of Psychoanalysis is well placed to make available to the English-speaking world psychoanalytic writings from other European countries and to increase the interchange of ideas between British and American psychoanalysts.

The Institute, together with the British Psychoanalytical Society, runs a low-fee psychoanalytic clinic, organizes lectures and scientific events concerned with psychoanalysis and publishes the *International Journal of Psychoanalysis*. It also runs a prestigious and internationally admired training course leading to qualification in the British Psychoanalytic Council and in the International Psychoanalytic Association, the body which preserves internationally agreed standards of training, of professional entry, and of professional ethics and practice for psychoanalysis as developed by Sigmund Freud. Distinguished members of the Institute have included Michael Balint, Wilfred Bion, Ronald Fairbairn, Anna Freud, Ernest Jones, Melanie Klein, John Rickman and Donald Winnicott.

ALSO IN THIS SERIES

Impasse and Interpretation Herbert Rosenfeld
Psychoanalysis and Discourse Patrick Mahony
The Suppressed Madness of Sane Men Marion Milner
The Riddle of Freud Estelle Roith
Thinking, Feeling, and Being Ignacio Matte-Blanco
The Theatre of the Dream Salomon Resnik
Melanie Klein Today: Volume 1, Mainly Theory Edited by Elizabeth Bott Spillius
Melanie Klein Today: Volume 2, Mainly Practice Edited by Elizabeth Bott Spillius
Psychic Equilibrium and Psychic Change: Selected Papers of Betty Joseph Edited by Michael Feldman and Elizabeth Bott Spillius
About Children and Children-No-Longer: Collected Papers 1942–80 Paula Heimann. Edited by Margret Tonnesmann
The Freud–Klein Controversies 1941–45 Edited by Pearl King and Riccardo Steiner
Dream, Phantasy and Art Hanna Segal
Psychic Experience and Problems of Technique Harold Stewart
Clinical Lectures on Klein and Bion Edited by Robin Anderson
From Fetus to Child Alessandra Piontelli
A Psychoanalytic Theory of Infantile Experience: Conceptual and Clinical Reflections E. Gaddini. Edited by Adam Limentani
The Dream Discourse Today Edited and introduced by Sara Flanders
The Gender Conundrum: Contemporary Psychoanalytic Perspectives on Feminitity and Masculinity Edited and introduced by Dana Birksted-Breen
Psychic Retreats John Steiner
The Taming of Solitude: Separation Anxiety in Psychoanalysis Jean-Michel Quinodoz
Unconscious Logic: An Introduction to Matte-Blanco's Bi-logic and its Uses Eric Rayner
Understanding Mental Objects Meir Perlow
Life, Sex and Death: Selected Writings of William Gillespie Edited and introduced by Michael Sinason
What Do Psychoanalysts Want?: The Problem of Aims in Psychoanalytic Therapy Joseph Sandler and Anna Ursula Dreher
Michael Balint: Object Relations, Pure and Applied Harold Stewart

Hope: A Shield in the Economy of Borderline States Anna Potamianou
Psychoanalysis, Literature and War: Papers 1972–1995 Hanna Segal
Emotional Vertigo: Between Anxiety and Pleasure Danielle Quinodoz
Early Freud and Late Freud Ilse Grubrich-Simitis
A History of Child Psychoanalysis Claudine and Pierre Geissmann
Belief and Imagination: Explorations in Psychoanalysis Ronald Britton
A Mind of One's Own: A Kleinian View of Self and Object Robert A. Caper
Psychoanalytic Understanding of Violence and Suicide Edited by Rosine Jozef Perelberg
On Bearing Unbearable States of Mind Ruth Riesenberg-Malcolm. Edited by Priscilla Roth
Psychoanalysis on the Move: The Work of Joseph Sandler Edited by Peter Fonagy, Arnold M. Cooper and Robert S. Wallerstein
The Dead Mother: The Work of André Green Edited by Gregorio Kohon
The Fabric of Affect in the Psychoanalytic Discourse André Green
The Bi-Personal Field: Experiences of Child Analysis Antonino Ferro
The Dove that Returns, the Dove that Vanishes: Paradox and Creativity in Psychoanalysis Michael Parsons
Ordinary People, Extra-ordinary Protections: A Post-Kleinian Approach to the Treatment of Primitive Mental States Judith Mitrani
The Violence of Interpretation: From Pictogram to Statement Piera Aulagnier
The Importance of Fathers: A Psychoanalytic Re-Evaluation Judith Trowell and Alicia Etchegoyen
Dreams That Turn Over a Page: Paradoxical Dreams in Psychoanalysis Jean-Michel Quinodoz
The Couch and the Silver Screen: Psychoanalytic Reflections on European Cinema Edited and introduced by Andrea Sabbadini
In Pursuit of Psychic Change: The Betty Joseph Workshop Edited by Edith Hargreaves and Arturo Varchevker
The Quiet Revolution in American Psychoanalysis: Selected Papers of Arnold M. Cooper Arnold M. Cooper. Edited and introduced by Elizabeth L. Auchincloss
Seeds of Illness and Seeds of Recovery: The Genesis of Suffering and the Role of Psychoanalysis Antonino Ferro
The Work of Psychic Figurability: Mental States Without Representation César Botella and Sára Botella
Key Ideas for a Contemporary Psychoanalysis: Misrecognition and Recognition of the Unconscious André Green

The Telescoping of Generations: Listening to the Narcissistic Links Between Generations Haydée Faimberg
Glacial Times: A Journey Through the World of Madness Salomon Resnik
This Art of Psychoanalysis: Dreaming Undreamt Dreams and Interrupted Cries Thomas H. Ogden
Psychoanalysis as Therapy and Storytelling Antonino Ferro
Psychoanalysis and Religion in the 21st Century: Competitors or Collaborators? Edited by David M. Black
Recovery of the Lost Good Object Eric Brenman. Edited and introduced by Gigliola Fornari Spoto
The Many Voices of Psychoanalysis Roger Kennedy
Feeling the Words: Neuropsychoanalytic Understanding of Memory and the Unconscious Mauro Mancia
Projected Shadows: Psychoanalytic Reflections on the Representation of Loss in European Cinema Edited by Andrea Sabbadini
Encounters with Melanie Klein: Selected Papers of Elizabeth Spillius Elizabeth Spillius. Edited by Priscilla Roth and Richard Rusbridger
Constructions and the Analytic Field: History, Scenes and Destiny Domenico Chianese
Yesterday, Today and Tomorrow Hanna Segal. Edited by Nicola Abel-Hirsch
Psychoanalysis Comparable and Incomparable: The Evolution of a Method to Describe and Compare Psychoanalytic Approaches David Tuckett, Roberto Basile, Dana Birksted-Breen, Tomas Böhm, Paul Denis, Antonino Ferro, Helmut Hinz, Arne Jemstedt, Paola Mariotti and Johan Schubert
Time, Space and Phantasy Rosine Jozef Perelberg
Rediscovering Psychoanalysis: Thinking and Dreaming, Learning and Forgetting Thomas H. Ogden
Mind Works: Technique and Creativity in Psychoanalysis Antonino Ferro
Doubt, Conviction and the Analytic Process: Selected Papers of Michael Feldman Michael Feldman. Edited by Betty Joseph
Melanie Klein in Berlin: Her First Psychoanalysis of Children Claudia Frank. Edited by Elizabeth Spillius
The Psychotic Wavelength: A Psychoanalytic Perspective for Psychiatry Richard Lucas
Betweenity: A Discussion of the Concept of Borderline Judy Gammelgaard
The Intimate Room: Theory and Technique of the Analytic Field Giuseppe Civitarese

TITLES IN THE NEW LIBRARY OF PSYCHOANALYSIS TEACHING SERIES

Reading Freud: A Chronological Exploration of Freud's Writings Jean-Michel Quinodoz

Listening to Hanna Segal: Her Contribution to Psychoanalysis Jean-Michel Quinodoz

Reading French Psychoanalysis Edited by Dana Birksted-Breen, Sara Flanders and Alain Gibeault

THE NEW LIBRARY OF PSYCHOANALYSIS

General Editor: Dana Birksted-Breen

Betweenity

A Discussion of the Concept of Borderline

Judy Gammelgaard

Translated by Karen MacLean, Ph.D., and Caitlín Madden

Routledge
Taylor & Francis Group
LONDON AND NEW YORK

First published in Denmark in 2005
by Akademisk Forlag

First published in the UK in 2010
by Routledge
2 Park Square, Milton Park, Abingdon, Oxon OX14 4RN
605 Third Avenue, New York, NY 10017

Routledge is an imprint of the Taylor & Francis Group, an Informa business

Typeset in Bembo by RefineCatch Limited, Bungay, Suffolk
Paperback cover design by Sandra Heath

British Library Cataloguing in Publication Data
A catalogue record for this book is available from the British Library

Library of Congress Cataloging-in-Publication Data
Gammelgaard, Judy.
[Mellemværende. English]
Betweenity : a discussion of the concept of borderline / Judy Gammelgaard ; translated by Karen MacLean and Caitlín Madden.
p. ; cm.
Includes bibliographical references.
1. Borderline personality disorder. 2. Psychoanalysis. I. Gammelgaard, Judy. Mellemværende. II. Title.
[DNLM: 1. Borderline Personality Disorder. 2. Psychoanalytic Theory. WM 190 G193b 2010a]
RC569.5.B67G3613 2010
616.85′852 – dc22
2010001452

ISBN: 978–0–415–54389–7 (hbk)
ISBN: 978–0–415–54390–3 (pbk)

DOI: 10.4324/9780203847626

Contents

Preface to the English edition

The term borderline was originally intended to supplement the diagnostic gap between neurosis and psychosis. Robert Knight – one of the pioneers in the early psychoanalytic attempts to understand these borderland patients – states that 'there is a borderline strip in psychopathology where accurate diagnosis is difficult' (Knight 1986: p. 164).

For this reason, opinions were divided from the very beginning on how to understand such people existing on the border.

In the historical chapter that opens this investigation into a phenomenon and its concept, the term borderline is traced back to the middle of the nineteenth century, where those working in the field of psychiatry became aware of cases of mental illness which failed to display the symptoms of psychosis and yet could not be categorized as nervous disorders. These cases caused some confusion and challenged the hegemony of the positivist scientific paradigm that prevailed at the time. Scientific thinking was not the only thing challenged by borderline patients. In reading the earliest descriptions of these patients it becomes clear that they set psychiatry on a collision course with the system of justice, which found it impossible to agree on whether to treat or punish these people for the criminal actions which were frequently part of their clinical picture.

Later psychiatry and psychoanalysis approached this intermediate field from different angles – i.e. those of neurosis and psychosis, respectively. Attempts were made through the 1950s and 1960s to bridge the gap between psychiatry and psychoanalysis. Otto Kernberg is among those who have brought psychoanalytic thinking into the world of psychiatry and contributed numerous important views on theory and treatment within this field.

The present work has arisen from a curiosity regarding the history of a concept. I have opted to examine the borderline concept in a historic context and have simultaneously investigated the explanatory models used by psychoanalysis in the face of this group of patients. It is, however, also an attempt to get a perspective on my daily work of understanding and helping such patients, who still challenge not only psychoanalytic thought but the very framework and technique of psychoanalytic practice.

As will become apparent I have not wanted to limit myself strictly to psychiatric diagnostics and the term Borderline Personality Disorder. I prefer a structural approach and have opted simply to discuss 'borderline' as a term for that which Kernberg led us to understand as a personality organized on a borderline level of functioning.

This book was written just after the turn of the millennium and was first published in Danish in 2005. I cannot deny that contemporary readers may find parts of the book of limited interest in relation to current debate and the positions now defining psychoanalytic explanations of the borderline concept. Consequently I have been obliged to consider whether parts of the book should be wholly or partly reworked in light of the most recent research. However, I have chosen, instead to add a postscript presenting and discussing two scientific positions from the field of psychoanalysis which in my opinion sum up current debate on borderline pathology. On the one hand, there is *The Work of Psychic Figurability: Mental States without Representation* (2005) by French analysts César and Sára Botella. This book constitutes a significant contribution at both the theoretical and the clinical level and represents an innovation vis-à-vis borderline and heavily traumatized patients, inspired by André Green's thoughts on the negative. On the other hand, there is the theory of mentalization developed by Peter Fonagy and his colleagues, which has assumed the bridge-building role between psychoanalysis and psychiatry that was previously played by Kernberg's theories.

In a broader perspective we are dealing not only with two diverging perceptions of the phenomenon and concept of borderline, but with two entirely different scientific traditions defining the ongoing work of developing Freud's thinking.

Even today this group of patients on the border continues to highlight the fault lines of psychoanalytic science. Can we understand this group of patients with Freud's psychoanalytic theory derived from his work with primarily neurotic patients, or do we need a theory like the theory of mentalization, which directly targets the apparent flaw in these patients, namely a lacking of the capacity for mentalization?

The dominant angle throughout the book is the possibility of using classical psychoanalytical concepts to develop a theory on borderline. Thus the main, theoretical chapters of the book delimit the parts of Freud's work that define the field between neurosis and psychosis. There are two themes which have turned out to be particularly significant for a theory of pathology beyond neurosis if one is to continue working within classical metapsychology: these are firstly the defences of the ego and secondly its relationship to external reality.

In seeking to extrapolate a theory of borderline pathology from Freud's writings I have felt a great affinity with César and Sára Botella who write in the introduction to their book that when it comes to their task of managing Freud's legacy, what counts is not so much the literal letter of his writing, but the spirit of it, i.e. 'a revolutionary mode of thought that is independent of the knowledge of the moment' (Botella & Botella 2005: p. xiii).

In discussing the ego and its defences I encountered semantic and terminological difficulties that have in no way been minimized in translating Danish and German words into English, duly assisted of course by Strachey's standardized version of Freud's work.

We are dealing with defence mechanisms that may be summarized by the term negating. Freud used different terms to denote these: *Verwerfung* (translated as repudiation in English) is the most common; then there are *Verleugnung* (disavowal) and *Verneinung* (negation). Particularly *Verwerfung* and *Verneinung* will be used and discussed in the following. The concept of *Verwerfung* has played a significant role in Lacan's discussion of psychotic defence and he opted to translate the German term as 'foreclosure'. Since Lacan's theory of psychosis – particularly the concept of foreclosure – has played a significant part in my investigation of the particular defences of borderline patients, I have opted to maintain the term foreclosure as the preferred translation of *Verwerfung*.

While my work thus mainly attempts to use classical Freudian thinking to determine a number of theoretical anchor points for a psychoanalytic theory of borderline pathology, I have wanted equally to represent my experiences in working with these patients and have thus sought to describe those existential dilemmas that display what it means to struggle with border problematics.

In order to do so I have coined a term – which does not translate easily into English – to denote the area that is most problematic and fraught for borderline patients, namely interpersonal relationships. The Danish word *mellemværende* literally means 'being in between', or 'that which is in between'. Figuratively speaking, however, *mellemværende* also refers to demands – particularly financial – made by one party on another. Having a *mellemværende* indicates the existence of unsettled scores between two people. Thus, since the word also entails a dimension of being, indicating philosophical concepts of being for and with the other, I have used it to convey the highly characteristic encounters with these patients and the suffering they undergo in their relations to their being with others.

Finally the Danish term *mellemværende* provides connotations to the Danish translation of Winnicott's concept of the intermediate area, '*det mellemliggende område*'. Since Winnicott has been one of my most significant sources of inspiration, this reference is certainly intentional.

This is the richness of significance I have wished to indicate, also using the term in the titles of the Danish book and one of the chapters. I have attempted to use a phenomenological approach to outline the difficulties borderline patients encounter in relation to others. General experience would indicate that it is the actual encounter with these patients that presents the most significant challenge in any analytical setting.

In searching for an English title to match the multiple connotations of the Danish words my translators found the somewhat unusual and archaic word *betweenity*.

According to the IAAC Emergent Culture Glossary the word betweenity was coined by Horace Walpole in 1760 to evoke the twilight between documentation and dramatization. Today the term is useful in describing processes that are within the limits of documentation but still beyond. They are 'in between'. They could be betweenities in space, situations that are likely to become specific but are not yet, or even betweenities of body, in the way the body as a general system expands or accepts estrangement (e.g. through devices inserted into our body or extensions of our body to make it reachable in terms of physical distances). In these senses betweenities are extra-intra dermal situations. Betweenities exist in nature as a rupture of two different phases, a process of transformation from one stage to another.

The word betweenity thus understood captures both the scientific endeavour to understand and theorize on borderline pathology and the 'transit' situation, in which these patients frequently find themselves. We may need diagnostic manuals in order to clarify and delineate the pathology in question as we may also need empirical investigations to further our knowledge of borderline disorder, but we cannot do without theoretical speculations as well as phenomenological or even poetic descriptions of what it means to suffer from borderline conditions.

In other words, the term betweenity conveys the multiplicity of meaning – indeed, the paradox – which I believe to be reflected in the borderline phenomenon. In my opinion it should be possible to read such multiplicity and complexity into our theoretical speculations. In other words, we are better served by science which – while it may fail to accommodate traditional positivist ideals – compensates by offering theoretical explanations that stimulate our curiosity and inspire further thought, reflecting the complexity of the phenomena we investigate.

Finally, I would like to express my gratitude to my two translators, Caitlín Madden and Karen MacLean, Ph.D., for their support and fine collaboration and inspiration.

1

Introduction

From its inception psychoanalysis has been a 'talking cure'. Analyst and analysand use the spoken word to express and communicate thoughts and feelings. However, it would be inadequate to describe psychoanalytical work as mere conversation. The order of the spoken word is quite unequal to capturing the process by which two people attempt to understand something of an entirely different order or 'disorder'. There is a paradox inherent in the fact that we use the logic of language to attempt to capture something that follows a different, non-linguistic logic. It might also be said that during analysis one is '*hearing with one's primary ear, speaking with secondary language*' (Green 1997b: p. 263).

Poetic language or imagery is far better suited to expressing what happens in this particular form of conversation. D. W. Winnicott is one analyst who was capable of capturing and communicating the essence of psychoanalysis, largely because he chose a style of writing more closely resembling poetry than prose.

Sigmund Freud often used chess as a metaphor for the psychoanalytic process. I myself have compared psychoanalytic work to dance: two people attune their movements, following a rhythm reflecting the erotic games of the body in its choreography.

There are rules, both in chess and in dance. But ideally these should merely be a prerequisite for the free, uninhibited expression of the game, albeit a prerequisite with which the analysand must necessarily come to terms. Once this framework has been established the analysand comes in four times a week, lies on the couch and with reasonable ease proceeds to follow the basic rule of analysis: speaking of whatever spontaneously occurs to him, uninhibited by any censorship.

This frame, quite essential to the psychoanalytic process, is forgotten the second the analysand becomes submerged in the themes at hand. The analyst for her part feels secure in this process, presuming herself sufficiently assisted by her knowledge and technique. She listens empathetically, her attention smoothly suffusing the situation; noting any unexpected impulses, pauses or peculiar linguistic turns, watching attentively for any signs of transference while maintaining a running dialogue with her own affective and cognitive processes.

However, it happens – not infrequently – that the situation is quite different. The analyst may at first notice that her confidence in her analytical techniques and attitude fails her. She becomes confused and insecure when what should have been an unnoticeable frame becomes visible simply because it is not working. Her analysand is unable to settle into the frame and persists in breaking out of it – e.g. by failing to show up for appointments; finding it unnatural to relinquish himself to free association; or reacting to what was intended as a helpful intervention with indifference or irritation, as though experiencing rejection.

In these cases the psychoanalytic situation is apparently failing to function as the intended facilitative frame which works so effortlessly with other analysands.

Psychoanalysis has been shaken and challenged in several ways by these so-called difficult analysands – termed borderline.[1] Since the middle of the previous century, clinicians both within and beyond the psychoanalytic community have been carrying on a far-reaching discussion concerning the diagnostic positioning of this group of patients, who do not fit into the canonized diagnostic categories of neurosis and psychosis.

Borderline analysands have caused psychoanalysts to consider modifying Freud's technique for treating neurotic patients, particularly hysterics. Freud based not only his treatment technique, but his entire personality theory on the development of normal and neurotic personalities. Similarly these borderline analysands challenge our psychoanalytical technique, shaking our firmly rooted trust in our methods and our entire professional identity; they also force us to examine Freud's models of the psyche.

Freud himself did not use the term borderline, and it was not until his late works that he began to reflect on the psychological mechanisms of psychosis.

Today we might question whether Anna O, with her flamboyant, dissociative states of consciousness, deserves the label neurotic, and we would hardly hesitate to diagnose the Wolf Man as borderline. As regards the latter it should be noted that Freud's sole interest was in his patient's infantile neurosis; he centred his case study around it, leaving the impression that this patient's serious adult disorders could be understood solely in light of this childhood neurosis. Later I shall expand on this case study, which may be read as one of the earliest psychoanalytical studies of the borderline phenomenon.

All Freud's key concepts are based on neurosis: the Oedipus complex; castration anxiety; the idea of the unconscious as a separate system from the conscious; the notion of desire as a driving force that is resistant to censorship and responsible for a number of physical manifestations from hysterical symptoms to parapraxis, dreams and artistic creation. Furthermore Freud perceived so-called narcissistic neuroses (psychoses) as being unsusceptible to psychoanalytic treatment.

The problem was that, at the time, psychological disorders were divided into neuroses and psychoses. Therefore, when the borderline diagnosis first came into use in the late 1930s, there was a tendency to consider the phenomenon and the concept either from a neurotic or a psychotic angle. This is clearly reflected in the language used. Thus we find terms like pseudo-neurotic schizophrenia (Hoch & Polatin 1949), ambulatory schizophrenia (Zillboorg 1957), pseudo-psychopathic schizophrenia (Dunaif & Hoch 1955), schizophrenia without psychosis (Beck 1959), latent psychosis (Bychowski 1953) and larval psychosis (Glover 1956).

Generally one might say that while psychiatry tended towards defining borderline patients as a diagnostic group affiliated with psychosis, out of loyalty to Freudian metapsychology, psychoanalysts were inclined to understand it from a neurotic perspective.

The borderline concept has been used as a term both in relation to hospitalized psychiatric patients and to analysands undergoing analysis on the psychoanalyst's couch. Thus in more than one respect the concept reflects a border problematic.

The concept exists in the borderland between two scientific discourses. On the one hand we have a psychiatric discourse, based on an empirically positivistic, scientific paradigm and on the other a psychoanalytical paradigm, more closely related to a humanistic, hermeneutic, phenomenological scientific tradition.

Additionally, the borderline concept is characterized as a border problematic within the field of psychoanalysis. Both the phenomenon and the concept itself have rendered it necessary to reassess and rethink basic psychoanalytical concepts. There is no doubt that some of the most original and groundbreaking work in the last 30 years of psychoanalysis derives from attempts to understand these difficult border cases and from communicating experiences from this work in a language that in more than one sense reflects their borderland existence. There are pragmatic justifications underlying the concept of borderline, which additionally reflect a categorial problem: the word itself indicates delineation or a line of demarcation. Are we using this word in reference to a phenomenon in the world? In other words: can one be a borderline or have a borderline?

A border may denote a line or a surface, or it may refer to some form of overlap as happens when two clouds border on each other. The borders of neurosis and psychosis appear to be somewhat indistinct. In other words, we are not dealing with a clear line of demarcation but with an area lacking clearly delimited borders: a no man's land.

The French psychoanalyst Jean Laplanche (1976: p. 87) spoke of terminological 'slippage', indicating that this must be countered by a certain slippage in reality itself if these concepts are to hold any depth and originality. By extension the borderline concept could be said to reflect a phenomenon originating in the concepts of neurosis and psychosis but corresponding to a phenomenon distinctly delineated from both. If, however, this concept is to be more than a pragmatically justified in-between category, one might ask whether it is indicative of the psychological borders of borderline patients. What is a psychological border? Initially we might think of psychological structures or of the contacts or exchanges that take place though bodily delineations – between the somatic on the one hand and reality on the other (Green 1997b).

I suggest that the term borderline reflects a number of problematic borders relating to regulatory mechanisms or demarcation lines of the psyche; necessary partly for communication and making contact and partly for protection against what may be experienced as threatening invasion.

We are confronted with the necessity of delineation – of setting up limits – on a daily basis. This necessity becomes particularly obvious in expanding our perspective from the narrower position of psychopathology and adopting a global and political view (Anzieu 1989).

I shall briefly mention a number of phenomena where this border problematic appears to be of some considerable urgency: the limits of economic growth; the increasing gap between rich and poor countries; the rising populations of certain countries, and the insatiable consumption of others; the Icarian flight of science; the invasion of the private sphere by mass communication; and the boundless desire for new world records, leading to doping and rigidly enforced training, as the problematic costs of a sporting world which has become a prestige-ridden, financial necessity rather than a healthy competitive practice. We are reminded of the importance of imposing limits on the violation of earth, air and water. We feel this necessity to establish and regulate borders in the current confrontation between the western world – particularly the U.S. – and the desperately destructive battle of Islamic cultures to create a place for themselves in history, sensing our powerlessness in the face of attempts to stop this process in which we are ourselves agents.

However, the purpose of this work is not to investigate limits and borders at the political level, but rather the border problematic I encounter in my professional practice through people who have difficulty delineating and regulating borders. What these patients who we term borderline have in common is a certain insecurity concerning various borders: between fantasy and reality; between reality ego and ideal ego; between desire and fantasy. They also have difficulties in balancing what appear to be contradictory but equally urgent desires: the desire for intimacy and the fear of invasion; the desire for self-realization and the fear of defeat. The consequences of this lack of ability to achieve equilibrium – and to establish and regulate borders – are evident in a fluctuating sense of self, depressive feelings of emptiness and undefined or diffuse feelings of non-belonging in oneself. These people often feel like observers in their own lives.

This pathological picture is a far cry from the conflictual pattern noted by Freud in his patients a century ago, which led him to the assumption that a cure for these people must consist of a freer realization of libidinous desires in love, work, and other forms of sublimated activity. While Freud observed that the prevailing borders of his time were rather too narrow and prudish, today we see virtually the opposite situation. There are practically no limits on ambitions of individual realization and expansion, but this limitlessness is shrouded in paradox, both psychologically and in light of the development of individual persons. In contemporary families children are exposed to almost traumatic levels of attention within borders that are becoming ever more restrictive and insecure because they are played out within severely delimited familial spaces, where parents must nurse their own ambitions as well as trying to nurture their love life. This combination of concentrated attention and lack of continuity has the potential to create immature and highly fluctuating regulatory mechanisms in children, who must learn to adapt to a society that requires early competency while perhaps limiting the space in which children can play spontaneously. The result may be that in adulthood these children will have difficulty achieving fulfilling relationships. They yearn for intimacy but attack or flee when it is offered because intimacy appears to them to be an invasive and self-effacing bond. This problematic encompasses both ordinary ambivalence and pathological forms that turn every intimate relationship into a potential battlefield. In Chapter 2 I shall discuss the psycho-developmental preconditions for pathological development and show that this trauma is not necessarily characterized by the violent and sexual attacks so frequently described in the currently ongoing professional debate. There is a trauma of the immature ego that consists not of singular events but rather of a certain kind of contradictory and disastrous lack of ordinary care.

My investigation of borderline phenomena opens with a historical account of the development of the concept from the first steps in the late 1800s to the introduction of an actual borderline diagnosis in the 1930s right through to the manifold and diverse literature of today. This chapter focuses on the border problematic outlined between psychiatry on one side and psychoanalysis on the other. Even within the ranks of psychoanalysis there are indications of the technical difficulties created by Freud's neurosis-based theory when clinicians and researchers need to explain a psychological problematic beyond neurosis.

Chapters 3 and 4 describe the two currently dominant explanatory models relating to borderline aetiology. All theories have concentrated on the so-called pre-Oedipal phase in a conscious effort to find explanations beyond the presumed Oedipal conflict of neurosis. While some analysts have concentrated on early mother–child interaction, others – particularly in recent decades – have drawn attention to the frequency of sexual and/or violent childhood trauma in borderline patients. I have selected a few representatives of these two explanatory models, discussing their relevance for a psychoanalytical theory concerning both normal and pathological development of what I have termed respectively the mother–child interaction model and the trauma model. In other words, this is a discussion of two explanatory models, both identified – with various degrees of justification – with psychoanalytic theory. The argument goes that psychoanalysis inevitably leads back to childhood and to traumatic experiences that become determinants for our future lives. However, while this is not entirely erroneous, nor is it the whole truth. My work is an attempt at establishing a detailed understanding of the nuances of interplay between past and present and of how development – whether it be normal or pathological – may be understood not as a linear, causally defined sequence but as an ongoing transformational process.

In Chapter 5 I shall introduce the concept of *betweenity*, which is my contribution to the ongoing discussion of the manner in which borderline patients forge relations. In this chapter I make use of a selection of psychoanalytical theories, seeking inspiration in existentialist continental philosophy to outline some of the key dilemmas that these patients pose to us as therapists. At the same time I attempt to pave the way for a renewed theoretical examination of the psychological regulatory mechanisms that appear to be so fragile in these patients.

In Chapters 6 and 7 I begin by tracing the concepts of classical Freudian theory that may contribute to an understanding of psychopathology beyond repression and the return of the repressed in form of the symptom. I point to concepts such as foreclosure, disavowal and negation, which Freud himself introduced in his few discussions on the relationship between neurosis and psychosis and which have later been developed and systematized not least in French psychoanalysis. Then, in Chapter 7, I attempt to demonstrate the use of these concepts through the study of a specific borderline patient whom I worked with through ten years of psychoanalysis.

My work for this book has partly been inspired by contemporary French analysis and partly – and most significantly – by Winnicott's work, which gave rise to my fundamental assumption that the problematic relating to these patients appears in betweenity or, to use Winnicott's term, in the intermediate area. His work provides a vast amount of knowledge about the significance of this space, defined as between outer and inner, between fantasy and reality. With this concept of an intermediate area of experience, Winnicott has contributed to mending the subject–object polarization that has plagued western thinking ever since Descartes. The intermediate area is also where what Winnicott terms the 'me' and the 'not-me' come into being and it is in this potential space (as Winnicott refers to it) that the creative unfolding of spontaneous activities of the self may take place. Because some of these patients that we term borderline have had difficulties in forming experiences in this area, their selves have corresponding difficulties in finding a place to belong. Frequently the result is a feeling of not being 'at home' in oneself, and the patients complain of lacking an anchor, a place in themselves from which thoughts, actions, and ideas may emanate. Winnicott indicated that something has taken place in these patients that has failed to find a psychological location. The result is what Winnicott and others have termed 'negative experience'.

Chapters 8 and 9 are devoted to discussing this notion of negative experience, which turns out to be an essential form of experience in the psychological lives of borderline patients. While negative experience refers to experiences that have failed to find symbolic representation, play and the transitional area in which it arises indicate a positive experience that assists the child in the early differentiations of me/not-me, as well as facilitating experiences of its own creativity within an illusory space.

I previously referred to chess and dance as metaphors for what takes place in an analytical situation. Winnicott suggests that psychotherapy takes place where the play-areas of patient and therapist overlap. If a patient is unable to play, then the initial action must be one which enables him or her to do so.

This book is about how we may understand those analysands who are unable to play and about how we might bring them to a point where they can. However, this work with the borderline problematic has also been motivated by a desire to continue working with psychoanalytical theory and to participate in the discussion of what is termed the pre-Oedipal field, which Freud – in a form of recognition of his own limitations – termed the 'dark continent'.

In contemporary work on psychoanalytical theory and technique there are a number of choices to be made. I have opted to maintain the classical concepts – primarily those of the drive (instinct) and the unconscious – while choosing mainly to discuss contemporary theories which I feel expand classical theory while upholding Freud's central theoretical ideas. This also means that I take a critical stance on theories which have contributed a great deal of new knowledge to the field but where innovation has perhaps also had the effect of throwing the baby out with the bath water. Naturally this is a standpoint which is open to discussion, and I hope that this is the spirit in which readers will approach my book.

However, the idea of potential space – or betweenity – also indicates something beyond an understanding of therapeutic space. It points to that space in which creation may take place; a space not only for playing but also for dreaming and for what we generally understand by creative endeavour. This is the cultural space in which adults play.

Borderline analysands teach us the importance of this space through their difficulties in using it. However, I also want to move beyond the clinical in order to investigate how – and under what conditions – we may become creative and embark on creative agency in the betweenities we encounter. I discuss this in Chapter 9.

One of the intentions behind my work has been to introduce a discussion of the widely differing theoretical approaches to pathological form beyond neurosis. In the concluding chapter I shall gather the threads and attempt to unify them into the borderline concept I have been outlining throughout the previous chapters.

Note

1 As will become apparent from my investigation this is not about the term used in the official diagnostic systems. I use the term borderline to describe a certain psychological structure that we may find both among the so-called personality disorders and in patients with what is termed a borderline personality structure (Kernberg 1986). In other words, this examination does not concern a clinical diagnosis; rather it is an attempt to capture a psychological structure and manner of functioning in people who experience difficulties regulating borders. Therefore I allow myself to quite simply use the term borderline. For similar usage of the borderline concept see Green (1997b), Pontalis (1981) and Rey (1994).

2

The border between psychiatry and psychoanalysis

> Understanding is something one does best when one is on the borderline. It was a law, that was what one understood. It selected some, and some it stumbled into perdition. But for those on the borderline work was being done to alleviate the consequences.
>
> (Høeg 1994: p. 37)

This quote is from the novel *The Borderliners* by Danish author Peter Høeg. The title indicates that we are dealing with a group of people for whom survival is a struggle played out on the margins of society. The novel tells the story of three children and their attempts to survive in the no man's land inhabited by those who belong nowhere; neither within the school system nor outside it. They are borderliners. Yet in an informed democratic society, everyone deserves a chance, including those who are defined as being on the border. 'Biehl's Academy was that chance' (Høeg 1994).

Høeg's novel is a grim portrait of the systematic thought of modern, informed educational institutions and the consequences of this system for those children who do not immediately fall within its limits. Describing the profound, sterile problematic related to all categorizations, Høeg combines it with a sensitive depiction of a group of children who become the victims of this enforced categorization. The novel constitutes a provoking literary counterpart to what psychiatry terms borderline pathology, which also deals with people living on the border.

It was Adolph Stern who in 1938 introduced the term borderline to denote those patients who could not be defined within canonized diagnostic units (Stern 1986 [1938]). The first steps towards a diagnosis between neurosis and psychosis, however, were taken during the age of the 'birth' of modern psychiatry by Kraepelin (1986 [1905]) and Bleuler (1950 [1911]). While they did not use the term borderline, they did acknowledge that in the area between neurosis and psychosis we find conditions which cannot be unambiguously defined within either category. From initial descriptions of a group of patients, who neither fit into existing categories nor into those institutions intended to either treat or prosecute them, to the current discussions of the problematic and deeply disturbing issues that this group of patients deal with, we get a clear sense of a borderline problematic that concerns not only individual patients, but also the contradictory discourses characterizing the entire treatment system.

These patients outline a borderline problematic in more than one sense. They have occupied the line between neurosis and psychosis and they have rendered visible the border between the discourses of medicine/psychiatry and psychoanalysis. Their personality structures and their social relations highlight the difficulties they experience setting limits and regulating their internal borders. Like the three children in Høeg's novel, they have failed to fit into the dominant diagnostic culture and through their very existence as 'borderliners' they have disseminated doubts concerning its long-term validity.

As early as the mid nineteenth century, psychiatry became aware of people suffering conditions that neither displayed the symptoms familiar from psychosis – such as hallucinations and delusions – nor fitted the category of less serious nervous conditions. This caused some confusion and contested the unambiguous nature of a science asserting a fundamentally positivist standpoint and a predominantly genetic aetiology of mental illness. If we read the earliest description of these borderline patients, it is striking that the main border problematic being outlined is of a societal nature and involves two institutions apparently set on a collision course: psychiatry and the legal system. In 1835 J.C. Prichard coined the term 'moral insanity' (Prichard 1986 [1835]), while C.H. Hughes referred to a morally affective insanity, which he defined as 'insanity of conduct, feeling or impulse, or all combined' (Hughes 1986 [1884]: p. 23). If it had not been for their blatantly affective impulsiveness, these people – lacking that intellectual disturbance so characteristic of the truly mentally ill – would not be considered mentally ill at all. These are the morally insane, who half a century later were to be termed borderline patients. They did not really fit into the domain of psychiatry, since they lacked the symptoms defining psychosis. Meanwhile, since they frequently displayed criminal behaviour, the question arose of whether they could be prosecuted for what symptomatically speaking appeared to be a moral shortcoming. What was required here: treatment or prosecution? Psychiatry and the legal system were indeed in opposition.

Modern psychiatry, writes Michel Foucault (1973), took over the power and position that the great reformists Philippe Pinel and Daniel H. Tuke had previously held in liberating the mad from their chains and introducing humane methods of treatment. Meanwhile, he continues, rather than acting as 'homo medicus' psychiatry wished to approach the mad more like a 'pater familias'. Thus using the bourgeois family as a role model, modern psychiatry was able to unfold a power whose deeply moral function mysteriously vanished behind a sober, medical gaze: 'What we call psychiatric practice is a certain moral tactic contemporary with the end of the eighteenth century, preserved in the rites of asylum life, and overlaid by the myths of positivism' (Foucault 1973: p. 276). Foucault here draws attention to the moral point of view hiding behind what aspires to be medical objectivity, and which means that in the final analysis it is disturbances of the moral order as well – he adds – as the gender order which characterize the field that from here on defines the borders of normality; distinguishing the normal from the borderliners. Sociopaths and hysterics are the prototypes of these impulsive, maladjusted patients, who do not benefit from milder methods of treatment, yet are not suited to hospital treatment either. Irving Rosse (1986 [1890]) succinctly refers to them as

> a class of persons standing in the twilight of right reason and despair – a vast army whose units, consisting of individuals with minds trembling in the balance between reason and madness, are not so sane as to be able to control themselves, nor yet so insane as to require restraint or seclusion.
>
> (Rosse 1986 [1890]: p. 32)

This moral stigmatization of un-reason did not only apply within the field of matters that legally challenged public morals, for up through the nineteenth century the mess of sexuality was made visible through that condition which Freud later described as having a particular affinity with the female. Freud was not alone in seeing through the prejudice which had for several millennia linked hysteria to female fertility. Yet he was the one to develop a psychological 'talking cure' that made it possible to enter into dialogue with this particular form of un-reason, which had been silenced by medical science throughout history.

Before Freud both Jean-Pierre Falret (1890) and Pierre Janet (1898) had described this '*folie hystérique*' with its '*idées fixes*' in a manner foreshadowing later psychiatric descriptions of typical borderline symptoms: impulsivity and emotional lability, which in more recent diagnostic cultures have been described as histrionic personality disorder. Today these early, insightful case studies are mainly of historical interest, since it was psychoanalysis, rather than psychiatry, that dominated the illustrations and explanations of borderline psychopathology for the next half-century. This psychopathological field was only later to be recalled into the fold of medical discourse, initially with the introduction of the American DSM diagnostic system, and later with the establishment of an actual diagnosis of Borderline Personality Disorder. The initial steps towards a diagnosis between neurosis and psychosis, pioneered by Emil Kraepelin, Eugen Bleuler, Falret and Janet, remained preliminary because they were not able to see through the semblance of madness. It was to be Freud and psychoanalysis who eventually managed to coax the hysteric's secrets from her, revealing the passion hidden in the deranged language of her body.

When psychiatrists with connections to psychoanalysis began taking an interest in these border phenomena, the amount of available literature on this increasingly evident border pathology exploded. During the last third of the twentieth century we see increasing effort on the part of psychiatry to systematically differentiate the borderline group descriptively, thereby scientifically and empirically underpinning what had hitherto been assumptions as to the aetiology. Descriptive diagnostics and theories emphasizing genetic factors gained ground at the expense of psychoanalytic and psychodynamic explanations. Meanwhile, there was also a colossal bridge-building effort going on in an attempt to adapt psychoanalytic theory and treatment to descriptive psychiatry while adjusting the Freudian model of neurosis to encompass an understanding of these patients on the borders of traditional diagnosis. Otto Kernberg was one such bridge-builder; due largely to his work, psychodynamic thought has gained a certain acknowledgement within a diagnostic system which has little else in common with those differentiations of psychopathology begun by Freud with his work on hysterics in the late nineteenth century.

In this chapter I shall narrate the story of the borderline concept and how it came to be positioned between psychiatry and psychoanalysis. On the one hand we have a theory and a method based on neurosis, particularly hysteria and compulsive disorders, on the other a theory of schizophrenia and manic-depressive psychosis. These are the polarities of the no man's land inhabited by borderliners. It has been interesting to observe how both psychiatry and psychoanalysis have sought – based on entirely different discourses – to extrapolate a concept of something which could not be captured within the foundational explanatory models of neurosis or psychosis. These historic studies raise the question of whether our understanding of borderline problematics might not have been better served by a more phenomenological approach beginning in that strange no man's land where these patients find themselves.

From psychiatry to psychoanalysis

As psychoanalysis developed its own theory, taking its cue from the conditions of hysteria and compulsive neurosis, it freed itself from psychiatry and an aetiological understanding emphasizing genetic factors and relying on concepts such as degeneration and moral flaws. Freud listened to patients' complaints, taking them seriously and thereby shaming any talk of moral judgement. He transposed the '*folie*' of hysteria onto another stage, so to speak – the unconscious. Using the psychodynamic theory of repression and the return of the repressed in the form of symptoms, psychoanalysis had not only distanced itself from theories of moral degeneration, it had also relegated all genetic assumptions to the background with its confidence in the explanatory value of psychological theory. It is understandable that psychoanalytically minded psychiatrists – in encountering borderline patients – wished to utilize a theory of neurosis, which was at once consistent and practical in terms of treatment.

We may discern this ambition in Stern's 1938 article mentioned above (Stern 1986 [1938]), which can be seen as the initial contribution to a discussion of the concept of borderline from the angle of neurosis. Stern's work inspired a number of analysts who had been obliged to emigrate to the U.S. by the rise of Nazism, and who went on to revolutionize American psychiatry. This is part of the explanation of why the borderline concept gained such a central place in American psychiatry while it was barely utilized in Britain and on the Continent.[1]

Stern suggested – as would Kernberg[2] and others – that borderline must be considered a reasonable delimited clinical phenomenon with a typical symptomatology. Stern drew attention to the particular transference phenomena so characteristic of this group of patients, thus designating a theme which for many analysts was to prove a cardinal point in their work with these patients, forcing psychoanalytically oriented therapists to question classic techniques when confronted with borderline patients.[3]

Stern described the difficulties these patients experience in obeying the basic rule of psychoanalysis. Their need for self-protection is so overwhelming that the invitation to say *everything* must appear to them as total capitulation, as one of my borderline patients expressed it.

In his description of these patients, Stern emphasized ten characteristics. The most significant among them are narcissism, primitive defence mechanisms, and problematic object-relations. The ego-functions of these patients, he says, are considerably more disturbed than is the case with neurotic patients. Unlike those who posit trauma as the basis of borderline pathologies, a view which appears to be enjoying increasing attention (Gabbard & Wilkinson 1994, Johnson *et al.* 1999), Stern chose to emphasize an insecurity in these patients which is so fundamental in character that it approaches a basic fault (Balint 1979).

Stern concluded that presentation of this group is confounded by the fact that the material points in two different directions – towards both psychosis and neurosis. This serves as a clear indication that we are operating in a diagnostic borderland, or, according to Robert Knight (1986 [1953]), a 'borderline strip': 'Without defending the term "borderline state" as a diagnostic label, I have thus far developed the argument to show that there is a borderline strip in psychopathology where accurate diagnosis is difficult' (Knight 1986: p. 164).

In her classic 1942 article about the 'as if' personality type Helene Deutsch attempted to use psychoanalytic metapsychology to understand the pathology of these patients. In so doing she initiated the work that was to culminate in Kernberg's extensive literary production on borderline pathology.

Deutsch emphasized the object-relations of borderline patients. These are people, she writes, who function in a reasonably normal manner in many situations, but who prompt others to ask: 'What is wrong here?' They are, as the term indicates, strangers to themselves. They suffer from a form of depersonalization of which they are unaware. They lack warmth and behave in an excessively formal manner, as if they are acting a part to protect themselves against deep-seated insecurities and fragile self-esteem. Deutsch indicated a personality trait that many have emphasized as a characteristic of borderline personality disorder. Erikson (1986 [1956]) called it identity diffusion; Kernberg (1986 [1967]) made this identity disturbance the cornerstone of his theory on borderline pathology; and Winnicott (1990c [1960]) coined the term 'the false self'.

> We see primitive and archaic drives returning from the depths of the unconscious in a dramatic manner. Regression takes place because the ego has failed. We speak of this as a 'weakness of the ego' and assume that the reasons for this failure are psychological, constitutional, or organic. Psychoanalysis can investigate the first of these, especially in prepsychotic conditions to which these cases belong.
> (Deutsch 1986 [1942]: p. 91)

Good superficial adaptation later appears in the DSM description of the schizotypal patient. Gunderson and Singer (1986) also indicated this apparent adaptation. But where both the American DSM and the European ICD-10 classification systems highlight the aggressive tendencies of borderline patients, Deutsch's group identifies so closely with the expectations of others that they will be more likely to repress their aggression. We recognize Winnicott's 'false self' in Deutsch's 'as if' personality.

Feelings of emptiness are another trait that Deutsch – and many psychoanalysts after her – have emphasized in borderline patients. The same can be said of their relatively stable reality testing, which associates this group with neurotic patients while distinguishing them from the psychotic group.

Even these early descriptions give an impression of a group of people suffering from a hidden form of madness. Every term which has been suggested indicates a serious disturbance – which has been found comparable to psychosis – behind a comparatively well-adjusted facade. Still, these patients do not exhibit the noticeably bizarre behaviour so characteristic of psychotic patients, at least not those in out-patient treatment. In light of Foucault's (1973) exposition of the history of madness it is tempting to put forth the assumption that madness – after the liberation of the mad by scientific psychiatry – has increasingly become an internalized and private phenomenon. The psychological resources of each patient and the care capacity of each family have taken over the structuring function of the large institutions, thereby turning madness into a private matter. André Green (1997b) used the expression 'private madness' in reference to a double movement of madness away from the domain of large institutions into the private sphere and away from public visibility to become a hidden, private pathology, playing out its nature only in close relations. It would be interesting to pursue this thesis on the privatization of madness and examine the conditions that create it as well as the demands it posits on the psychological resources of each individual.

The popularity of the borderline concept and its incorporation into the DSM has removed it from psychoanalytical discourse, but also from the notion of its affinity with schizophrenia. In the late twentieth century, psychiatrists tended increasingly to consider borderline pathologies as a symptomatic expression of bipolar disorder and hence indicated a kinship with manic-depressive psychosis (M. H. Stone 1986). This may be one of the reasons that affect rather than thought has been emphasized in contemporary descriptions of borderline patients. Today a typical psychiatric borderline patient displays anger, sadness and a tendency towards acting-out – far from the isolated, schizoid patient to whom the world and the self are strange, unreal, and devoid of meaning (Gabbard 2000).

While Deutsch's article is an attempt to describe borderline pathology in the structural and dynamic terms of metapsychology, Melitta Schmideberg (1986 [1947]) has provided a specific, compassionate description of a group of patients who distinguish themselves by exceeding all traditional boundaries within psychoanalytic treatment because of the impulsive acting-out characterized by substance abuse, criminality and generally highly destructive behaviour. Despite considerable difficulty Schmideberg manages admirably to maintain her psychoanalytic attitude, intervening interpretatively and where possible creating a minimum of space for the psychotherapeutic alliance.

When psychiatrists in the 1940s began to seriously study borderline patients, the dominant idea was that of a particular affinity with schizophrenia. Hoch and Polatin's (1949) article on 'pseudoneurotic schizophrenia' was seminal, as was the theory represented in Denmark by Vanggaard (1979).[4] Hoch and Polatin took their cue from the claim that there is very little in psychiatric literature to help us differentiate diagnostically between schizophrenia and psychoneuroses. Not even Bleuler, who devoted his life to the study of schizophrenia, mentions the subtle indications of psychotic mechanisms displayed by patients suffering from, for example, compulsive neuroses or hysterical symptoms. Hoch and Polatin assume that we may find psychotic mechanisms at work even in predominantly neurotic personality structures, thus indicating the overlap which has always existed between the two major groups of conditions. This assumption has been repeated by contemporary psychoanalysts, not least by Bion (1988) and Rosenfeld (1990), and has made it possible to take a more nuanced view of some of the classic cases. I shall return to this later.

Hoch and Polatin drew attention to a group of patients who were mistakenly diagnosed as neurotic, but on closer examination turned out to have characteristic traits of schizophrenia, although they displayed them somewhat more discreetly. This applies to autistic withdrawal and thought disturbances. They do, however, admit that these traits are more distinct in hospitalized borderline patients than among those we encounter in private practice. These so-called pseudo-neurotic patients are more withdrawn than typical neurotic patients and are clearly ambivalent. This ambivalence is not focused – as is the case with neurotics – but rather more diffuse, and includes all aspects of patients' lives. In these patients we also encounter expressions of unveiled hatred, targeting particularly close relations. We also find a form of anxiety that is quite different from neurotic anxiety, which has prompted many to suggest the term pan-anxiety or pan-neurosis. Although these patients lack the grossly disturbed thinking of schizophrenia, their speech displays both condensation and displacement, and above all there is characteristically catathymic thinking.

In this context it seems reasonable to turn to Freud's 'Rat Man' and his catathymic rat fantasy, to consider whether Freud was in fact guilty of defending his model of neurosis, and in so doing overlooked that a madness of a more private and serious nature lurked within the generally neurotic personality structure of this and other patients. Presumably these are the discrete thought disturbances which later prompted Kernberg to claim that borderline patients display thinking which follows the mechanisms of primary processes. It is interesting to note that Hoch and Polatin are critical when it comes to using psychoanalytical regression concepts to explain borderline behaviours. They claim that neither schizophrenic nor borderline patients can be said to display regression in the purely quantitative sense, and that here we are dealing with disintegrative rather than regressive processes. Generally speaking they cannot condone the idea of a continuum from neurosis to psychosis where movement along this spectrum is marked by the depth of regression. I shall return later to a discussion of the mechanisms that characterize psychotic thinking in patients who are not obviously psychotic. Here I shall merely foreshadow this discussion by mentioning that I do not share Kernberg's view of primary process thinking. According to my understanding it is more relevant to speak of a particular logic of the unconscious which leaves traces in patients' ego function. The result is what is termed splitting, as evidenced in associations that fail to follow the logic we are accustomed to in our work with neurotic patients. This particular form of representation, characteristic of these patients, is repeated without mediation in an analytical situation. This may explain the violent psycho-physical reactions we as analysts may experience in the presence of these patients.

A final characteristic of these patients is that their thinking is neither bizarre nor eccentric but rather vague and contradictory.

Phyllis Greenacre (1941) summarized the image of a typical borderline patient as depicted up through the twentieth century. These people, she says, have an:

> organic stamp of suffering (consisting of) a genuine physiological sensitivity, a kind of increased indelibility of reaction to experience which heightens the anxiety potential and gives greater resonance to the anxieties of later life. The increase in early tension results in or is concomitant with, first an increase in narcissism, and later an insecure and easily slipping sense of reality. I referred especially to the increase in the sense of omnipotence which may occur in a compensatory way to overcome or balance the pre-anxiety tension state of the organism, and to the increased mirroring tendency arising partly from the primary narcissism and partly from the imperfectly developing sense of reality. This increased mirroring tendency is the antecedent of the tendency towards overfacile identification . . . Libidinal attachments are urgent but shallow. . . .

> The patient is not well individuated . . . with the libido quickly and urgently invested and withdrawn.
>
> (Greenacre 1941: pp. 610–611)

Throughout the 1950s there was a shift from a generally descriptive to a more dynamic understanding of borderline personality disorder as psychoanalysis became more widespread. Robert Knight's work (1986) denotes the movement away from psychiatry in an exemplary fashion. His article on 'borderline states' started the movement that was to attempt to explain borderline problematics using the neurosis model. Up through the 1950s it was common to consider borderline states as pre-psychotic and pseudo-neurotic, but a decade later borderline personality disorder was generally considered a distinct phenomenon. Although it had not yet become entirely clear what borderline actually bordered on, the descriptive characteristics had fallen into place, and so the term remained. Today there is general agreement on what constitutes a description of borderline personality disorder, and – to a certain extent – on the treatment required. There are great divergences, however, at the theoretical level, as will become apparent in the ensuing chapters. Kernberg (1986) and Masterson (1990) were highly influential in creating consensus at the levels of description and treatment. They consider borderline personality disorder a clearly delimited, clinical phenomenon and are convinced that it is of an essential nature. In other words, borderline personality disorder has come to be recognized as a well-defined and clearly delimited phenomenon.

> Until recently, much confusion in the literature was caused by the fact that the term 'borderline' was used to refer both to the transitory acute manifestations of patients who were rapidly regressing from neurotic symptomatology to an overt psychotic reaction, and also to patients who function chronically in a stable way at a level which was on a borderline between neurosis and psychosis.
>
> (Kernberg 1986: p. 281)

Kernberg suggested reserving the term borderline for the latter group. I shall return to this after a quick glance at the psychoanalytic contributions that preceded Kernberg's work, and which quite clearly inspired it.

The first metapsychological descriptions of borderline pathology

Psychoanalysts working in the 1950s and 1960s not only had to describe borderline pathology, they were also faced with the challenge of providing an explanation at the structural, dynamic, and genetic level. Freud's theoretical model constituted an obstacle in this context, for Freud's metapsychology rested solidly and consistently on the theory of neurosis. Looking back on the numerous psychoanalytical writings on borderline disorders, it becomes apparent that they are generally limited by two mistakes. One dates back to Freud and the fact that he based his theory of personality on studies of the structure and psychic mechanisms of neurosis. The other originates in the attempt to expand the theory of the particular mechanisms of psychosis to include a broad borderline spectrum ranging from hospitalized patients to those on the analyst's couch. Numerous significant clinical observations notwithstanding, literature on borderline personality disorder was characterized by loyal attempts to adapt a theory on this disorder to classical metapsychology.

Knight's pivotal article on 'borderline states' is the fruit of a metapsychological delimitation of borderline pathology. He argues that borderline disorder is best characterized as a severe disturbance of normal ego functions, secondary process thinking, reality testing and defences against primitive unconscious drive impulses. Knight suggests a multi-factorial model of explanation consisting of constitutional factors, predisposing events of a traumatic nature, disrupted object-relations, and current stressors, all of which render the ego of a borderline patient weak and dysfunctional. Certain ego functions are severely disturbed, such as the capacity for integration, concept formation, judgement, realistic planning and defence against primitive drive impulses. Other ego functions such as conventional adaptation and superficial albeit stable object-relations may however appear quite unremarkable. Finally, the clinical picture may be characterized by hysterical, phobic, obsessive-compulsive or psychosomatic symptoms. Knight concluded – based on this description of the varying and fluctuating ego functions of borderline patients – that these neurotic structures should be understood as a defence against the more regressive levels of the personality structures of these patients. Caution should therefore be exercized when it comes to therapeutic interventions vis-à-vis what appears to be a neurotic defence mechanism.

Freud believed – and this was the reasoning behind his conservatism – that the so-called narcissistic neuroses (psychoses) were inaccessible to psychoanalytic treatment. His argument was that these patients were unable to establish transference. Thus, according to this line of thought, the narcissistic dimension presents an obstacle to psychoanalytic work outside the area of neuroses.

Leo Stone (1986 [1954]) and other pioneers who attempted psychoanalytic treatment of borderline and narcissistic patients have had to struggle against this assumption, which has as its foundation the entire Freudian metapsychology, and its consequences for treatment.[5] On the basis of these attempts to augment the number of possible patients for psychoanalysis, Stone concluded that the problem lies in the intense and overwhelming nature of narcissistic transference. This can lead patients to withdraw into themselves through fear, thus letting their dramas play out on an inner stage rather than within the therapeutic relationship. For the therapist, of course, this leads to equally powerful counter-transferences. Yet these patients do in fact develop transferences – they are simply very different from those of neurotic patients, and hence the emotional and personal integrity of the therapist is essential to the outcome of working with them.

Kernberg's achievement was to gather these various contributions into a psychoanalytical description and explanation of borderline pathology and the personality structure on which it is based. Prior to concluding this historical description of psychoanalytical theories on borderline disorders with a brief overview of Kernberg's highly systematic work, I would like to refer to a work by John Frosch (1990 [1964]) which in many ways foreshadows Kernberg's descriptions.

Like Kernberg, Frosch was convinced that we may from this borderland distinguish a syndrome which he termed the 'psychotic character', a well-defined unit corresponding to neurotic character. Rather than focusing on the immediately apparent symptoms, Frosch delimited this clinical unit using criteria almost identical to those suggested by Kernberg: he proposed focusing on the ego and its functions with regard to reality assessment, the nature of object-relations, and the relation to the other psychic structures. Just as a neurotic personality is dominated by traits characteristic of neurosis, the psychotic character is dominated by corresponding traits of psychosis. There are, however, important differences. Unlike the obvious psychotics, these psychotic characters retain an intact capacity for reality assessment and function at a more mature level of object-relations.

Regressions are reversible and psychotic episodes are of a transient nature. Finally, these patients display ego-syntonic adaptation.

Through his work Frosch contributed a nuanced understanding to the frequently rather vague concept of reality testing and has suggested that we distinguish between 1) relations vis-à-vis reality, 2) the sense of reality, and 3) the ability to test reality.[6] The latter ability remains intact in people with a psychotic character, while they may well display symptoms of disturbances both in relation to reality and in their sense of reality. When it comes to relations between the ego and other psychic structures, Frosch writes that we may observe the same unstable borders with the id as in psychotic patients and that in this type of patient it means that all ego functions are disturbed by aggressive and libidinous impulses that overwhelm the ego. With psychotic characters, however, these episodes are of a transient nature. Frosch emphasizes precisely this transient aspect of the dysfunctional egos of borderline patients, and warns against perceiving it as a passing phase en route from neurosis to psychosis.

Kernberg (1985, 1986) was instrumental in finally determining this 'stable unstable' way of functioning – to paraphrase Schmideberg (1986) – in borderline patients, arguing for the existence of a group of patients with a well-defined and remarkably stable pathological ego structure on the border between neurosis and psychosis. He suggested the term 'borderline personality organization' to denote this group of patients, who display a certain form of ego-weakness, certain primitive defence mechanisms and problematic internalized object-relations. Kernberg delimited this borderline personality structure in terms of descriptive, structural and genetic-dynamic analysis, respectively.

At the descriptive level we are dealing with patients displaying multiple symptoms, which may – initially – appear reminiscent of those of neurotic patients. Kernberg observed varying degrees of a chronic, diffuse, free-flowing form of anxiety; obsessive-compulsive symptoms; multiple phobias; dissociative reactions; conversion symptoms; hypochondriac speculations; paranoid tendencies; polymorph perverse sexuality; and substance abuse problematics in these patients. He believes that personality disorders may be grouped on a continuum. At one end we find hysterical, obsessive-compulsive, and depressive personality disorders as well as certain masochistic disorders in relatively well-integrated people. At the opposite end we find infantile disorders as well as the majority of narcissistic ones,

Deutsch's 'as-if personalities' and finally the antisocial personality disorders – all of which are structured at a borderline level.

Although Kernberg believes it is possible to diagnose a borderline personality structure purely at the descriptive level, he simultaneously warns against basing a final diagnosis purely on this descriptive level. For this reason he has supplemented his descriptive diagnostic with a more sophisticated structural analysis, in which he has outlined four main areas.

Non-specific weaknesses of the ego constitute the first structural area. One aspect of what we understand to be the function of the ego is to channel drive impulses and control anxiety; borderline patients, however, lack this ability due to a constitutional weakness of the ego. Furthermore, their capacity for sublimation is limited, as is their ability to be led by the superego, which remains unintegrated into their personality structure. The second main area is the regression of these patients to a psychotic mode of thinking, as also emphasized by Knight. This regression to primary-process thinking occurs in unstructured situations or under severe, affective stress. This phenomenon is the reason Kernberg and others have recommended a different form of therapy to classical analysis, whose unstructured nature may lead to undesired regression. Unlike what we observe in psychotic patients, these shifts to primary-process thinking occur without disturbances in patients' reality testing.

Unlike neurotic patients, borderline patients make use of primitive defence mechanisms, particularly splitting, which Kernberg (1986) defines narrowly as an active process separating introjections and identifications. Clinically speaking, splitting manifests itself by alternating and contradictory behaviours, attitudes, and affections. Other people are perceived as either thoroughly good or thoroughly bad, and the patient may either show little concern for these contradictions, or deny them entirely. Other defence mechanisms such as primitive idealization, omnipotence, and devaluation merely reflect this general tendency to splitting. Projective identification, through which ego- and object-representations are split and projected into the object in order to control it, is another of these primitive defence mechanisms, which Kernberg describes as typical of borderline patients.

Finally, a borderline diagnosis is based on the presence of pathological internalized object-relations. Just as these patients are liable to perceive others as 'all good or bad', they also suffer from highly polarized internal objects. Their clinical manifestation may be frightening experiences of being pursued by notions of 'all bad', which makes it difficult for them to find peace in good, calm, inner objects. Similarly, these people have difficulty integrating positive and negative images of their ego, expressed as a diffusion of identity. According to Kernberg, this is one of the most characteristic traits of borderline patients.

Thus Kernberg's perception of borderline pathology is not based purely on the descriptive level. He consciously seeks to characterize this group of patients from a psychoanalytical point of view, using a combination of ego-psychological theories and theories of object-relations. His justification for this standpoint is that he considers borderline pathology not so much to be an isolated disorder, but rather a number of disorders which – in spite of their symptomatic differences – share an organization at a fairly primitive borderline level.

Back to psychiatry

We have Kernberg to thank for the popularity of the term borderline in American psychiatry. His work has led to the phasing out of old terms such as pseudoneurotic schizophrenia (Hoch & Polatin 1949), ambulatory schizophrenia (Zillboorg 1957), pseudopsychopathic schizophrenia (Dunaif & Hoch 1955), latent psychosis (Bychowski 1953) and larval psychosis (Glover 1956), and the toning down of the supposed affinity with schizophrenia.

In contrast to Kernberg's psychodynamic exposition, other contemporary American psychiatrists have sought a more stringently descriptive delimitation of this group of patients.

In the late 1960s Grinker (1968) and his co-workers presented such an attempt at a more precise delimitation of this group of patients. The empirical foundation of this work was a detailed examination of 50 hospitalized patients. It was the first quantitative investigation, and it was followed by a series of biometric, psychometric, and physiological studies up through the 1980s and 1990s, again mainly of hospitalized patients. Naturally this means that the literature available on these patients is far more extensive than that on less severe cases (Gabbard 2000). Grinker found that there were several subgroups of borderline syndromes within what he perceived to be a borderline spectrum. Meissner (1984, 1988) categorized the borderline population differently than Grinker, but he, too, felt that it would be misleading to refer to a single borderline personality disorder. He believed that it was necessary to descriptively account for different groupings of patients in the borderline spectrum and proposed a hysterical and a schizoid continuum. In one retrospective study of 180 hospitalized patients who were all diagnosed as borderline according to DSM-III, Fyer *et al.* (1988) found that 91 per cent of these patients had one additional diagnosis, while 42 per cent had several. In conclusion, these attempts to descriptively delimit the borderline diagnosis have been used to describe a highly heterogeneous group of patients, and the symptoms described as typical of borderline patients may also be found in patients with other diagnoses.

In the mid 1970s John Gundersen and Margaret Singer (1986) wrote a seminal article for the ongoing work of delimiting the descriptive characteristics of borderline symptomatology. Based on a thorough reading of recent literature describing borderline symptoms, they suggested a new diagnostic definition based – as was Grinker's – on descriptive criteria. However, Gunderson and Singer's work was more precise, featuring criteria for inclusion as well as exclusion. Their diagnostic criteria were based on direct observations and on anamnestic material. Their work has been of enormous significance to the spread of the borderline diagnosis among clinicians with no psychoanalytical training. Gunderson and Kernberg paved the way for the inclusion of the borderline diagnosis in the American diagnostic system. However, ironically, over time this spread has also entailed an increasing superficialization of the concept, which has become further and further removed from its original psychoanalytical and psychodynamic meaning (M. H. Stone 1986).[7] Gunderson and his colleagues (Zanarini *et al.* 1990) were able to clearly identify differential diagnostic criteria for borderline pathologies based on descriptive studies of borderline syndromes. They emphasize traits such as quasi-psychotic thinking, self-mutilating tendencies, manipulative suicidal behaviours, experiences of abandonment and destruction as well as the opposite – fear of invasion – as characteristic of borderline personality disorder. These are patients who become regressively demanding in a therapeutic situation, thus provoking strong counter-transferential emotions in the therapist.

Descriptions in current psychiatric literature begin to trace the outlines of a pattern of typical borderline behaviours. These patients are constantly seeking exclusive relations without risk of abandonment. They demand such relations with an air of entitlement which repels others, while at the same time being afraid of losing their identity through what they perceive as invasion. They may be so terrified of abandonment that they resort to self-mutilating or suicidal behaviour. Clinical observations of borderline patients also report cognitive difficulties such as transient disturbances in reality testing and quasi-psychotic thinking (Gabbard 2000). Gabbard and his colleagues (Gabbard & Wilkinson 1994) have provided a detailed description of the counter-transferences that inevitably result from working with these patients. These might include rescue fantasies, feelings of guilt, breaches of professional conduct, rage, hatred, anxiety and terror, as well as deep feelings of helplessness and impotence.

In contrast to this pessimistic image Harold Searles (1979) has contributed a series of highly engaging descriptions of sessions with borderline and schizophrenic patients, with particular reference to the counter-transferences they provoke. Unlike Kernberg and Gabbard, Searles is convinced that both groups of patients may benefit from psychoanalytic treatment.

Early attempts at understanding borderline patients through psychoanalytic theory centred on dynamic and structural views on their pathology, while genetic considerations and the affinity with psychosis were toned down.

Margaret Mahler's (1971) studies of the early development of psychotic and normal children made it possible to link descriptive studies of borderline patients with explanations founded in developmental psychology. Numerous psychoanalytic borderline theories are indebted to her fine observations of the developmental phases of early childhood, not least the theories of Kernberg, Rinsley, and Masterson. Their work has led to suggestions that borderline pathology is a result of disturbances in early mother–child relations, particularly the so-called rapprochement subphase, where the process of detachment from the mother is at its most vulnerable. Here an explanatory model of borderline pathology emerges that we may term the early mother–child interaction model. Recent infant research has opened the field for study of child development in the so-called pre-Oedipal phase, showing that both normal and pathological development is dependent on early interactions between the infant and its primary caregiver.

The finer nuances of mother–child interaction gleaned from this research tradition have given rise to a hypothesis of cumulative trauma

(Khan 1996a [1963]) as an aetiological explanation of borderline pathology.

On the other hand, we have theories indicating serious physical and sexual assaults on young children as a significant condition for the development of borderline pathology. In Chapter 4 I shall discuss the trauma model which – as the title indicates – views the development of borderline pathology in the light of early trauma.

The psychoanalytically inspired debate on borderline pathology dominated from the late 1930s to the 1960s and 1970s. However, this does not mean there was no critique of these explanatory attempts. Mahler (Mahler & Kaplan 1977) has herself been critical of those who have tried to localize the developmental disorders of borderline patients in the rapprochement phase. She objects that it is too simple to limit an explanation of borderline pathology to a single phase of infant development in the belief that there exists a direct link between an infantile developmental phase and the particular symptomatology of adult borderline patients.

Masterson and Rinsley (1975) have been criticized for singularly blaming the mothers of borderline patients, while Kernberg's account has been charged with unduly emphasizing constitutionally conditioned aggression in borderline patients (Atwood & Stolorow 1993).

Psychoanalytic and psychodynamic theories have mainly been under attack from more empirically oriented researchers. Thus Masterson and Rinsley's hypotheses of the overly involved mother have been countered by a number of empirical studies, while others have demonstrated a high frequency of early experiences of separation and loss among borderline patients (Zanarini & Frankenburg 1997). Yet other studies (Gabbard & Wilkinson 1994, Gabbard 2000) have documented a high rate of infantile trauma among the borderline population. Thus Gabbard (2000) has found sexual assaults among 60 per cent of the borderline cases examined, but yet he warns against unilaterally traumatological explanations, claiming that sexual trauma is neither a necessary nor a sufficient explanation for the development of borderline pathology.

While some parts of current empirical research aim to chart the infantile preconditions of borderline pathology, focusing especially on mother–child interaction and trauma, a number of researchers have attempted to chart the biological and genetic factors involved in the development of borderline personality disorder. Thus Cloninger and colleagues (Gabbard 2000) took their cue from the somewhat dubious observation that 50 per cent of human personality is founded in temperament, and 50 per cent in environment, to develop a psychobiological personality model. Similarly Zanarini and Frankenburg (1997) suggested a multi-factorial aetiology based on the presumption of a constitutionally conditioned vulnerable temperament and a traumatic and chaotic family background, combined with a series of trigger factors such as broken relationships, failed attempts to leave home in early adulthood, and other potentially traumatic events.

I shall not detail the extensive literature available on genetic and biological explanations, but merely indicate the development undergone by research on borderline pathology since the introduction of the DSM system and the first attempts at descriptive categorization at the symptomatic level. Empirically oriented research which includes genetic, biological, environmental, and traumatological aspects conforms to a general interest in and tendency to prioritize this form of evidence-based research.

However, it does not stand alone. As American scholars attempted – from the 1960s up to the present day – to systematically descriptively differentiate the borderline group and underpin aetiological assumptions with an empirically scientific foundation, British and French psychoanalysts and psychiatrists sought to qualitatively describe the life-world of borderline patients. It is interesting to note that those who made the greatest contributions to borderline theories rarely used the term themselves. Fairbairn (1994 [1952]), Federn (1977), Balint (1979), Guntrip (1983), Laing (1990 [1960]), Winnicott (1990b, 1990c, 1990e, 1992b), Rosenfeld (1990), Green (1997b) and Pontalis (1981) have shown less interest in descriptive, systematic accounts of borderline symptomatology, than in seeking to approach the life-worlds of these patients through empathic, insightful phenomenological descriptions. In the attempt to bring these observations of the experienced world of borderline patients into accordance with the dynamic, structural and genetic views of psychoanalytic theory, these researchers have been obliged to move beyond the traditional model of neurosis. The following chapters will deal with these attempts to link phenomenological observations from work with borderline patients in a therapeutic setting to theoretical explanations of their thoughts, feelings, and actions.

Thus we leave behind this overview of the nosographic delimitation of borderline disorders and attempt to define a structural concept with the theoretical capacity to encompass the phenomenological observations of borderline behaviours afforded by an analytical setting.

I shall now briefly summarize the mainly descriptive approaches of the last century to the study of borderline disorders. We may conclude that theories on borderline pathology have passed through three phases. The concept arose in psychiatry in the middle of the nineteenth century through observations of patients whose pathology – while not obviously psychotic – was assumed to have an affinity with psychosis, particularly schizophrenic psychosis. When psychoanalysis was established, the neurosis model – and in particular the model of personality which Freud developed based on his studies of hysteria and obsessive neurosis – became the foundation of several decades of speculation as to the development of borderline pathology. Towards the end of the twentieth century psychiatry appeared once more to be gaining ground. In keeping with a general tendency to uphold evidence-based scientific criteria as the only valid standard, psychoanalysis of necessity appeared speculative. This tendency to emphasize evidence-based research is evident in the increasingly empiricist literature on borderline pathology, and in the explanations stressing external factors as decisive in its development.

We may now distinguish the contours of three explanations for the development of borderline pathology. According to one, represented by Masterson and Rinsley and in part by Kernberg, borderline pathology is understood as a product of disturbances in early mother–child interaction, to which Kernberg would add a constitutionally conditioned increase in the potential for aggression.

The second explanatory model emphasizes the observation of sexual traumas in borderline patients, while the final view presents a multi-factorial model based on a combination of genetic vulnerability and trigger events originating in patients' family background.

In the following chapters I shall pursue the two models I refer to respectively as the mother–child interaction model and the trauma model. My main focus, however, will be on attempting to develop an alternative model based on a modification of the Freudian neurosis model, and to delimit the specific characteristics of borderline patients' particular mode of being as it unfolds within what I have termed betweenity.

Notes

1 Besides Adolph Stern this includes Helene Deutsch, Franz Alexander, Frieda Fromm-Reichmann, Gregory Zillboorg, Sandor Rado, Heinz Hartmann and Otto Kernberg. In this particular context Peter Hartocollis, James Masterson and Glen Gabbard should also be mentioned.

2 I do not discuss Kohut in this context as his main works on narcissism (1971, 1977, 1984) centre on a group of narcissistic patients, whom I – in accordance with Kohut's own views – shall define as a delimited field within the structural concept of borderline being discussed here.

3 The issue of transference and counter-transference in borderline patients was already being dealt with by several analysts in Freud's own era. Sándor Ferenczi's experiments with active techniques (Ferenczi 1988, Freud & Ferenczi 1993), relaxation and mutual analysis must be considered spurs to discussing the necessity of modifying classical techniques in treating these severely disturbed patients.

4 In this context Aarkrog's (1994) considerable contribution to bringing the borderline concept into juvenile psychiatry merits mention.

5 Alfonse Maeder and the Swede Poul Bjerre began utilizing psychoanalytic principles in treating paranoid patients in 1911 and 1912 respectively (M.H. Stone 1986) and obtained good results. Thus they may be considered pioneers for the numerous subsequent analysts who have found it possible to treat severely disturbed patients using psychoanalytic therapy.

6 In the literature available on this topic there is a certain inconsistency in the use of the concept of reality testing. This is unfortunate since this criterion is frequently used to distinguish neurosis from psychosis. In the following chapters I shall argue that reality testing is not so much about delimiting external reality as about inhibiting and binding internal, mental processes, to prevent them from interfering in our experience of reality. It is this inhibiting and binding function which is partially disturbed in patients with borderline pathology (see the Postscript for further discussion).

7 Yeomans, Clarkin and Kernberg's (2002) latest published work clearly demonstrates how this bridge-building to psychiatry has removed Kernberg from psychoanalytic thought when it comes to communicating an understanding of borderline pathologies and suggesting treatment of hospitalized patients.

3

Early mother–child relationships

Psychoanalytic explanations of borderline pathology are almost all based on the relationship between infants and their primary caregivers. Analytical work with such patients has taken us beyond the Oedipal triangle with castration anxiety as the dominant form of anxiety. The key problematic of these patients plays out within dyadic relations and their dominant anxiety is twofold: the fear of loss and separation and an equally great fear of invasion and annihilation.

However, while most clinicians agree on ascribing early mother–child relations great significance in the development of borderline pathology, there are divergent opinions as to what specific aspects to ascribe particular significance. Presumably this is linked to the fact that theories on mother–child relations rest on quite different basic assumptions. This is especially relevant to the dyadic concept itself and the significance ascribed to it in forming the psychic structure of the child.

Masterson and Rinsley (1975) focused directly on the contradictory behaviour of the mother towards her child in their explanation of the development of borderline personality disorder, while Kernberg (1972, 1985, 1986) focused on internalized object-relations while emphasizing a constitutionally conditioned potential for aggression as a significant aetiological factor in people who develop a borderline personality structure, entirely in accordance with his theoretical stance on object-relations. Adler (1975) and Adler and Buie (1979) attempted to build bridges between Winnicott and these ego-psychologically inspired object-relations theorists, and work from the assumption that borderline patients have regressed to a phase where object constancy has yet to be firmly established, and where the ability to recall the supportive image of a caregiver figure has been temporarily lost.

In recent years Fonagy *et al.* (2002) have worked at expanding their model of children's development of the capacity for mentalization and reflexivity (Fonagy & Target 1996a, 1996b, 2000) to include examinations of adult borderline patients.[1] Fonagy and Target position themselves in contemporary psychoanalysis between classical attachment theory and ego psychology.[2] Their explanation of borderline pathology is based on observations of a normal child's development of the ability to make thoughts and emotions the object of reflection and in consequence to be able to distinguish the subjective world from the objective one. They argue that reflexive functioning and the capacity for mentalization require the child's primary caregiver to be able to mirror the child's mental states in such a way that the child learns to understand the difference between experienced (interior and exterior) reality and its representation. Like Winnicott they indicate play as an important location of the child's initial attempts to grasp the difference between interior and exterior, between reality and imagination. In Chapter 9 I shall return to Fonagy and Target's interpretation of children's play and later in this chapter I shall be expanding on their explanation of the aetiology of borderline pathology.

In his theory of child development, Winnicott also emphasized the mother's capacity for empathy and intimacy, and believes that it is of vital importance to the child's later development. However, comparison with the work of Masterson and Rinsley or Fonagy and Target makes it clear that Winnicott's focus is located somewhere else entirely, and that what we summarize as object-relations theory turns out to cover a number of highly diverse views on the significance of the object to the development of the child's psyche. In spite of his belief in the significance of the good-enough mother, Winnicott is preoccupied with the mother–child relationship, with an emphasis on the relationship between them, while Masterson and Rinsley emphasize the object, or the empirical mother and her behaviour towards the child. Fonagy and Target have further developed early attachment theories and supplemented Bowlby's (1980) assumption that early relationships generate the prototypes for later relationships. The theories mentioned here share as their foundation the concept of a self in relation to an object and the consequent idea that the object is in a sense internalized to become a psychic structure within the child. The influence of empirical infant research combined with an ego-psychological starting point constitutes the shared theoretical framework for these theories, regardless of their significant observable differences.

It is not until Winnicott proposes his idea of an intermediate area that we encounter a concept capable of dissolving the duality between object and self.[3] Winnicott's idea of the intermediate area has inspired the basic assumption of my own work, namely that borderline is a symptom that arises when transitional phenomena and the paradox of the intermediate area cannot be sustained. While Masterson and Rinsley speak in unambiguous terms of the real mother, and Fonagy and Target emphasize the 'intersubjective process between infant and parent . . .' (Fonagy & Target 1996b), Winnicott underlines the *function* of the mother in maintaining this intermediate area. In other words the mother cannot be reduced to an object, and her significance for the child's development cannot be limited to that which can be gleaned from her behaviour, just as we cannot limit our understanding of early infant development to anything that can be read in even the most thorough empirical studies of the interactive processes between mother and child.[4]

Like Bion, Winnicott has convinced us that the mother, rather than being an object, is a continuity and a functional entity. We are no longer dealing with the affirmative or rejecting reactions of a specific mother to the individualization of her child, but with a far more subtle relationship, which in short consists of the holding or containing function of motherly care for the spontaneous and creative unfolding of the true self within a potential or illusory experiential field. I shall expand on these different theories on mother–child relations and the disturbances that are assumed to form the basis of the development of borderline pathology. All the so-called object-relations theories and the approaches based on them take their cue from the internalization of object-relations, focusing on the psychic representation of self and object and paying only peripheral attention to the drive aspect involved in mother–child interaction. Theories of object-relations have been right to emphasize the significance of the object to the development of the child. Yet they often forget that this significance is deeply embedded in the passionate 'language' spoken by mother and child. French psychoanalysis has supplemented the concept of the object as we know it from object-relations theory with the idea of the mother as a significant mediator of sexual discourse. In other words, the mother leads the child into the psychosexual register. Laplanche (1989, 1997, 1999) has argued for a theory he calls general seduction, Aulagnier (2001 [1975]) spoke of a form of verbal violence against the childish psyche, and Green (2000b) has consistently upheld the classical theory of the drives, without which he believes we would never be able to fully understand the reactions – be they normal or pathological – of children to their surroundings.

This chapter deals mainly with object-relations views on early mother–child relations and their significance for the development of borderline disturbances. The theories of Bion and Winnicott make it possible to expand our understanding of the significance of the mother as an object whose function it is to create a potential space between herself and the child.[5] Winnicott is arguably the psychoanalyst who has proven most insightful in depicting mother–child relations in a manner that captures the child's experiential world. However, he spends very little time on drives, so I have found it necessary to supplement his account of mother–child interaction with the work of French analyst Piera Aulagnier, whose work can be said to form a bridge between Lacan and Winnicott. Like Laplanche she has formulated a theory of motherly care as a necessary seduction of the infant psyche. This means that her work, like that of Laplanche, features a sharp distinction between ordinary and pathological seduction. In this and the following chapter I shall therefore be supplementing the object-relations views of mother–child relations with the assumption that the dialogue between mother and child is passionate and as such dependent on the taming and channelling of the mother's repressed drive representations.

I have chosen to take my cue from the theories of Kernberg, Masterson and Rinsley. Leading figures in the current discussion of both diagnostic and aetiological views of borderline pathology, they represent the object-relations standpoint developed on the basis of ego psychology and Mahler's empirical research on infant pathology.[6] They are remarkable for their theoretical simplicity and have undoubtedly been highly instrumental in allowing psychoanalytical viewpoints to penetrate American psychiatry. At the same time this simplicity is a weakness. Explanations are reduced to a key conflict in mother–child relations at a particular phase of child development. Kernberg, Masterson, and Rinsley have all placed particular emphasis on the child's development in what Mahler termed the rapprochement phase. However, it appears unlikely that borderline pathology with its complex symptomatology can be reduced to a single key conflict played out in the rapprochement praxis of the separation–individuation phase.

Another essential critique that may justifiably be levelled, and which is connected to the above statements, is that they elevate a definite and general problematic of mother–child relations and turn it into a pivotal point in explaining borderline pathology. Firstly, such an explanation fails to capture the many subtle details of the problematics of borderline patients. Secondly, it becomes difficult to distinguish the numerous variations of normal development from what must be termed deviant and actually pathologic. A psychoanalytic discussion of mother–child relations encompassing the unconscious and the irrational phenomena of drives have the benefit of rendering normality more capacious and pathology more comprehensible.

An object-relations explanation

Kernberg, Masterson and Rinsley display a great many similarities and significant areas of agreement in their work on borderline pathology. This is presumably due to their inspiration from Mahler, which may be seen in their emphasis on the central significance of the separation–individuation phase to the healthy separation of the child from the mother, as well their references to the child's differentiation of self and object and its experience of entirely good and entirely bad self-object representations. However, whereas Kernberg emphasizes the internal psychological pressure of great aggressive potential, Masterson and Rinsley concentrate on investigating the mother's rewarding and rejecting behaviour towards the gradual separation of the child during the rapprochement phase.

Mahler was among the psychoanalytical pioneers – with Bowlby and Spitz – who were able to demonstrate empirically and specifically the great significance of the mother's emotional availability to the child's psychic development. While Mahler's work was based on studies of psychotic children, Spitz and Bowlby witnessed the immediate and subsequent effects of physical separation from the mother – caused by her illness or death. Based on these specific experiences of separation and loss, Spitz and Bowlby established the foundations of the concept of attachment, evident in its current form in the research of Fonagy and his colleagues.

Although Mahler – as mentioned in Chapter 2 – warned against extrapolating from adult psychopathology to infantile developmental phenomena, she nevertheless believed that there was sufficient clinical evidence to support the assumption that borderline patients were fixated in the rapprochement phase, which she defines as the age from 16 to 25 months.

Similarly, Kernberg's work contains few references to a specific, empirical mother. We encounter patients' family background only in case reports and anecdotes. In keeping with his object-relations standpoint Kernberg expresses himself in more general metapsychological terms in order to describe how interpersonal relations are internalized to create internal psychic structures. Kernberg's theoretical account of the personality structure of borderline patients is organized around the three coordinates detailed in Chapter 2: descriptive, structural, and dynamic-genetic. I shall be focusing on the latter. Kernberg (1982, 1993) describes childhood development from a basic matrix which he denotes S-O-A (subject, object, affect). The idea is that every self-experience is always linked to an object and coloured by an affect. Similarly affects are linked and developed from primitive affective parts to a complex and finely differentiated affective structure. In other words Kernberg posits affect as primary representation of drive within the psyche, i.e. that which contributes a given quality to relations between object and self. In early development, where affects are few and unsophisticated, they are denoted as either bad or good and are as such indistinguishable from the identically labelled object and self. Kernberg (1972) imagines the development of internalized object-relations to take place in four stages, working on the presumption that borderline patients are fixed in the third stage. At this point the child has developed separate self and object representations, gathered into a unit termed 'all good'. The process of self and object differentiation within the 'all bad' unit does not take place until much later, and is complicated by early forms of projection, in that the child seeks to externalize that which is experienced as bad. Kernberg (1986, 1993) emphasizes pregenital and, in particular, oral aggression as a significant aetiological momentum in the development of borderline pathology. He simultaneously indicates a condensation of pregenital and genital conflicts and a premature development of Oedipal conflict. The high level of aggression in these patients must either be ascribed to extreme frustration or to a constitutionally conditioned aggressive defence, or to both. In consequence, however, the child projects these aggressive affects, which then appear as paranoid distortions of object experiences, particularly in relation to the mother. She is experienced as dangerous, and hatred for her is extended to the father. The result is a contaminated image of a terrifying parental configuration, underpinned by fragile object differentiation and excessive splitting. The premature development of the Oedipal conflict must – amongst other things – be understood as an attempt to escape from pregenital, oral aggression. This splitting of the libidinously cathected good self and object images from the aggressively cathected bad self and object images, and the structural consequences of this, is responsible for the clinical manifestations of the borderline problematics to which we were introduced in Chapter 2.

Masterson and Rinsley (1975) and Rinsley (1977) agree with Kernberg's view of oral aggression as a characteristic of borderline personality disorder. However, they cannot condone the idea of excessive aggression as a constitutional condition. Instead they follow in Mahler's footsteps, emphasizing the importance of the mother's emotional availability and her empathy for the child, particularly during the phase when the child is experimenting with separating from her. Masterson (1972, 1973, 1990) has introduced the term 'abandonment depression' as a key conflict in the personality structure of borderline patients. This is a form of separation anxiety with a depressive note. Masterson and Rinsley base their theoretical considerations on Mahler's concept of separation–individuation, believing that the sub-phase to which the particular difficulties of borderline patients may be localized is the rapprochement phase. The mother's reaction to the child's attempts at freedom and independence are vital, and form the base of the development of borderline personality disorder.

> Our contention is that the determining cause of fixation of the borderline individual is to be found in the mother's withdrawal of her libidinal availability (i.e. of her libidinal supplies) as the child makes efforts towards separation–individuation during the rapprochement subphase; and further that the fixation comes into existence at exactly that time because the child's individuation constitutes a major threat to the mother's defensive need to cling to her infant and, as a consequence, drives her toward removal of her libidinal availability.
>
> (Masterson & Rinsley 1975: p. 165)

In their exposition of the consequences of this pattern they utilize familiar object-relational terms, speaking of a split in the basic self-object-affect matrix along the lines of Klein (1987b [1946]) and Kernberg (1966). In borderline patients the object-relations unit is split into two, each constituted by a part-self representation and a part-object representation held together by libidinous or aggressive affect. These two units are the result of an internalization of specific interaction with the mother, in that the mother of a later borderline patient has rewarded regressive, clingy behaviour and rejected the child's attempts at liberation and independence. They term the two internalized units the rewarding part-unit and the withdrawing part-unit. The former is cathected by libidinous energy and is experienced by the child as good; the latter is cathected by aggressive energy and is experienced by the child as bad. The inspiration from Fairbairn is obvious.[7]

However, there is one detail of Fairbairn's theory of a split inner world to which Masterson and Rinsley fail to pay attention. What Fairbairn terms the 'exciting object' may appear in borderline patients as a need for inner excitement, which serves to calm feelings of abandonment, emptiness and nothingness. I shall return to an example of this phenomenon in Chapters 7 and 8.

In the rapprochement phase, the child begins to experience itself as separate from the mother. It can now tolerate the accompanying separation anxiety and exploit this tolerance to develop and underpin its individuality, on the condition that previous interactions with the mother have afforded opportunities to introject predominantly good object representations, which have in turn supported the foundation of good self representation. Rinsley (1977) and Adler and Buie (1979) have indicated the phase-appropriate ability of the child for 'evocative memory' (Fraiberg 1969), corresponding to what Winnicott (1971) called the soothing function of the transitional object. Rinsley has ascribed this ability a decisive role in allowing repression to begin to replace the more primitive splitting mechanism.[8] In cases where there is an excess of bad introjects, i.e. aggressively cathected objects, the child will be forced to rid itself of them using projective and splitting mechanisms, thereby exposing itself to the risk of these bad introjects returning as primitive persecuting objects.

Summing up, it may be said that an excess of bad introjects causes splitting mechanisms; prevents phase-appropriate development of evocative memory; inhibits the experience of whole objects and – to use Klein's (1992 [1935]) terminology – arrests the development of the depressive position. In consequence, both self and object are experienced as either entirely good or entirely bad. Thus it is precisely the mechanism of splitting, as well as the differentiation of self and object, which distinguishes borderline patients from psychotic patients. Add to this the fact that the separation anxiety observable in borderline patients does not have the same diffuse, Pan-like nature which may be observed in psychotic patients. For borderline patients anxiety is bound up in a psychic structure. Borderline patients – as emphasized by numerous researchers – experience an anxiety containing moments of a form of guilt which expresses the fragile, primitive, and isolated structure of their superegos. This is the image which prompted Masterson (1972, 1973) to suggest the term abandonment depression, which proved a very succinct description of the complex emotional register of these patients, who often give the impression of concealing or masking a depressive mood below their 'noisily' aggressive and anxious surface.[9]

Masterson and Rinsley's theory on the aetiology of borderline pathology – repeated and discussed in countless writings – does not manage to avoid a touch of simplification, most clearly evident in Masterson's 2000 publication. This applies particularly to the conviction that it is the mother's rewarding or punishing behaviour, vis-à-vis the child's attempts at independence, which become the explanatory factor in every case history referred to by the authors.

However, by introducing the term abandonment depression Masterson captured the complexity of the affective lives of borderline patients, which are precisely composed of separation anxiety and depressive, guilt-marked affect. Using leads including abandonment depression, Masterson and Rinsley have contributed vivid and illustrative images to Kernberg's more abstractly metapsychological work. Yet, like all theories which set out to explain the multitude of human differences using a limited theme, theirs also has its limitations.

Masterson and Rinsley have selected a specific theme within the mother–child relationship and used it as an exclusive explanatory tool. The weakness of this form of argument can be summarized in two points, both of which not only display the fact that our understanding of borderline personality disorder is limited, but that our considerations on treatment are subject to the same limitations:

1 It is true of all object-relations theories that the term 'object', with its connotations to 'objective', must of necessity call to

mind a specific mother. Similarly, it becomes difficult to free the idea of an internalized object from the idea of an external object.[10] This misses the fact that the mother – prior to becoming an object – is primarily important to the child because of her function. Furthermore, it is through this function that she becomes internalized in what might be termed a form of primary identification, which I believe to be prerequisite to the child's internalization of the whole gallery of self and object representations.

2 In consequence of object-relations theories minimizing the importance of drives and the unconscious, these theories fail to capture that every child contains the oppositional inner images, which are emphasized as typical traits in borderline patients.

Turning a phase-specific phenomenon in early mother–child relationships into a universal explanation for borderline pathology is not only of limited value, but is bound to have consequences for potential treatment techniques. It is no coincidence that both Masterson and Kernberg have found a confrontational and expressive technique beneficial in treating borderline patients. There is clear agreement between a theory of internalized object-relations, with the use of splitting and projection, and treatments which, in Kernberg's words, 'follow the patient's affect as an indicator of what the predominant object relation dyad is likely to be at any given moment' (Yeomans, Clarkin & Kernberg 2002: pp. 109–110) – treatments whose main techniques are clarification, confrontation and interpretation, and whose focus is clearly on transference in the current situation.

Masterson similarly proposes a confrontational technique aimed at current transferences:

> The therapist is not treated as a separate person . . . but as the actual maternal figure on whom the patient can engage in a kind of instant replay of the abandonment scenarios imprinted in childhood.
>
> (Masterson 1990: p. 131)

He agrees with Kernberg that '*transference analysis* directed at a systematic analysis of primitive defences . . . is important in the long-term strengthening of the ego in that it brings back to the patient what he has been projecting or denying' (Yeomans, Clarkin & Kernberg 2002:

p. 137). Here we are clearly dealing with a form of therapy which differs significantly from classical psychoanalysis. I will not discuss the usefulness of this form of treatment, which may well be justified in a psychiatric ward with severely disturbed borderline patients. I shall merely indicate the observable connection between a theory of internalized object-relations and the idea that these are played out in transference, thus becoming available to conscious acknowledgement. Within the object-relations tradition transference is understood as simple repetition of previous relational patterns. Transference may be more precisely expressed as displacement from an infantile to an analytical object. Laplanche (1989) drew attention to the fact that this is much too simple an understanding of transference. He suggested a distinction between 'full transference' and 'hollow transference', where the former refers to the classical understanding of this phenomenon, and is a positive repetition of 'forms of behaviour, relationships and childhood imagos' (Laplanche 1989: p. 161). A hollow is also a repetition, but one which is not filled out, where the answer is not given, but must be sought. In Laplanche's words 'it is the childhood relationship that is repeated, it regains its enigmatic character, and the imagos are not really full' (Laplanche 1989: p. 161). For an elaboration of this view on transference, see also Gammelgaard (2003a, 2003b).

Winnicott's work offers yet another alternative, and not only to the classical understanding of transference in the analytical situation. His idea of borderline pathology, aetiology and treatment is quite different from what we encounter in the work of Kernberg and Masterson. A closer investigation of Winnicott's theory of early mother–child relationships provides, firstly, a piece of the puzzle of understanding the particular difficulties of borderline patients; and secondly, a decisively different understanding of the subsequent treatment required by these patients. However, before discussing Winnicott we shall cast a glance at Fonagy and Target and their theory on mother–child relationships and the development of borderline pathology. They also combine an ego-psychological stance with a developmental point of view, yet these authors have also contributed important perspectives to the understanding of the particular disturbances observable in the ego functions of borderline patients.

The capacity for mentalization

Mentalization[11] is a key concept in Fonagy and his colleagues' theory of child development. The idea of mentalization is centred around the development of the child's self and its ability to relate reflectively to the difference between inner and outer worlds, between reality and imagination. This is also central to the authors' understanding of borderline pathology, which is explained precisely in light of the lacking capacity for mentalization displayed by borderline patients. In accordance with their extensive work on the development of attachment patterns in early mother–child relations, Fonagy and his colleagues have emphasized the mother's behaviour vis-à-vis the child in explaining the development of mentalization.

The capacity for mentalization, which might also be termed the capacity for thinking about thinking, or what the authors term 'meta-cognitive monitoring' (Fonagy & Target 1996b), depends on the child's ability to integrate two modes of experience, which in pre-Oedipal children alternate and are isolated from one another. They do not become integrated until around the age of four, and stabilize the ability to distinguish between mental and physical reality. There is a differentiation between a mode of experience in which what is subjectively experienced is identical to the outer reality – 'equivalent mode' – and one where the child withdraws into the 'pretend mode'. In this world, the child may experiment with the difference between what things are, and what they may be imagined to be. However, the child can only maintain pretend mode on the condition that it is entirely separated from external reality. Under normal conditions, the ability to integrate these modes of experience arises through the child's experience of its own mental states being mirrored and reflected by another consciousness. Play is an important medium for such experiences, because this is where another person can connect the child's mental states with an external reality, for example, by demonstrating the child's mental state to exist within the other. This is what imbues subjective experience with a certain reality momentum, which, so to speak, renders it real in a world external to the child.

Fonagy and Target (1996b) claim that the ability to reflect thoughts and emotions is built up through intersubjective processes between the child and its parents and between the child and older siblings. The relative strength of this ability is significant not only for the child's capacity for reflection, but also for its sense of self, which is created and underpinned by these experiences. Parents support the child's budding sense of its own mental self through a behaviour which lets the child know that its mental state may be understood using concepts such as emotions, desires and ideas. 'Thus at the heart of the child's relationship to the object lies the object's capacity to create a world for the child in which he may experience himself as a feeling, wanting, thinking being' (Fonagy & Target 1996b: p. 461). The primary caregiver ascribes certain mental states to the child in an all-inclusive and largely unconscious way and these states are subsequently internalized by the child. The attitude of the primary caregiver is essential to the child's success in mastering the difference between the subjective and the objective through this playful exchange. The adult must be able to mirror the mental states of the child as accurately as possible for the child to recognize them, without making them so realistic that the child becomes overwhelmed by their reality: 'If the adult's attitude precludes the duality of holding the frame of external reality while accurately re-presenting the child's mental state, the transition towards integration and mentalization may be jeopardized' (Fonagy & Target 1996b: p. 472).

Fonagy and Target believe that this is precisely what happens in the development of borderline pathology. The capacity of borderline patients for mentalization has been disturbed in that the two modes of experience have not been integrated, but continue to exist side by side.[12] This may explain the obviously contradictory behaviours which are so characteristic of these patients, as well as their fear of thinking thoughts and having emotions which may become too overwhelmingly realistic because they cannot be reflected. Fonagy and Target explain the frightening sensation of an internal bad object, which also troubles these patients, by referring to the fact that they have internalized something alien. In other words, they have internalized the image of the mother rather than the mother's image of the child's own mental state (Fonagy & Target 2000).[13]

Fonagy and Target borrow many ideas from Winnicott, for example, the idea of a delicate balance between interior and exterior, and between imagination and reality, which the child gradually learns to master in the process of developing a sense of self. Similarly the idea of the decisive influence of the environment on children's overall development as well as on their particular mastery of the abyss between interior and exterior is also a key concept in Winnicott's theory. The absence of empathy and devotion can retain the child in either a continuous defensive use of equivalent experiences according to the precept that 'all must be real' or in a withdrawal to an imaginary world that cannot touch on reality. Finally, their debt to Winnicott is apparent in their reference to the importance of play to the child's attempts at mastering the gap between internal and external worlds. Yet because the starting point of their work is a mental model that operates with a self divided from an object and subsequently with a theory of object-internalization within the ego, they cannot move beyond the dyad, and hence find it difficult to utilize Winnicott's concept of an intermediate area of experience. For the same reason there is a significant difference between their perception of play and 'pretend mode' and Winnicott's concept of the illusory nature of play. I shall return to the latter in chapter 9, but for now I shall introduce Winnicott's theory on mother–child relations.

Mother–child relations according to Winnicott

'There is no such thing as an infant', claims Winnicott (1990f [1960]: p. 39) with his usual sense of the power of paradoxical statements. In making this one he wished to express the complete dependence of the small child on its primary caregiver, which part he never doubted was best fulfilled by the biological mother. Yet the relation between a mother and her infant referred to here by Winnicott cannot be satisfactorily expressed within the self–object matrix.

> It is generally acknowledged that a statement of human nature in terms of interpersonal relationships is not good enough . . . if there is a need for this double statement [inner and outer reality] there is also a need for a triple one: the third part of the life of a human being, a part that we cannot ignore, is an intermediate area of *experiencing*, to which inner reality and external life both contribute.
>
> (Winnicott 1971: p. 2)

Winnicott's interest lies in this intermediate area, and to him this is what represents the precondition necessary for healthy childhood development. This is also the experiential area which borderline patients have difficulty utilizing. The unfolding of our true selves requires us to have experiences of this intermediate area. Yet it is paradoxical: it is neither subjective, nor objective, but potential in character. The paradox of understanding which Winnicott is focusing on here is quite clearly expressed in his little postscript to his book *Playing and Reality*:

> I am proposing that there is a stage in the development of human beings that comes before objectivity and perceptibility. At the theoretical beginning a baby can be said to live in a subjective or conceptual world. The change from the primary state to one in which objective perception is possible is not only a matter of inherent or inherited growth process, it needs in addition an environmental minimum.
>
> (Winnicott 1971: p. 151)

Thus Winnicott assumes a gap between ideas and perception; he believes that the child's ability to exploit this potential space is of vital importance to its health and vitality, and that it is the mother's function to help the child utilize this space. This potential space entails a form of creativity. Winnicott defines it within the mother–child relationship, considering it an illusory space:

> The mother, in the beginning, by an almost 100 per cent adaptation affords the infant the opportunity for the *illusion* that her breast is part of the infant . . . the breast is created by the infant over and over again out of the infant's capacity to love or (one can say) out of need. A subjective phenomenon develops in the baby . . . The mother places the actual breast just there where the infant is ready to create, and at the right moment.
>
> (Winnicott 1971: p. 11)

Thus from birth onwards the human being is concerned with the difference between objective perception and subjective imagination. The intermediate area is a place which – from the child's point of view – exists between primary creativity and objective perception. From our point of view it comes from the outside, although – as previously mentioned – this is not the case for the child. The intermediate area is paradoxical. Winnicott believes the necessary acceptance of this paradox to be significant for the child's development. The false self, as Winnicott terms borderline pathology, indicates a flaw in the ability to experience this paradox. Borderline patients are unable to make use of the illusory in this intermediate area: they are, so to speak, unable to play. This observation was to prove decisive to Winnicott's understanding of therapy with borderline patients, to which I shall return later.

There may appear to be only subtle differences distinguishing Fonagy and Target's understanding of play as the site of the child's pretence coming into contact with reality, and Winnicott's intermediate area. I am convinced, however, that these subtle differences disguise two entirely different theories concerning mother–child relations. Winnicott makes the area of play a particular mode of experience, preconditioned by the elimination of the difference between the subjective and the objective, rather than seeing play as the place where children experience and experiment with this difference.

Winnicott's description of play provides a certain sense of what is entailed in his distinction between subjective and objective objects and, for that matter, his understanding of objects. Although he does not say so directly, the object to Winnicott is not the same as what object-relationists would refer to as an object. As previously indicated it cannot be encompassed within the duality of interior and exterior. Thus it is not a mental representation, nor does it refer to a real mother. Winnicott may be unambiguous in his references to the specific mother, with her holding, handling and presentation of object, but it is nevertheless essential to understand that Winnicott's investigation of the mother's significance to the child focuses on the child's use not of the mother but of her function, or motherliness. Winnicott is far more in line with classical psychoanalytical thought than Masterson, Kernberg or Fonagy. He wishes neither to focus on the empirical mother nor on the internalized object, choosing instead as his focal point those motions of psychic life that can be observed in the spontaneous unfolding of play.

According to Winnicott the first object is created by the child itself. It has no independent existence, but is created over and over according to the needs of the child, thus reflecting its basic creative ability. The status of this object is captured in the following paradox: the breast exists precisely in that place where the child is prepared to create it, and at the right moment. Following the child's growing ego integration the objects of the outside world are constituted. These will always be marked, however, by the very first created, subjective objects. Then we have the transitional objects, at once me and not-me. It is worth noting, however, that what are being referred to as subjective objects and transitional objects are in fact objects devoid of objectivity.[14]

> It is interesting to compare the transitional object concept with Melanie Klein's (1934) concept of the internal object. The transitional object is *not an internal object* (which is a mental concept) – it is a possession. Yet it is not (for the infant) an external object either.
> (Winnicott 1971: p. 9)

Winnicott's indication of the difference between relating to an object and using that object (see Chapter 8) provides us with yet another illustration of the fact that – in his terminology – object-relations are not a representative process so much as a functionality. Through the destruction of the object – that is, through the removal of the object from omnipotent control – a person may begin to use another person. I shall return later to the consequences this may have for therapy, but first let us reconsider the significance of the mother on the child's development.

Primary maternal preoccupation

Winnicott developed his theory of the particular psychic state of a mother whose child is in the completely dependent phase as a critique of the viewpoint that seeks to place 'the blame for the infantile neurosis on the mother's shortcoming in the oral phase . . .' (Winnicott 1975b: p. 300). He argued that frustration is inevitable as well as necessary to the child's development and that it would be an expression of 'facile 'misleading generalization' to posit this frustration as an explanation of disturbed development. With his concept of 'primary maternal preoccupation' Winnicott refers to the dreamlike state that Bion (1988) termed reverie – a certain psychic state which a healthy mother gradually develops during pregnancy and immediately following birth. By using the word 'devoted' and the term 'normally devoted mother' Winnicott wished to indicate a state in the mother which is a precondition for her ability to meet and support the coming-into-being of the childish psyche in the optimum manner. If the mother is able to tune her mind to the child, and follow its rhythm as described by Stern (2006), she will be able to function as the necessary framework or screen needed for the coming-into-being of the childish psyche – which Winnicott refers to as 'undisturbed isolation'. Only on condition of the mother's reverie is the child able to gain experiences of this state. This description is reminiscent of Freud's (1911b) explanation of the primary narcissistic state, which he also realizes has the facilitating presence of the mother as its precondition.

Aulagnier (2001) has expanded the idea of the primary narcissistic state by suggesting that the child's narcissism is really parental narcissism, in the sense that the parents wish to be, have, and become all which they put into the child, and imagine the child to want. This depends on the parents (or the mother in the earliest developmental phases) acting towards the child under the influence of what Aulagnier termed the 'spoken shadow'. This is the shadow cast across the child's body through the mother's preconceived ideas of her child and of her own motherly behaviour. This shadow addresses the child in accordance with what Winnicott (1971) called the normally devoted mother, and which Fonagy and Target referred to as the mother's mirroring representation of the child's mental state. British and French analysts emphasize the mother's drive impulses very differently; the latter consider them an essential assumption if we are to understand normal and particularly abnormal mother–child relationships.

To supplement Winnicott, Aulagnier emphasizes firstly that the devoted communication of the normal mother requires repression of her own infantile drive impulses, secondly that she has sublimated them into what Winnicott terms normal devotion, and thirdly that she acts towards her child in accordance with what her culture considers normal maternal behaviour. Maternal love, Aulagnier claims, requires the barrier of repression to be maintained. Hereby she believes that the interpretation or seduction which the mother is obliged to carry out towards her child, as long as it is unable to express its needs itself, requires a barrier of repression to prevent her behaviour from being controlled by repressed drive impulses. The helpless infant is at the mercy of maternal care as it has yet to develop the barrier of repression, which it is hence obliged to presuppose in the mother. In healthy parents, the helplessness and dependency of the child supports the repression of primitive sexual, aggressive, or narcissistic drive impulses, thereby preventing 'confusion of tongues' (Ferenczi 1982 [1933]) from emerging between adult and child. In the next chapter I shall expand on what happens when this barrier of repression cannot be maintained, and the child becomes exposed to a perverted form of seduction.

The maternal referred to by Winnicott cannot be captured by the concept of the object. At this early stage of childhood development the mother is more of a continuity; a background which the child presumably experiences as the silent ground of its own existence. With Winnicott we can assume that it is this holding function that is internalized through a primary form of identification and later constitutes the framework or screen necessary for the unfolding of the psychic processes of inner life. In several of her writings, Winnicott's close colleague, Marion Milner, has elaborated on the idea of the silent background, a 'preconscious matrix', which she believes we all experience as an undifferentiated bodily experience, one of which we are not normally aware, but of which we may become conscious if we let go of the 'figure' constituted by ideas to find the 'ground' (Milner 1969: p. 53). In a beautiful metaphor gleaned from D. H. Lawrence she expresses that fragile form of being which has the primary maternal state as its crucial prerequisite: 'It is a fearful thing to fall into the hands of the living God. But it is a much more fearful thing to fall out of them' (Milner 1969: p. 52). Prior to internalizing object-relations and before the object even comes into being, we must assume that the small child internalizes the holding function of the mother and that in early interactions with the mother the child does not register anything that in any way outlines an object, but simply the maternal function which may be best expressed using a 'substantivized adjective'. According to Gantheret, 'substantivizing an adjective [motherliness] corresponds to moving from particular or random qualifications to the idea of a substance, which in this case should not be confused with the object of the mother' (Gantheret 1983: p. 123; translated from Swedish)[15].

The mother never adapts herself one hundred per cent to the needs of her child, nor should she do so. Not even in the beginning, when the mother is biologically designed for her highly specialized function, is the adaptation perfect (Winnicott 1975d). It is the gap between complete and incomplete adaptation with the needs of the child, which – in giving rise to the development of thought, symbolization and imagination (see page 189) – helps the child to tolerate the gap and exploit the creative potential of the intermediate area. As we shall see in the following chapter, French analysts – who are very much inspired by Winnicott's thought – take this one step further in assuming that the explanation for the gap between complete and incomplete satisfaction depends on the inner world of the mother, whose unconscious fantasies prevent complete 'biological adaptation'. Milner (1969) appears to have been aware of this in her assertion that the child's outer world is comprised of the mother's inner world.

For Winnicott the resistance encountered by the child's impulses and spontaneous gestures is what creates the first differentiation between me and not-me. When the mother adapts to the needs of the child, this is not registered by the child, but gives rise to that experience of illusion without which it would be impossible to bring about an exchange between the child and its surroundings. The child registers the motherly adaptive flaw not as a flaw in the mother, but as a threat against its own existence; this gives rise to the first ego-structure and to the silent construction of a true self. Presuming that external resistance does not cause a reaction in the child, the child will permit a repetition of this resistance, and the first differentiation between interior and exterior will solidify without leading to any form of anxiety. When there is an excessive failure to adapt to the child's needs, the child will experience this as an invasion against which it is obliged to defend itself by reacting. Such reactions entail a temporary loss of self, which can only be regained when the child returns to a state of isolation.

In extreme cases the child experiences little other than such reactions. This means that the child must develop a false self as the only way to adapt to an invasive world. Hereby the first intimation of an isolation or splitting of the true self or 'a psychotic distortion of the environment–individual set-up' is created (Winnicott 1975d: p. 222).

Again it may be beneficial to supplement Winnicott's theory of the insufficient adaptation of the mother with the needs of the child and the resulting invasive experience of the child with the French analysts' emphasis on the sexually charged communication between the child and its primary caregiver. In normal cases, this takes the form of normal devotion. In disturbed relations this communication may assume a sexually perverted character. Accordingly, Aulagnier (2001) speaks of necessary and exaggerated violence, while Laplanche (1989) refers to general and perverted seduction, and Green underscores that some kinds of play may be 'impregnated with destructiveness' (Green 2005: p. 12) and proposes that Winnicott idealized the concept of play in his idea of the 'good-enough mother'. If we are to understand those parts of themselves with which our borderline patients struggle, it is important to keep in mind that the shortcoming of maternal care is insufficiently described by Winnicott's idea of the not-good-enough mother. Following the French analysts, we should add that the mother as the privileged word-bearer (Aulagnier 2001) communicates to the child a world already interpreted by her. There are three particular issues which the mother in her role of interpreter passes on to the child, and of which the child is only gradually able to grasp the significance. One issue is gender; the second is family relations centring on the questions 'Who am I?' and 'How did I come into the world?'; and the third is about how to understand relations between my parents.

There will always be an insurmountable chasm between the needs of the child and the mother's anticipated ideas of how to satisfy them, which enforces a primary form of violence. Aulagnier defined this violence as an action whereby one person imposes a thought, action or choice on another person, motivated by the desire of the latter, yet based on an understanding of this desire that derives from what the first person perceives as necessity. This may be expressed somewhat more specifically with reference to the fact that we always interpret expressions of the child's needs as want – want of food, want of sleep, want of thought, want of growth – and prepare ourselves to be the one to fulfil this want. We feed, wash and dress the child, we rock it to sleep and talk to it using the words it does not itself have at its disposal. Seen in this light maternal care consists in the necessity of the mother's interpretation of the child's needs. To optimize this interpretation, the child must necessarily appeal to something that is very close to the mother's primary impulses while at the same time repressing and sublimating them into normal devotion.[16] The mother is obliged to interpret the child's needs, and her desire therefore becomes whatever the psyche of the child demands and expects. This corresponds to Milner's statement that the internal life of the mother becomes the external life of the child. In psychotic and borderline patients we see the result of a failure to uphold this barrier, and the mother's own infantile impulses mingle with her attempts to provide the child with normal care. The result is confusion regarding the three previously mentioned coordinates normally communicated by motherly discourse: 'How did I get here?' 'What gender am I?' and 'How am I to understand the relationship between my parents?'

Hanne was five years old when her father died. The mother wished to conceal the fact that the father had died at his own hand, and therefore chose to remain silent not only on the subject of his death, but on his entire person. Hence there was no funeral, no gravesite, and he was never mentioned. This left a void which was difficult for Hanne to express symbolically. This meant that she found it difficult to use him in her attempts to seek answers to the basic question of her own becoming, her gender, and relations to her mother. At the same time the mother bound Hanne to her in a form of symbiosis, which was presumably partly based on a desire to protect her daughter, but was undoubtedly also motivated by the mother's own needs for an intimacy which positioned the daughter in the void left behind by the husband. Hanne knew – with the intuitive knowledge of a child – that something did not correspond to what was being said. She registered – through the hidden messages of the mother – a number of desires which did not correspond to her childish need for motherly attention, and failed to obtain an explanation that could help her grieve and work towards a positioning of the father in a relation between him, the mother, and herself. This had serious consequences, not only for Hanne's experience and understanding of her own becoming and gender, but for her ability to distinguish between reality and imagination and between her own wishes and those of others.

Fonagy *et al.* (2002) have provided a number of illuminating examples of mothers who due to their own complicated and unprocessed emotions are unable to perform the containing function that mirrors and modulates the child's emotions. The result is that the child – in order to protect itself against its own frightening inner feelings – either withdraws from or clings to the mother or another object in an attempt to externalize a destructive part of its own self.

In the next chapter I shall delve into the psychological consequences of trauma and in Chapter 8 I shall deal with Winnicott's theory of the development of borderline pathology. Here I shall provide another image of the great significance attributed by Winnicott to spontaneity and play in the unfolding of the true self, and conclude by indicating how these thoughts of early childhood development have left their mark on Winnicott's ideas on psychotherapy for borderline patients.

The capacity to be alone and the ability to play

The child's capacity to rest in being is supported by what Winnicott refers to as 'I am alone' experiences. At the beginning of psychic life the ego – this initial organization of an interior separate from an exterior – is a necessary condition for the experience of being or 'I am' experiences. In this state of pure being the child is unprotected, exposed and vulnerable, and entirely dependent on a protective caregiver. When the child subsequently experiences being alone, it has learnt to perceive its own being as implying the presence of another existence. The capacity to be alone and enjoy it requires the child to first learn to be alone in the reliable presence of the mother. In other words the child must have plenty of experience in spending time with a person who does not make demands, in order to acquire the ability to feel joy in being alone. Borderline patients have great difficulty in being alone – in fact it is frequently impossible for them, and in light of Winnicott's views we see that they have presumably had few experiences of being alone in the reliable presence of another.

> When alone in the sense that I am using the term, and only when alone, the infant is able to do the equivalent of what in an adult would be called relaxing. The infant is able to become unintegrated, to flounder, to be in a state in which there is no orientation . . . In the course of time there arrives a sensation or an impulse. In this setting the sensation or impulse will feel real and be a truly personal experience.
>
> (Winnicott 1990a: p. 34)

A child who has repeated experiences of this nature learns to appreciate its own personal impulses and is able to repeat them whenever it is alone, because this experience is associated with the presence of another. As time goes by this is also possible without the physical presence of the other. The child has learned to use evocative recognition (Adler) or a 'soothing' internal object (Rinsley).

Winnicott's emphasis on the significant difference between spontaneity and reaction as well as of the potential of intermediate space for creativity and mental growth is, as previously mentioned, clearly evidenced in his considerations on treatment, particularly for those patients who do not possess the ability to play.

> Psychotherapy takes place in the overlap of two areas of playing, that of the patient and that of the therapist. Psychotherapy has to do with two people playing together. The corollary of this is that where playing is not possible then the work done by the therapist is

> directed towards bringing the patient from a state of not being able to play into a state of being able to play.
>
> (Winnicott 1971: p. 38)

In order to understand the implications of this statement for psychoanalytic technique, we need to take a closer look at what Winnicott means by play and the area of play.

In English there is a clear distinction between *game* and *play*. While the former refers to a structured form of play according to certain rules, *play* refers to the opposite: unorganized, spontaneous, free display. It is worth noting that Winnicott, in his book *Playing and Reality* (1971), uses verbal nouns (Pontalis 1981). While this is a frequently used inflectional form in English, Winnicott uses it with particular frequency, especially when he wishes to emphasize the unusual use of traditional words. He refers to *dreaming*, *fantasying*, *living*, *object-relating*, *holding*, *using*, *being*, *interrelating*, and *communicating*. All these terms denote a motion, a process, in contrast to a finished product. Play is constituted by such unorganized, free expression. This is what we should strive to provide for our patients within the framework of the psychoanalytic setting. Winnicott defined playing as follows: 'The experience is one of a non-purposive state, as one might say a sort of ticking over of the unintegrated personality' (Winnicott 1971: p. 55). Winnicott also termed it 'formlessness'. In other words, it is necessary to distinguish between purposeful activity and its opposite, purposeless being. Referring to Balint's (1979) differentiation between benign and malign regression, Winnicott goes on to characterize the condition desired for the patient as relaxation. What we term free association on the couch or child's play on the floor requires a relaxed state, where ideas, impulses and sensations can be given free rein without any requirements as to orderliness or purpose. We must accept, says Winnicott that:

> there are patients who at times need the therapist to note the nonsense that belongs to the mental state of the individual at rest without the need even for the patient to communicate this nonsense . . . Organized nonsense is already a defence, just as organized chaos is a denial of chaos.
>
> (Winnicott 1971: p. 56)

It is the idea of crucial respect for the spontaneous expression of the small child that is reiterated, here in relation to the therapeutic process. Like the normal, devoted mother, the therapist must adopt a listening, wait-and-see attitude, which does not interfere with the patient's spontaneous narration.

> The therapist who cannot take this communication becomes engaged in a futile attempt to find some organization in the nonsense . . . An opportunity for rest has been missed because of the therapist's need to find sense where nonsense is.
>
> (Winnicott 1971: p. 56)

Naturally this does not constitute a request for the therapist to become entirely passive, but is simply a reminder that any intervention must take its cue from whatever material the patient puts forth at any given time. No patient will feel helped by the therapist bringing new material into the patient's narrative, such as comments on significant persons in the patient's past: 'Your mother was not good enough', 'your father really seduced you', 'your aunt dropped you out' (Winnicott 1990h: p. 37). Change can only arise when traumatic events – regardless of their character, or of where they have arisen – are brought into the patient's material, or, as Winnicott puts it, within the patient's omnipotence: 'In psycho-analysis as we know it there is no trauma that is outside the individual's omnipotence' (Winnicott 1990f: p. 36). While the small child is entirely dependent on what takes place around it, adults have taken all events into what is termed psychic reality. We shall fail to make contact with this reality if we try to make it approximate external reality, regardless of whether we do so by transferential interpretations or through so-called genetic interpretations: 'Changes come in an analysis when the traumatic factors enter the psycho-analytic material in the patient's own way, and within the patient's omnipotence' (Winnicott 1990f: p. 37).

Just as the mother respects that the child creates its reality, so the therapist must make room for ideas that follow their own order 'not assuming the existence of a significant thread' (Winnicott 1971: p. 55). Winnicott seems to explicitly use – as does Bion (1984) – Keats' concept of 'negative capability' (1952 [1895]: p. 277) as a metaphor for the professional, i.e. neutral therapist. Like Bion (1981), Ogden (1997) and Bollas (1993), Winnicott, too, has indicated that the therapist may steal the patient's creativity by knowing too much. Note that Winnicott emphasizes that both patient and therapist must be willing to play. New and valuable things arise only in that area where the play of both patient and therapist coincide. Winnicott's answer to the 'How?' of psychotherapy would appear to be the creation of the conditions necessary for this to take place. This question is not answered by referring to specific techniques, as was illustrated by the object-relations school. The only procedure Winnicott is willing to indicate is one which affords 'opportunity for formless experience, and for creative impulses, motor and sensory, which are the stuff of playing' (Winnicott 1971: p. 64). The idea of an overlapping area is not only relevant to the therapeutic setting. In Chapter 9 I shall try to link the potential space of psychotherapy to the creative display that takes place in the special experiential spaces of playing and dreaming.

For now I shall return to Winnicott's remarkable definition of trauma. He says of the psychoanalytic setting, vis-à-vis trauma, that it is always within the omnipotence of the patient. This is to be understood as follows: while the infant's situation is one in which good or bad befalls the child – in other words it is entirely beyond the child's reach and control – and infancy itself is the period where these external factors are gathered within the omnipotent area of the child, the latter is all we deal with in adult individuals. It cannot be underestimated that what Winnicott is referring to here is diametrically opposed to the view we find defended in contemporary traumatological literature, where trauma is defined as something exterior – an event or assault. Winnicott turns this definition upside down and says that traumas belong to the external world only in childhood and that paradoxically it helps the child that it can let this external trauma appear as a projection.

> The paradox is that what is good and bad in the infant's environment is not in fact a projection, but in spite of this it is necessary, if the individual is to develop healthily, that everything shall seem to him to be a projection. Here we find omnipotence and the pleasure principle in operation, as they certainly are in earliest infancy, and to this observation we can add that the recognition of a true 'not-me' is a matter of the intellect; it belongs to extreme sophistication and to the maturity of the individual.
>
> (Winnicott 1990f: p. 38)

For adult individuals, however, infantile trauma will always be internal in character. Like all events, traumas have become part of a complex internal structure. Trauma may rise again and be repeated, but never as a copy of original events. With these remarks the foundation is laid for a discussion of the influence of trauma on borderline pathology.

Notes

1 Since then, Anthony Bateman and Peter Fonagy have collaborated (2004, 2006) to further develop the theory of mentalization, particularly in relation to borderline pathology. Moreover, they have created a practical guideline – based on mentalization – to treating borderline pathology.

2 In this context I would like to draw attention to Paul Federn, who in 1953 wrote about schizoid patients from an ego-psychological standpoint, as well as to Harry Guntrip (1983 [1968]), who combined the ego-psychological explanation with the theoretical paradigm of object-relations in his examination of schizoid phenomena. In the process of this investigation I shall be referring sporadically to these early ego-psychological studies of borderline pathology.

3 For a critical discussion of the concept of the object in psychoanalytic theory, see Green (2000a) and Gammelgaard (2003a, 2003b). For a suggestion of a developmental theory beyond the dyad, see Muller (1996).

4 For a discussion of the relationship between empirical and clinical research see Green and Stern (2000).

5 Although Fonagy and Target refer to Winnicott's concept, I do not think they use it as an intermediate area of experience. Despite providing a significant and nuanced explanation of the child's gradual mastering of the relationship between interior and exterior, Fonagy and Target consistently adhere to the thought of an interior as separate from an exterior. Winnicott however dissolves this dichotomy in the paradoxical statement that the intermediate area of experience cannot be understood as a place for either subjective or objective experience.

6 Since the publication of this book in Danish, research on infants has progressed significantly. In addition to scholars such as Fonagy and his colleagues, Daniel Stern merits mention. As opposed to Fonagy *et al.*, however, Stern (1995, 2006) has not bridged the gap to a theory of developmentally specific borderline pathology, neither in his theory of the child's interpersonal world and development nor in his book on the present moment (Stern 2004). Hence he is only referred to sporadically in this context.

7 Fairbairn must be emphasized as one of the first object-relationists to

systematically describe the split self and object ideas of the inner world. Fairbairn (1994 [1952]) distinguishes between on the one hand an 'exciting object' with a corresponding *libidinous ego*, and coinciding with Masterson and Rinsley's rewarding part-unit; and on the other a 'rejecting object' with the corresponding *internal saboteur*, which is the equivalent of the withdrawing part-unit.

8 Fraiberg distinguished between recognition and evocative memory. Recognition is a developmental precondition for the ability to recall an image of the mother, even in her absence.

9 Abraham (1982 [1912]) was the first analyst to draw attention to the feelings of pain and emptiness suffered by depressive patients with ensuing feelings of insufficiency and a lack of ability to love, combined with the need to project aggressions into others and to create what Klein (1986 [1932]) later termed 'persecuting objects'. Freud (1916) saw depressive self-blame as an expression of identification with a lost object, which – because relations with this object had been of a narcissistic nature – continued to exist as part of the ego at its expense, so to speak. Rey (1994) described a particular form of depression, which he calls 'depersonalized depression'. He refers to the feelings of emptiness, boredom, and general lack of interest which often make these patients seek stimulants, develop substance abuse problems, or resort to acts of perversion, promiscuity or self-mutilation.

10 In French there is a distinction between *objective* and *objectale*, where the latter relates to the nature of a relationship, thereby referring to an intersubjective phenomenon and thus allowing the possibility of imposing other connotation on the idea of the primary object (Green 2000a).

11 While Fonagy refers to Lecours and Bouchard (1997) in his use of the term mentalization, the two French authors indicate that their mentalization concept is not to be confused with Fonagy's. One significant difference between the authors of the so-called Marty school and Fonagy is that the former have integrated the theory of drive into their theoretical framework, while Fonagy's mentalization concept clearly rests on a cognitive foundation, and his theory on mother–child interaction rests on the idea of a social bio-feedback model (Fonagy & Target 2000, Fonagy *et al.* 2002).

12 To my knowledge, the authors do not define what they mean by the crucial term integration, e. g. how two different kind of epistemology might be thus integrated.

13 There may appear to be an initial similarity between this perception of the internalization of the alien and Laplanche's idea of otherness. Both theories distinguish between the moment of otherness which is also contained in normal development on the one hand, and the brutal intrusion on mental structure, which is the result of early trauma, on the

other. In spite of these descriptive similarities, the fundamental theoretical preconditions are so different as to permit a reference to two entirely different 'metapsychologies'. I shall return to this difference in the next chapter, where I shall discuss the psychoanalytical idea of trauma in relation to borderline pathology.

14 See Note 10 on page 59, on *objective* and *objectale.*

15 '*Substantiver un adjectif, c'est passer des qualifications particulières ou fortuites à l'idée d'une substance; laquelle ne se confound pas avec cet objet qu'est la mère*'.

16 Bollas (2000) has written a series of fascinating essays on hysterical patients emphasizing the erotic dimension of early mother–child relationships. He believes that the reason for the desexualization of the body encountered in hysterical patients is to be found in the mother's lack of ability to naturally and spontaneously stimulate and confirm the pleasure experienced by the child when the erogenous zones of its body are touched.

4

Psychic trauma

The psychoanalytic theories of borderline pathology discussed in the previous chapter were all based on early mother–child interaction and situated the causality of pathological development in disturbances during the pre-Oedipal phase. Significant theoretical differences between American, British and French psychoanalysis aside, Kernberg, Winnicott and Aulagnier all combined developmental theory with metapsychological standpoints in their respective attempts to understand severe psychopathology.

During the late 1970s, a new explanatory model surfaced, based on quantitative empirical studies, typically comparing the borderline population with associated diagnostic groups. These studies concluded that the group of borderline patients displayed a significantly higher prevalence of childhood trauma than other patient groups, i.e. sexual, physical and verbal abuse of children from a very early age.

A family study carried out by Walsh in 1976 (Gabbard & Wilkinson 1994) showed that 64 per cent of the population examined had severely dysfunctional relationships with their parents. These were characterized by outright abuse, hostility, and devaluation. Since this original study, numerous reports have confirmed a high occurrence of childhood abuse in borderline patients. Gabbard and his colleagues have summed up the results of these empirical studies.

Some of them reported significantly higher occurrences of physical and sexual abuse in borderline patients compared with patients with adjacent diagnoses, while others found verbal abuse to be significantly more common among borderline patients than among the other diagnostic groups.

Judith Lewis Herman's work (Herman *et al.* 1989, Herman 1992) may be considered representative of these empirical studies which unequivocally indicate sexual or physical abuse as a significant aetiological factor in the development of borderline pathology. In an early study Herman *et al.* (1989) documented that patients with a diagnosis of borderline personality disorder or borderline traits had a significantly higher occurrence of backgrounds featuring physical abuse (71 per cent), sexual abuse (68 per cent) and severely dysfunctional and violent family patterns (62 per cent) compared with non-borderline patients with associated diagnoses. A few years later these studies were incorporated into a book on trauma (Herman 1992). However, this work no longer constitutes a scientific, neutral study, but an ideological feminist indictment centering on a victim/perpetrator problematic. Herman is not alone in succumbing to the temptation to side with the victims, particularly in discussing sexual abuse of children, a subject which – understandably – arouses strong counter-transference reactions in analysts, yet also often results in an over-simplification of the trauma theories involved. I shall venture no further into this debate on the truth of traumatic memories,[1] but merely limit myself to pointing out that trauma once again appears to have gained terrain in attempts to explain the development of severe psychopathology. In dealing with physical, verbal or sexual abuse, trauma is often defined in the physical sense of an overwhelming event.

> The most powerful determinant of psychological harm is the character of the traumatic event itself. Individual personality characteristics count for little in the face of overwhelming events. There is a simple, direct relationship between the trauma and its psychological impact.
>
> (Herman 1992: p. 57)

It is conceivable that there may be some truth to this statement when it comes to the infliction of physical damage to the human organism. In dealing with abuse and damage inflicted on the human psyche, however, this is an overly simple viewpoint. It is this distinction which is frequently overlooked in all these studies that epitomize physical and psychic damage under the shared heading of trauma.

When dealing with sexual abuse of children it can be difficult not to succumb to morally indignant judgement, which can enhance the tendency to believe that physical abuse provides the entire and natural explanation for the development of psychopathology. However, this is a 'category mistake' (Ryle 1990 [1949]). It does not present an actual explanation but postulates a link between external factors and psychic effects. We must inquire into the traumatic nature of sexual abuse (Bollas 1989). In other words, what is it that is so highly disruptive to later development? Is it physical abuse in and of itself or is it the psychic representation, and how may we more precisely understand the connection between external occurrences and their effect on psychic structures?

I supervised a therapeutic process where the patient had been subjected to sexual abuse by her father for many years. One day she told her therapist that the greatest violation had actually been the sudden cessation of this abuse when she reached sexual maturity and registered a sense of pleasure for the first time. The abuse stopped at that moment, and she felt humiliated and debased. Gabbard (Gabbard & Wilkinson 1994) refers to a patient whose father subjected her to ten years of perverted sexual acts. Naturally this story produced anger and indignation in the therapist. He showed empathy through an interpretation linking the sexual abuse to the depressive and suicidal behaviours of the patient. The patient reacted with great wonderment, claiming that this made no sense. On the contrary her father had made her feel special and loved, unlike her mother who had been cold and distant. Her depressive and suicidal behaviour had arisen when the sexual relationship with her father had ceased. This vignette serves to emphasize a not uncommon state of affairs when women speak of the abuse they have been subjected to by their fathers. The ensuing hatred is frequently aimed at a mother who appears cold and insensitive, which forces us to pose the question of how fantasies of the mother enter into the child's attempt to understand what is going on, and why. Is this because the mother is spared unwanted intimacy with her husband, as I heard one patient describe in another supervised therapeutic process? Or do the actions of the father represent a penetration which in the child's imagination becomes the work of the mother (Bollas 1989)?

These examples unambiguously indicate that when it comes to phenomena of psychic and sexual life, matters are far more complicated than theories of the traumatic character of mere events would lead us to believe.[2] With reference to sexual relations between adults and children, we must firstly remember that the child is also a sexual being, reacting to incestuous abuse with thoughts and fantasies based in his or her level of psychosexual maturity. Secondly, this is an interplay that cannot be comprehended in behaviourist terms, but must be understood as actions communicating something which child and adult presumably understand quite differently. Theories of trauma which fail to take these factors into account will all too easily reduce complex psychic states to overly simple physical states.

In this chapter I shall indicate a theory of psychic trauma capable of explaining why and how sexual assault has traumatic effects. Subsequently I shall pave the way for an attempt at linking psychic trauma with the development of borderline pathology.

The theory of seduction

Psychoanalysis originated as a theory of trauma, which – as most readers know – was defined as seduction. The 'theory of seduction' refers to the theory that Freud developed and abandoned even before 1900, which briefly postulated that painful events – often of a sexual nature, and frequently from early childhood – underlay the symptoms of hysterical patients.

Freud's theory of trauma and seduction was an attempt to resolve the mystery of hysteria, which Freud linked to sexuality at a very early stage in his career. Even in early studies of hysteria Freud realized that the time at which events occur and the time at which they are repressed do not coincide. Thus he worked on the assumption that there was a certain dynamic relationship between sexual events and their return in the form of memories which defined psychic trauma. This means that psychic trauma was linked to sexuality from the outset and considered in the light of two defining moments: the event and the ensuing (*nachträglich*) memory. Psychic trauma may of course be triggered by external events, but the actual traumatization takes place at the psychic level through the memory of external events. This psychic trauma – henceforth understood as memory – is a kind of 'foreign body' which continues its activity long after installation, only now according to the laws of the psyche. The familiar conclusion from Breuer and Freud's *Studies on Hysteria* (1895b) is that hysterics suffer from 'reminiscences'. But why do memories function in this manner?

The answer is not simple but entails the entire theory of psychosexual development and seduction. Thus the answer may be formulated in terms of a presentation of this theory. In fact it may be summed up with the provocative message from the opening line of Joyce McDougall's investigation of human sexuality: 'Human sexuality is inherently traumatic' (McDougall 1995: p. ix). Freud, however, did not pursue the question of the relationship between seduction and psychosexual development. He changed his mind and gave up on the theory of the sexually seduced child, replacing it with a theory of the anxiety-provoking effect of sexual fantasies. In other words, trauma was removed from the exterior to the interior scene as Freud developed his theory of an inner psychic life, underlining the fantasies and psychic mechanisms that regulate the interplay of forces in conscious and unconscious psychic processes. Trauma was no longer a relationship between internal and external but was internally anchored, and basically consisted of the return of traumatic memories as opposed to events.

This development in psychoanalytic theory has created something of a stir among later generations of therapists. The typical argument runs that Freud committed a fatal error in turning his attention from real events to the child's supposedly hyperactive imaginary life (Ulman & Brothers 1988). Herman's feminist discussion of the theory of seduction reads:

> Out of the ruins of the traumatic theory of hysteria, Freud created psychoanalysis. The dominant psychological theory of the next century was founded in the denial of women's reality . . . Psychoanalysis became a study of the internal vicissitudes of fantasy and desire, dissociated from the reality of experience.
>
> (Herman 1992: p. 14)

The fact that Freud wrote off the theory of seduction created a dilemma for many of his followers between a theory of a brutal reality with sexual and violent assaults on children, and a theory which – to use Herman's words – regards 'hysterical patients' accounts of childhood sexual abuse [as] untrue' (Herman 1992: p. 15). Clearly, actual events are indisputable in a theory of trauma when the opposite is lying, cheating or pure, phantasmatic inventiveness in the traumatized patients.

This dilemma rests on a false opposition which has proven fatal to psychoanalytic theory. Many therapists have simply written off psychoanalytic explanations first of hysteria and later of borderline. Psychoanalysis has not only been considered useless, but an actual failure and a form of treason towards the patients. Freud himself is not without blame in this respect. He desisted from working the issue of seduction into his later theory on psychosexual development and sexual fantasies. In the following I shall try to demonstrate how a psychoanalytic theory of seduction might dissolve the unfortunate polarization between truth and lies, while simultaneously seeking to uphold the discussion of trauma at the level of psychic processes. We owe it to Jean Laplanche (1989, 1997, 1999) to have maintained Freud's original theory of seduction and built it into the theory of normal psychosexual development.

Physical and psychic trauma

The frequently polemic discussions on the real or imaginary nature of sexual assaults tend to overlook an important but necessary distinction for dealing with trauma.

The word trauma is Greek and means wound or injury, or the verbs to injure, penetrate or torture. The concept originated in medicinal discourse where trauma is defined as physical damage inflicted on the organism, usually through violent blows or attacks from an external party. From there it slid into psychological terminology and psychic trauma – analogously to physical trauma – has been defined as a violent external event that threatens the normal functioning of the human organism.

In speaking of the human organism, we must be clear on whether we mean the biological organism or the function of the psychic apparatus (Laplanche 1989). Physical assaults that threaten our biological survival, such as traffic accidents and muggings, are traumatic in the physical sense. Conversely, when dealing with other forms of physical violence, for instance torture, we already find ourselves in a borderland, and when it comes to sexual attacks, we are completely unable to comprehend the traumatic moment unless we relate it to the psychic apparatus. There may be analogies between physical and psychic traumatization, but the differences are so great that it is meaningless to speak of any real analogy or identity. It could be claimed that physical and psychic trauma, rather than complementing each other, actually exclude one another (Laplanche 1989). This is a hypothesis which means that physical trauma relates to physical pain inflicted on the physical organism. I shall try to justify this in the following discussion. Conversely, psychic trauma relates to overwhelming, significant impressions that impact the psychic apparatus.

In other words we are dealing with phenomena defined at entirely different levels of the human organism, and which must thus be handled and treated differently. In a traumatic situation physical damage may prevent rather than augment psychic trauma.

The distinction between physical and psychic trauma can be seen already in Freud's early work in a place where he appears to be working on a model of the biological organism. In reality this is an attempt to understand the constitution of psychic trauma. It is not always clear, however, when Freud theorizes at the level of the organism and when he is working at the psychic level. One example is the important concept of the protective shield (*Reizschutz*), a protective membrane on the surface of the living organism. Besides maintaining different levels of input and output of energy, this shield plays a decisive part in everything related to pathology. Depending on the actual circumstances, the energetic flooding of the protective shield is converted to pain or trauma. The question is, however, what the implied model refers to. An unambiguous reading of Freud could easily lead the reader astray, since we are clearly dealing with several things at once. The notion of the protective shield refers on the one hand to the organism in a biological sense. Understood as such this model may explain pain: physical pain appears as an effect of a delimited penetration of the protective shield. Yet we may also perceive it as a protective membrane surrounding our psychic apparatus, which we should consider as a specialized organ which has evolved from an organismic or biologic basis, and finally we may perceive it as an ego function, which is only indirectly based in biology.[3]

Thus our theory on trauma must respect these different levels to avoid confusing the organismic level – where we deal with an organism vis-à-vis an overwhelming external world – with the ego level, where we deal with an ego vis-à-vis a world of desire to be interpreted and managed.[4] I believe that those who have advocated reintroducing the theory of sexual trauma discuss it at the organismic level. In consequence psychic trauma is understood as analogous or even identical to physical trauma.

Trauma and the psychic apparatus

We encounter Freud's first theoretical model (1895a) of the psychic apparatus and the first theory of trauma in his posthumously published

'Project for a Scientific Psychology', written in 1895. However, this work cannot stand alone if we are to understand psychic trauma. Here we must add the contemporary theory on psychopathology and treatment techniques from *Studies on Hysteria* (1895b).

In the 'Project', the starting point is a simple model of the nervous system and a couple of assumptions concerning its function. In the context of this study, the significant issues are the so-called principles of constancy and inertia, defined as the primary tendency to discharge tension by the shortest possible route. The primary function of the psychic apparatus is to keep itself free of tension, partly by keeping tension out, and partly by enabling discharge of incoming tensions.

However, the tendency towards inertia turns out to be more ambiguous than was initially supposed. One case where the initial assumption appears to be erroneous is in reference to the experiences of pain, particularly that which returns through memory. The argument in the 'Project' claims that the tendency to get rid of tension as quickly as possible appears differently depending on whether we are dealing with augmentation related to an experience of satisfaction or of pain.[5]

Experiences of satisfaction and their memories pose no explanatory problem. When a need – once satisfied – re-emerges to cathect the memory of satisfaction, the tension or cathexis, as we call it, will find either motile or hallucinatory discharge. Thus the assumption is that young children hallucinate the satisfying breast, and we all know the desirous tendency to cathect memories that have brought us satisfaction and confirmation. Yet how do we explain that we apparently also cathect painful memories, thus releasing pain we would rather be without?[6]

In order to answer this question we must account for the significant difference between the experience of pain and the memory of pain. Freud says of the experience of pain that it confirms the assumption of the primary tendency of the psychic apparatus to keep itself free of tension:

> Everything that we know of pain fits in with this. The nervous system has the most decided inclination to a *flight from pain*. We see in this a manifestation of the primary trend against a raising of Ωή tension, and we infer that pain consists in *the irruption of large Ωή into ψ . . .*
>
> (Freud 1895a: p. 307)

Confronted with violent, irresistible penetration, the apparatus is helpless: 'It can do nothing to divide it up into acceptable portions and assign it ways to go: pain does as it wishes and goes its own ways' (Reitan 1994: p. 70, translated from Danish).[7] In other words pain is an illustration of the frailty of the psychic apparatus. Freud works on the assumption of a form of violence towards the psychic apparatus, and it is easy to imagine that the likelihood of such reckless and violent penetration of the psychic apparatus is greater the less evolved is the apparatus itself. In Winnicott's words we may add that in psychoanalytic work there is no such thing as trauma outside the patient's omnipotence. By this he means that, as time passes, the trauma becomes integrated within the psychic system, thereby losing its external properties. This is similar to Freud's early distinction between pain as experience and pain as memory.

The model of the psychic apparatus developed by Freud based on the assumption of the principles of constancy and inertia faces something of a challenge in seeking to explain why the recollection of pain carries particularly large amounts of energy. It seems entirely counterproductive to repeat the experience of pain as a memory, one that indeed requires large amounts of energy which would typically be experienced as anxiety at the psychic level. In order to explain the origin of this energy, Freud introduced the idea of special neurones, which he termed 'key neurones':

> Just as there are motor neurones which, when they are filled to a certain amount, conduct Ωή into the muscles and accordingly discharge it, so there must be 'secretory' neurones which, when they are excited, cause the generation in the interior of the body of something which operates as a stimulus upon the endogenous paths of conduction to ψ – neurones which thus influence the production of endogenous Ωή and accordingly do not discharge Ωή but supply it in roundabout ways. We will call these [secretory] neurones 'key neurones'. Evidently they are only excited when a certain level in ψ has been reached. As a result of the experience of pain the mnemic image of the hostile object has acquired an excellent facilitation to these key neurones, in virtue of which, [facilitation] unpleasure is now released in the affect.
>
> (Freud 1895a: pp. 320–321)

In order to understand what is being discussed here, we must remember that through these apparently abstract and neurophysiological speculations, Freud was working on assumptions that were to position sexuality within the psychic apparatus, and that he was in the process of exposing the trauma of hysteria. As I mentioned earlier, Freud wanted to solve the riddle of hysteria, and to that end he worked on two hypotheses: firstly that sexuality is the decisive factor in the aetiology of psychoneuroses, and secondly that psychic illnesses in particular are an effect of the sexual seduction of children by adults. Transferring this to the above observations on that mysterious discomfort associated with painful memories, we can therefore add that what Freud is aiming at in the 'Project' is not so much pain in general, nor is it pain in a physical sense. Rather it is that pain or anxiety, which is associated with the activation of what Freud termed key neurones; 'glands' that release 'sexual substances' and produce psychic tension or anxiety. We are now no longer at the level of physical trauma. The trauma is sexual. In other words, what lies hidden in Freud's apparently neurophysiological speculations in the 'Project' is a discussion of the psychic consequences of seduction. The key to this understanding lies partly in the contemporary *Studies on Hysteria*, and partly in the only clinical example described by Freud in the 'Project', the important story of Emma. All clinical examples show that the traumatic moment of seduction is not only the sexual assault, but also – and not least – the memory of it, which becomes associated with particularly strong anxiety because it activates sexual tensions through so-called key neurones.

To express all this in somewhat more specific terms we may imagine a situation where a small child is subjected to sexual assault which can find no psychic correspondence in the child. The seduced child does not understand the sexual desires expressed by the seducer, nor the diffuse sensations it feels itself. The tension thus produced can no more be psychically discharged than the physical pain. Its violence undermines the structure of the psychic apparatus. When the child recalls this experience later in life it is accompanied by great tension or anxiety. Unlike the actual experience of pain, which may be understood in purely quantitative terms as being of that overwhelming nature we associate with physical trauma, the memory of pain is not only quantitative and as such cannot be removed through motile deflection or hallucination, as is the case with memories of experiences of satisfaction. If tensions arise through input from life drives, they may be released though hallucinations of the experience of satisfaction, but if their source is the cathexis of key neurones with the memory of pain, tension cannot be released in this manner. The excitation may of course leave a hostile memory image. This is what takes place in phenomenological terms when we displace our thoughts in order to avoid thinking of something unpleasant. But these memories of pain do not disappear; they are foreign bodies that remain active long after their installation. They are merely lying in wait for sexual energy to be liberated from key neurones in order to be activated as an internal assault. In other words psychic trauma always has two elements: one is the experience of pain or the sexual assault itself; the other is the recathexis of the experience or the memory of the experience, which is experienced as an assault whose intensity is partially attributable to the person's own sexual tensions. In other words we are dealing with a form of re-traumatization.

This account of the experience vis-à-vis the memory of pain has served to demonstrate that in dealing with sexual trauma we cannot limit them to the assaults themselves, since they constitute only one element in the traumatization process. It is followed by a psychic traumatization, when the sexual energy reoccupies images of memory, and the person is assaulted from the inside by his or her own sexual impulses, which cannot exist without disturbing the dormant memories.

Meanwhile, we need to add another element in order to fully understand psychic trauma. This has to do with the ego and its development. The human ego turns out to be the secondary function capable of keeping hostile memory images at bay. The ego is equipped with an attention function, which above all inhibits new cathexes of traumatic memory images. This inhibition may as we said take the form of displacement, for example when we try to think of something else. But if this function aimed at the inhibition of unpleasure-releasing memories were able to avoid the attention of the ego – simply moving around it, so to speak – then the ego would be too late in its attempts to displace it. This is precisely where Freud refers to the psychosexual development evidenced in the formation of hysterical symptoms and which perhaps more generally describes the development of human sexuality. The story of Emma is a case in point.

At the age of twelve Emma experiences two young shop assistants in a grocery store laughing. Previously she had registered a certain attraction towards one of them, but when they laugh she thinks they are laughing at her clothes and rushes out of the shop in a severe fit of anxiety. This anxiety, which develops into a phobia, turns out to be based on an earlier experience. At the age of eight Emma had visited a different grocery store on a couple of occasions, where the shop-keeper had groped her genitals through her clothes. When her own sexual impulses re-awaken the memory image of the grinning grocer she is assaulted from within by something which had lain dormant and which was activated by the experience years later. Twelve-year-old Emma's attention is unambiguously directed towards the external world, which is generally the case since the purpose of attention is to avoid the release of unpleasure for which the ego is normally prepared, providing its origin is external. In Emma's case the discomfort comes from the inside, because the released sexual energy cathects an unpleasurable memory image. There is a paradox built into the psychic apparatus, constituted by the production of sexual energy by the key neurones which cathect memories, which then mount assaults from the inside, and cause the release of unpleasure. The paradox lies in the fact that the development of the ego is not synchronous with the development of sexuality. The premature development of sexuality and the delayed development of the ego allow sexual energy to cathect unpleasurable memories without encountering resistance from the ego, and to mount attacks from within through this connection. Sexual substances are constantly being produced and are merely waiting for a memory to set them in motion. Only the relatively late-developing repressive capacities of the ego enable it to render these processes ineffectual.

Infantile and general seduction

For a number of years, from the age of nine until around the age of 13, Finn was subjected to a number of paedophile assaults, which he only acknowledged as such during our analytical work, haltingly and under great protest. While they went on, of course, Finn experienced the pain and terror at what was happening to his body, but his childish longing for the fatherly affection he had never received intervened and made these experiences more complex than evidenced by the physical assaults alone. Finn's story is the grim story of a perverted adult exploiting a boy's trusting and expectant experience of what he believes to be fatherly affection. It is the story of the desecration of a child's body in an encounter with perverted adult desire. Yet it is also the general story of the possibility of seduction, and here I refer not to perverted seduction, but to that seduction which is a prerequisite for the sexual development of any child.

Unfortunately the latter may be exploited, leading to perverted seduction that threatens the child's entire psychosexual development. Naturally sexual assault on children is traumatic in the original sense of the world. Psychic traumatization, however, contains a moment which cannot be reduced to physical assault. In Finn's case pain, humiliation, and not least confusion were all associated with sexual exploitation, but only later does Finn become aware of what happened, or rather, he realizes that what is now associated with shame and horror is related to something that has already happened, not to something that is about to happen. Finn contracted a serious venereal disease and the humiliation and stigmatization he was obliged to endure during treatment, combined with his own sexual maturation, revealed their sexual significance even as they labelled his own sexuality as bad and dirty. It is impossible to understand the difficulties Finn later encountered without moving beyond the sexual assaults per se. They are assigned re-traumatizing significance through Finn's attempts to find a way to appropriate his own sexuality. The stigmatizing association between the venereal disease, the condemnation, and his awakening sexuality play a large part in this process. Nor is it possible to understand Finn's reactions to the sexual assaults without understanding the child he was prior to their occurrence. However, this is another story to which I shall return in Chapter 7.

In an autobiographic account Ditlev Jensen (2001) has detailed in a highly absorbing manner the paedophile seduction to which he was subjected for three years.[8] His story is comparable to Finn's in a number of ways and is interesting in its clear demonstration of the difference between psychic and physical traumatization. Jensen has quite unambiguously illustrated why sexuality is particularly vulnerable to traumatization and why it can be so easy to seduce a child. The sexual assaults by a man named Gustav lasted for three years and of course the boy experienced both pain and confusion, but he only later realized what had happened. All is revealed through a single word telling him what it all means. At this point he is experiencing an increasing aversion to the sexual and verbal assaults that Gustav subjected him to, and at the peak of such a bout of antipathy, another small boy visiting Gustav naively and openly talks about a 'faggot camp' he is about to visit. The word 'faggot' hit Jensen like an 'electric shock'.

> I went into the sitting room. Something was happening. It was coming right from my stomach; rumbling in my brain like violent intellectual diarrhoea about to explode. I walked back and forth in the sitting room. I was out of breath and flushing scarlet. Faggot camp. What did it mean? What the hell did it mean? My subconscious was screaming. Come on. Work it out. This is life or death. COME ON!
>
> (Jensen 2001: p. 139; translated from Danish by KM[8])

What Jensen needs to work out is what has happened, not what is about to happen. The word faggot sealed his fate through the past three years. The word faggot denotes his relationship with Gustav, and the word is every bit as brutal as the rape, because it symbolizes not the boy's world, but that of the perverted adult, entering the child's world like poison.

> The more he talked the less I listened. I was in a kind of shock. The earth disappeared beneath me in an existential sense. My entire world collapsed. I was in a state of paralysis, rage, and fear of death.
>
> (Jensen 2001: p. 140; translated from Danish by KM)

This understanding, arrived at too late, and naming something that has already taken place, is the traumatization point for both Finn and Jensen. The painful experiences are connected to something that can be interpreted, but too late, and their interpretation brands these experiences.

> What happened that Sunday was that everything fell into place. And it all happened in the space of a few minutes. When Gustav gave me the word I needed – faggot – it all fell into place. That word was the formula for the rest. As soon as it was in place everything else simply had to be filtered through it: Yes, that was it, and that's it, and that's it. It all fits together. That was precisely why I entered that state of shock, and I've experienced nothing like it before or since.
>
> (Jensen 2001: pp. 144–145; translated from Danish by KM)

Here the author formulates what in psychoanalytic terms would be called *Nachträglichkeit*[10] – the causality of deferred action. It postulates that nothing is inscribed into the human unconscious unless it relates to at least two events separated in time by a moment of mutation, permitting the subject to react differently to the latter event than he or she did to the former, or rather to react to the memory of the first experience in a way that is different from the reaction to the experience itself.[11]

The story of Emma was Freud's prototypical example of the two elements of psychic traumatization. The first element may be termed the experience of pain or the time of fright, where the subject is confronted with this highly significant sexual act the significance of which he or she is unable to assimilate. The memory of this event is neither pathogenic nor traumatic in and of itself. This only becomes the case when it is re-experienced in another scene which becomes associated with the first. However, because the subject now has new possibilities it is the memory itself rather than the new scene that becomes the traumatizing source of energy. The concept of *Nachträglichkeit* implies that the actual traumatic effect has the character of re-traumatization. Recalling Freud's description of the release of unpleasure that results from the activity of the key neurones, we see that both Finn and Jensen begin to understand the extent and the significance of the sexual assaults at a time when their own sexual development allows an interpretation that was previously impossible. At this point the discovery hits them with considerable force because it comes too late and from within, catching them by surprise, retroactively – *nachträglich*.

> I keep forgetting how little I was when it all started, and I still have difficulty accepting that I couldn't *possibly* understand it from the start. When you're nine years old, you're a little child, when you're thirteen you're a big child.
>
> (Jensen 2001: p.144; translated from Danish by KM)

Re-traumatization does not end with the obliteration of memory. Nor is it possible to simply put it behind oneself or forget. Ideally this activates a pathological defence termed repression. During the first assault by the adult – the first sexual scene – the child has no adequate means of defence. It has no weapons, no right answers, and is at best able to encapsulate the experience. The second time, however, the child is able to understand what is going on. Yet now it finds itself under attack from an unexpected angle. It is attacked from within by its own memories, not by an event. Freud makes place for the ego between interior and exterior. For the way in which an individual can be assaulted from within, where an inner border is under attack, may only be understood from the moment when the individual has found a substitute in its beginning ego: there is no protective shield here other than what the ego can manage. Yet this also means that the gravity of the consequences of such a psychic re-traumatization for the psychic apparatus depends on the functioning of the ego, and not least on the development of its defence mechanisms. In light of this we can understand Winnicott's remark that '[i]n psycho-analysis . . . there is no trauma that is outside the individual's omnipotence [and that e]verything eventually comes under ego-control' (Winnicott 1990f: p. 37). It is precisely in this sense that we cannot trust our patients' accounts of traumatic events. Nevertheless we must welcome them as attempts to understand something which is in any event positioned in a place that is neither interior nor exterior. When it comes to traumatic sexuality we must abandon all attempts to account for the difference between external and internal factors. In these cases everything is at once internal as well as external, since every effect is due to an internal reactivation of a memory that originates in external reality.

As previously mentioned it was Laplanche who continued developing the original theory of seduction and contributed a viewpoint capable of dissolving the unfortunate and simplistic opposition between a theory emphasizing the human imagination, and one equally unambiguously positioning causality in external events.

What we in psychoanalysis understand as the psychosexual development of the child presupposes the seductive element of motherly love. Childish sexuality is coaxed forth providing that the mother has sublimated her desire in a loving, caregiving function. This was, as previously mentioned, what Aulagnier termed the 'spoken shadow'; the anticipation of the child and its needs are cast on the child like a speaking shadow similarly to the way a lullaby eases a child to sleep. This healthy seduction furthermore requires the child's openness towards the world, the receptiveness of its senses and mind to adult care. Unfortunately this is the same openness which makes the child an easy victim of adult exploitation, as described by Jensen.

A trip to Provence became a watershed in Jensen's life since it revealed a world of sensorily sated experiences and stimulated a thirst for knowledge he barely knew he possessed. This was the trip on which he met Gustav, who became the source of a bombardment of sensory impressions, taste, music and not least encounters with the unknown. Gustav stimulated all this, coaxing it forth, yet Gustav was also the one who scared him and ruined everything with his perverse, sadistic assaults on these very things he had called forth. There is a particular asymmetry in the relationship between child and adult, which Laplanche has formulated as the passive position of the child versus the active one of the adult. The child is passive in the sense of being less complete and '[o]ne created thing is more perfect than another when we find in the first that which gives an *a priori* reason for what occurs in the second. This is why we say that one acts upon the other' (Laplanche 1989: p. 124). The knowing more of the adult and the superior content of his messages define the relationship between adult and child as an active–passive relationship, which means that the adult communicates more to the child than it is immediately capable of understanding – and often more than the adult understands. The adult world is not just a world of things, but a world of signifiers in the broadest sense of the word. The adult addresses the child with this entire world of sexual significances which the child must attempt to imbue with meaning and respond to, although it is only able to do so to a limited extent.

Sándor Ferenczi (1982 [1933]) was one of the first to understand that communication between parent and child is not always as harmless as we are inclined to believe. He spoke of a 'confusion of tongues' between child and adult, thus referring to the possibility that the messages of the adult may be traumatizing to the child, because they contain the language of adult desire, while the child encounters the adult with the language of tenderness and vulnerability, which is the only language at its disposal.[12] The confrontation between child and adult contains this asymmetry, referred to by Laplanche, which means that the adult psyche is richer than that of the child. This richness is not unambiguous, however, and far from perfect. It also encompasses the frailty of the adult, i.e. the split between conscious and unconscious, creating the basis for what Laplanche termed primal seduction. 'I am, then, using the term *primal seduction* to describe a fundamental situation in which an adult proffers to a child verbal, non-verbal and even behavioural signifiers which are pregnant with unconscious sexual significations' (Laplanche 1989: p. 126). Laplanche calls these expressions 'enigmatic signifiers'. They inscribe themselves in the unconscious of the child with potentially traumatizing effects, which may only be cancelled out by comprehension. Clearly we must distinguish between general and perverse seduction. However, perverse seduction does not cancel out general seduction. Rather, the latter is the ground on which the former stands. The adult leads and seduces the child into this world, coaxing forth its senses and desires in the process. In this sense seduction is a prerequisite if the child is to feel joy in sensuousness and sexuality. Yet the adult also seduces through his or her own unconscious. In Jensen's case this turned out to be fatal and disastrous. General seduction became sick, perverse seduction.

Gustav was fond of telling stories and jokes, but this was where perversion expressed itself through its own mysterious language.

> Almost all the jokes had a 'naughty' twist. An unusual number of the things he said were about sex or genitals or bodily secretions. I never thought about it at the time. I was just happy that I was suddenly allowed things that were forbidden at home. I was glad to receive the attention I had been missing.
>
> (Jensen 2001: p. 50; translated from Danish by KM)

Yet the unconscious will not settle for expressing itself through jokes. One day things go wrong and Gustav communicates a side of himself that the boy does not understand, but which he nevertheless feels in the depths of his soul, and which it takes him many years to comprehend and overcome. Gustav wants him to eat olives, but the boy dislikes the look of them. This spontaneous reaction, which clearly showed the child in the boy, provoked sadism in the adult who then ridiculed and devalued the boy with a violence that scared and confused him. What happened to his friend? One day, many years later, when Jensen is a young student, he buys a glass of olives on impulse.

> It took me a full fifteen minutes to get up my courage after unscrewing the lid. It took me two minutes to finish chewing it. I was over twenty years old. This was the first time I had tasted olives since my childhood. In earlier years I almost experienced spasms whenever I saw olives. I would leap up from a table . . . Ever

> since that trip to the south of France I completely overreacted anytime someone served black olives . . . In reality I was still reacting to that first time Gustav assaulted me . . . That was the first pure violation . . .
>
> (Jensen 2001: p. 54; translated from Danish by KM)

The story of the olives may be read as an allegory of seduction. Its necessary condition is a passive or exposed child without sufficient knowledge to understand the extra meaning – the 'more' so to speak – contained in the adult's message and with insufficiently developed ego-functions to protect itself and set limits. The child is dependent on the adult setting limits, yet it is neither aware of nor prepared for the necessity of setting limits. It is open and trusting. In the middle of this seduction, which arouses joy and desire, stimulating the senses and a thirst for knowledge, something leaps out of the dark of the other's unconscious to present the boy with a mysterious message which cannot immediately be understood – mainly because the adult cannot or will not understand it. For a long time the child does not know what the adult wants, but in spite of this lack of understanding, the child feels that this message is addressed to him.

As the story of the olives shows, general and perverse seduction are interwoven. Primal seduction is a prerequisite to perverse seduction. This does not make it any less brutal. The openness of the child towards the world, its sensuality – or to use Freud's words its presexual sexuality – render it susceptible to the 'more' of the adult's sexual messages. Indeed it is the non-synchronicity of the child's sensually sexual development and its ego development that define the adult's messages as seductive in the sense that they are not transparent, but rather abstruse bearers of enigma. Laplanche's double concept of seduction contains the acknowledgement that the child – even within the relationship to a good-enough mother – must struggle with a communication containing both the child's own sensuous, presexual–sexual impulses and the hidden 'more messages' from the mother's unconscious. When we are dealing with a mother who is unable to maintain the barrier of repression it is clear that the child must struggle to understand not only itself, but also the mother. This drive dimension is often overlooked in object-relations theories. While they rightly emphasize the significance of the object, they overlook the fact that this significance is embedded in and stems from the drives. The result is chaos and confusion, since the child is unable to understand whether the tensions originate internally or whether their source is external – deriving from within the other.

The child is now in a situation where it must relate to the madness within itself as well as to that of the other's drives. In this situation destructive forces are mobilized as the child's ultimate attempt at maintaining its own existence in the situation and as a response to the fact that the ego can no longer perform its binding function. My patient Hanne, to whom I referred previously, remembers how – after the death of her father – her relationship to her mother became turbulent, alternating violently between hateful physical and verbal assaults and equally emotionally exhausting reconciliations. It cannot be sufficiently emphasized that it is the child's attempts to create meaning in something that is false – and therefore meaningless – in relation to ordinary logic that create the particular form of thinking which is characteristic of our borderline patients. Something becomes inscribed within the child's body which does not match the child's primary desire: to be loved and wanted. Ambivalence and hostility, or unveiled sexual desires resulting from a flaw in the mother's capacity for repression and sublimation, inscribe themselves within the child's body with the result that it becomes difficult for the child to cathect its own body, which bears the mark of motherly penetration. As I mentioned earlier, destructivity may be an expression of the attempt to bind something against which the ego has been defenceless, and once the child develops the capacity for thought, this ability – which the mother cannot penetrate in the same way – becomes the secret place in which the child desperately seeks to rescue itself from a chaotic situation. Ideally, thinking can be the salvation of the child. In the worst case the child will develop thought disturbances in an attempt to maintain the illusion of being protected by the mother's love in spite of experiences to the contrary.

During the assaults to which he was subjected, Jensen found a certain comfort in the oath he swore: that what he was experiencing would be told. He was able to do so first in therapy and later in his book *Det bliver sagt* (2001) – 'It will be told'. Hanne was unable to make this promise to herself simply because she did not have access to – and therefore was unable to formulate in thoughts and words – the terrible thing that had happened. Because the father did not exist in her and her mother's common language, Hanne had not only lost the opportunity to grieve for her loss, but had also lost the option of using him as a structuring figure for thoughts on her own existence.

Because he had disappeared from their language, he had left a void in it and was therefore only able to return in what Lacan has called the real. One day Hanne told me that she was sure that on this very day her father was going to stop in his car outside my house to wait for her. We do not hear all that much about Jensen's background and thus we are unable to assess whether it conceals issues that might explain the irresistible attraction that radiated from Gustav and the ensuing difficulty Jensen experienced in protecting himself and setting limits. Thus his story has served as a suitable illustration of general seduction as a common prerequisite for perverse seduction. The child's openness to the world conditions the adult's opportunity to exploit the child to satisfy his perverse desire. The story of the olives shows us that the violation entailed in this perversion goes beyond sexual seduction and captures a moment that should be referred to as the murder of the child's openness and trust.

Finn's story is the story of perverse seduction as part of more far-reaching neglect, long preceding the sexual dimension, and thus relating to existential issues. The same can be said of Hanne's story. Remaining in Laplanche's terminology we may say that it is about a failure of general seduction or a failure in the form of a basic and profound absence, what Winnicott (1990b) would term a form of death or nothingness. In these cases we may observe how the child through its psychosexual development desperately yet vainly searches for answers to fundamental questions related to the very fact of existence.

In my attempts to understand borderline pathology I have had to move beyond explanations limited to interplay in early mother–child relationships and beyond a theory of trauma defined as an exterior event. Yet as this chapter has indicated I have not wanted to walk down the same road as Freud in seeking the answer to questions on the aetiology of neurosis in the human imagination. In Chapter 6 I shall return to Freud once more, but this time I shall be investigating a theory that is not linked to the model of neurosis. First, however, I shall recapitulate what I have said on the issue of psychic trauma.

I have suggested a distinction between physical and psychic traumatization and linked the latter to psychosexual development. I have suggested that trauma is based in the non-synchronicity of the development of the ego and sexuality, respectively. This non-synchronicity means that development is not linear, and that events at the infantile level have far-reaching effects *(nachträglich)*. The concept of *Nachträglichkeit* implies not only a new understanding of the relationship between past and present but also dissolves the sharp distinction between internal and external and between what we term psychic reality and reality, where the latter is understood as that which has effect. For a theory of trauma this means that trauma is constituted though two moments. Due to the subject's new options for reaction it is the memory rather than the new scene which becomes traumatizing. The concept of *Nachträglichkeit* means that traumatic reactions are only associated with trauma if trauma becomes re-traumatizing.

I have used Laplanche and Aulagnier to suggest a distinction between the two moments of seduction. Seduction refers to the child's openness to the world and to the fact that the adult cannot avoid awakening the child's senses and feelings of desire. Sexuality is awakened by the care and attention provided by the adult. This awakening of the child's sexuality through the adult and the adult's unconscious is a fundamental condition. The child communicates with primary caregivers from the beginning of life, and the child registers messages from the adult, but does not understand them until much later. These mysterious messages have been inscribed and lie dormant as memories ready to be awakened by sexual impulses. They are active as the foreign bodies of which Freud spoke, and they remain active long after their installation. Thus we must distinguish between primal seduction and perverse seduction. This does not mean, however, that primal seduction chronologically precedes perverse seduction, but it does constitute its foundations. Hopefully this serves to illustrate why it is insufficient to refer to external or physical trauma in explaining, for instance, the development of borderline pathology. If we define psychic trauma using these two moments we may maintain an aetiology of trauma even in cases that do not feature severe physical traumatization. As is also evident, it is necessary to pursue both the question of mother–child interaction as trauma and the aetiological conditions surrounding borderline pathology using somewhat more complex psychological concepts and theories.

This I shall do in the following chapters. However, prior to theorizing on the psychic mechanisms of borderline pathology, I shall present a phenomenological description of therapeutic encounters with these patients.

Notes

1 For a nuanced, critical discussion of this topic, see Zeuthen (2002).
2 See Postscript.
3 In Chapter 7, where I introduce Anzieu's concept of the 'skin ego', we shall see an example of a use of Freud's term that defines it on a purely psychic level.
4 The ego is not identical with the organism. Its functions cannot be reduced to these or considered analogously. Nor is the ego the entirety of the psychic apparatus. The ego is a specialized organ within this apparatus, and its function is justified in relation to the apparatus as a whole. This means that the danger to which the ego reacts is different from that which prompts a reaction of the organism. Laplanche clarified this difference in the aphorism: 'The "drive" is to the ego what pain is to the body' (Laplanche 1999: p. 209).
5 When Freud speaks of the experience of pain in the 'Project', we may assume – in reference to the theory of seduction in *Studies on Hysteria* – that he is referring to sexual assault.
6 In order to negotiate this problem Freud was obliged to supplement his original model and the principle of constancy with a theory of something 'beyond pleasure'. This something became the assumption of the death drive.
7 I am indebted to Reitan (1994) for his thorough account of Freud's 'Project for a Scientific Psychology'.
8 My thanks to Katrine Zeuthen for drawing my attention to this valuable narrative.
9 KM denotes Karen MacLean, one of the translators of this book.
10 English translation 'deferred action'.
11 One example of the fact that the theory of sexual trauma may be discussed without referring to classical drive theory derives from the in many ways insightful descriptions of traumatization and its psychic consequences carried out by Fonagy and his colleagues (2002). They introduced the concept of 'ego-destructive shame' to denote the shame resulting from brutal assaults by the original attachment figures. If the child has not developed the capacity for mentalization prior to such brutal assaults, because the parents have not been able to mirror the child, the feeling of shame will attach itself to the child's self in a frighteningly real manner. However, it is thought-provoking that the authors do not distinguish between sexual assault and other forms of physical assault, and therefore fail to observe that sexual assaults address the child in an entirely different manner than do other forms of violence.
12 Dominique Scarfone (2002) has taken up Ferenczi's concept of the 'confusion of tongues' with a view towards renewing the meaning of the Freudian (1905) theory of infantile sexuality.

5

Betweenity

As we have seen, the borderline concept was brought in to denote a condition somewhere between neurosis and psychosis. This definition has proved to be fraught with problems even on a semantic level and does, on closer inspection, in fact appear to be a contradiction in terms. If neurosis and psychosis are two distinct and mutually exclusive categories, how then may something be defined by existing on the border of these categories? The problem persists if we pursue another line of thinking currently dominating parts of the clinical world, which presumes that psychopathology cannot be defined by exclusive criteria, but should be positioned within a continuum. How are we in this case to define the borderlands that separate borderline from neurosis on the one hand and from psychosis on the other? When it finally comes to describing the particular problems of specific people, the concept reveals itself as a paradox. How can a border define a person and how does the mind of such a person work?

The borderline concept, as we saw in Chapter 2, arose from observations of certain patients who turned out to be difficult to position within the then current diagnostic groups. The term borderline refers to a condition where patients share certain distinctive characteristics with neurotic patients but without their relatively integrated and stable personality organization and who do not display the advanced and highly effective defence mechanisms characteristic of neurotics.

This terminological paradox counters another paradox inherent in the phenomenon itself, whereby we are reminded of the weaknesses and limitations inherent in our diagnostic categories and are forced to consider the rationales that are prerequisites to our criteria of inclusion and exclusion. It turns out that the people we characterize by a borderline problematic challenge the limits of our customary rational logic, illustrating that psychic life may assume forms defying so-called common sense.

Through psychiatric history, especially the work of Foucault (1973), we have been familiarized with that form of injudiciousness that has been termed madness, and recent investigations into psychosis in the fields of psychiatry and psychoanalysis have contributed to an understanding of important ego-functions such as thought, symbol formation, reality testing etc. In practical psychoanalysis, however, it is our actual experience with borderline patients' psychological difficulties that facilitates a multi-faceted understanding of ego-functions, revealing, for instance, nuances of the defence mechanisms of the ego when repression is not an option.

As psychoanalysts, we have become familiar with psychic disturbances founded on repression and thereby on the distinction between the conscious and the unconscious. We have become used to thinking in dichotomies and distinguishing between latent and manifest significances, primary and secondary processes, pleasure and unpleasure, sexuality and destructiveness. In our therapeutic work we have been able to ally ourselves with the healthy part of the ego, experiencing the value of beneficial transferences or working alliances. Psychoanalysts are increasingly referring to the significance of the actual relationship between patient and therapist, understanding the analytical situation as an intersubjective phenomenon (Ogden 1994a, 1994b, 1999; Renik 1998; and – for a more critical perspective – Green 2000c). In keeping with these developments, the analyst's counter-transference – previously a potential source of error, a blind spot – has become an important source of information about what is happening in the patient and is being enacted in the therapeutic setting. This paradigm of intersubjectivity appears to have re-established the optimism concerning treatment which Freud associated with his work, particularly in the early stages, and which he compared to a cultural labour enabling us to stem irrationality: 'Where Id was, there Ego shall be' (Freud 1933: p. 80). Towards the end of his life Freud became ever less optimistic. In the work that may be considered his clinical testament, he expressed doubts about the faith he had hitherto had in the cooperative abilities of the psychological ego.

> The ego, if we are able to make such a pact with it, must be a normal one. But a normal ego of this sort is, like normality in general, an ideal fiction . . . Every normal person, in fact, is only

> normal on the average. His ego approximates to that of the psychotic in some part or other and to a greater or lesser extent . . .
>
> (Freud 1937a: p. 235)

In an unfinished work written in London in 1938, Freud expressed the opinion that the rejection with which he predicted psychoanalysis would be met in the future would be caused by:

> a number of hypotheses – it is hard to say whether they should be regarded as postulates or products of sciences – which are bound to seem very strange to ordinary modes of thought and which fundamentally contradict current views.
>
> (Freud 1940: p. 282)

Here Freud is of course referring to the unconscious, which he had at this point come to understand not merely as a contained system, but as an aspect of all psychological structures. Freud appears to have recognized that psychic disturbances are not simply about repressed sexual secrets, but that disturbances may exist at the very core of our ego, giving rise to doubts concerning the cooperative abilities of this ego.

When Freud reworked his model of the psyche in the 1920s he did so in recognition of the fact that the ego could not unambiguously be considered a guarantor of common sense and reality adaptation, but had to a large extent shown itself to be irrational and unconscious as to its own modes of functioning. Towards the end of his life Freud realized that there remained a great deal of work to be done in examining the role of the ego in the configuration of morbidity. Anna Freud and the ego psychologists took it upon themselves to supplement Freud's theories on drives with a theory on the psychological ego. Ultimately, however, the chief contribution of ego psychology turned out to be a consolidation of the adaptive and autonomous ego, which Freud had increasingly come to doubt. It is only through working with borderline patients that we have gained some insight into the normal and pathological modes of functioning of the ego, confirming the assumption Freud apparently resisted for a long period: that in many cases the ego is blind to its own activity and in some cases even split in its innermost essence. Freud was initially aware of the existence of a form of pathology bordering on psychosis and the need to find a key to this condition through studies of the ego beyond repression, but throughout his life his writings provided only guarded intimation concerning this issue.

In one of his works where he reflects on the differing mechanisms of neurosis and psychosis Freud writes that:

> it will be possible for the ego to avoid a rupture in any direction by deforming itself, by submitting to encroachments on its own unity and even perhaps by effecting a cleavage or division of itself. In this way the inconsistencies, eccentricities and follies of men would appear in a similar light to their sexual perversions, through the acceptance of which they spare themselves repressions.
>
> (Freud 1924b: pp. 152–153)

These are the kind of remarks that have fuelled notions of a form of injudiciousness of the ego that we see in borderline patients. These patients teach us more about the ego's manifold methods of resolving psychological problems than the sound, sensible ego promoted by the ego-psychologists, and they force us to revise our views on the common sense we consider our ally when working with mental suffering. It is our work with these patients that tells us that the ego may display bizarre or perverted modes of operation similar to the ones that became known to Freud through the sexual life hidden behind the repressive barriers of the normal and the neurotic, and which caused him to claim neurosis to be the negative of perversion.

It is important to emphasize that these borderline patients are not psychotic; in fact they are people who in some ways live well-adjusted lives. They are often intelligent and creative, functioning well in a number of different social and workplace settings. However, their severe difficulties become apparent in close relations, and their ability to commit to and enjoy a relationship is seriously disturbed, not least in relation to their ability to tolerate ambivalence, suffer tension and frustration, and rejoice in closeness and intimacy. Here they reveal their psychological vulnerability, which differs greatly from the neurotic patient's capacity for renouncing satisfaction of the drives. Naturally this also means that the therapeutic setting itself exposes the difficulties experienced by these people. I have chosen the word betweenity[1] to describe that which these patients find so difficult. I intend no intersubjective or interactive theoretical claim in using this word. Nor can my angle of approach to understanding borderline be said to exist within the referential framework of object-relations theory. In other words I do not emphasize the conceptual self–object couple; instead I highlight a form of entity which unfolds as an act of being in a relation between the self and an Other. It is this facet of being or entity to which these patients so eminently draw our attention; and it is this dimension which exposes their weakness. Instead of speaking of difficult or fragile patients it is better to speak of 'difficult *encounters* between analyst and analysand' (McDougall 1995: p. 238).

It has been my desire to exploit the connotative ambiguity that may be read into the term betweenity. On the one hand the word refers to something *between* people, the mutual wants and demands prerequisite to entering into any relation. On the other it contains a reference to a particular mode of being in the space between us, which is dimensioned in both space and time.[2]

In my interpretation of Winnicott and my use of the concept of betweenity I shall refer repeatedly to Sartre's philosophical argument that being is contingent on otherness.

Above all, borderline patients experience difficulties being in relationships. The betweenity of their close relations to others is often marred by grave and conflicting difficulties; at the same time it is extremely difficult for them to establish and maintain relations in a mutually satisfactory balance of give and take. In other words, they have problems being or living in a creative relationship to other people, i.e. in a relationship involving mutual enrichment through a meeting between an I and a you. When they venture into relations – and they do – these are emotionally tempestuous and challenging; marked by mutual accusations in an expression of defensive attempts to avert the threat represented by the Other.

It is in large part the difficulties I have experienced working as an analyst with borderline patients that have motivated me to summarize my experiences and attempt to clarify the psychic problematic that makes relational life so desperately unhappy for them.

The following is primarily intended as an attempt to describe my experiences in the company of these patients. In this chapter, where I introduce the concept of betweenity, the objective is to specify the way of relating to the Other – what Sartre termed being-for-Others – that characterizes borderline patients. In the following chapters I shall attempt to theoretically outline the psychological structure and dynamics of the borderline patient and tentatively answer the question of the source of their difficulties. I will also broach the issue of how to structure our analytic techniques in order to reach these patients, creating the relation they so desperately want yet simultaneously flee from with the most destructive of efforts.

Withdrawal and the fear of invasion

I have already emphasized the importance of maintaining that these people are not psychotic and therefore I find it irrelevant to discuss larval psychosis or any other term for non-manifest psychosis. Nor do I find the term 'fault'[3] to be particularly apt, preferring to understand the term as an expression of the observer's theoretical standpoint rather than as comprehensively indicative of the patients' psychological mode of functioning. However, vital functions are affected in borderline patients, meaning that they experience significant difficulties in some of the most important areas of life. Nevertheless, as previously indicated, they may appear to function reasonably well and to be intelligent and creative, as indeed they often are. With the exception of hospitalized borderline patients, this group is characteristic in that their madness is revealed only in close personal relations – not in the desperate and manipulative way in which the neurotic seeks to satisfy hidden desires, but by either desperate or indifferent ways of being in the presence of the Other, which render the meeting itself the stage of their suffering. This is no hidden or suppressed wish, but a form of disturbance expressed in the act of being with others, an act that is blind, or blinds itself to the Other. It is this blindness to one's own functioning that confronted Freud with the necessity of formulating a theory of defence beyond neurosis. Throughout his work we find disparate hints of defence mechanisms that I would term negating, since they all strive to negate a condition of reality that is unbearable to the ego, and a defence that involves the ego sacrificing its integrity to this endeavour. Freud termed these defence mechanisms disavowal (*Verleugnung*), foreclosure (*Verwerfung*) and negation (*Verneinung*).

Most descriptions of the mode of functioning of borderline patients have made it difficult to position these people both structurally and genetically. I am, as described in Chapter 3, convinced of the futility and reductive nature of attributing this aetiology to a particular developmental phase within what we term the pre-Oedipal field. Some of these patients display a distinctly narcissistic dimension, whereas in others, a primitive separation problematic dominates their mode of functioning – and they all display peculiar, observable mixtures of Oedipal and pre-Oedipal problematics. These people are not characterized by fear of castration, but by a fear springing from their central dilemma: 'The fear of separation from the object and the desire to penetrate into it and fuse with it into a primal unity can be so intense that it surpasses human understanding' (Rey 1994: p. 12). Human relations offer both the possibility of relief from their suffering and of fear, since they appear as a threat of invasion. As Guntrip (1983) has already described so succinctly, the schizoid patient is captive: demanding love, but prevented from loving because he fears the destructive force of his love vis-à-vis its object. He dares not love because he fears that it will mean destruction of the object. Any indication of an actual meeting, every revelation or opening towards the Other, will inevitably lead to momentary 'inclosing reserve' to use an apt word from Kierkegaard's description of this despair of the self.

Existential philosophy – the work of Heidegger, Sartre and Kierkegaard – offers a wealth of insightful descriptions of a pathology that in psychoanalytical and psychiatric literature has been described as a pathology of the self. In much twentieth-century literature we find similar literary expressions of a problematic of being which reflects the vulnerability revealed to us in our meeting with these patients for whom – to paraphrase Winnicott – hiding is a vital necessity and not being found is a catastrophe.

> You can hold yourself back from the sufferings of the world, this is something you are free to do and is in accord with your nature, but perhaps precisely this holding back is the only suffering that you might be able to avoid.
>
> (Franz Kafka, quoted in Laing 1990: p. 78)

As early as the 1950s and 1960s Ronald D. Laing was inspired by existentialist literature and philosophy to describe the fear of implosion, petrifaction, and depersonalisation that characterizes this group of patients. Being met with understanding, or simply being watched, Laing writes, is synonymous with annihilation.

> To be hated may be feared for other reasons, but to be hated as such is often less disturbing than to be destroyed, as it is felt, through being engulfed by love.
>
> (Laing 1990: p. 44)

In order to protect themselves against what they experience as destructive intrusion, these patients withdraw, or hide behind an objectification of the self or the Other.

We feel this withdrawal and the fear of invasion in transference, where patients often experience our words as threats that strip them of their existence. Words may disempower them to the extent that they no longer feel their own existence. Our well-meaning words can make them feel powerless or rather driven out of their own existence. Not only the words of others; a mere glance can impact their vulnerable existence to a point where they feel unbearably exposed. We rarely encounter a carefree, actively engaging gaze on opening the door to these patients, and for many the analyst's couch offers some protection, although conversely it can also render the absent gaze of the analyst frighteningly indeterminable.

Sartre captured the secret of this power that emanates from an existential meeting with the Other in a highly apt metaphor. The gaze of the Other reveals my own self – my self – in my vulnerability, 'that I am vulnerable, that I have a body which can be hurt, that I occupy a place and that I can not in any case escape from the space in which I am without defense . . .' (Sartre 1995 [1943]: p. 259).

The gaze of the Other, says Sartre, is a field of betweenity, where I refer from me to myself. This betweenity, where I become self-aware as myself, is not to be understood merely as seeing myself as the Other sees me. The gaze of the Other fastens me mercilessly in space as well as time. In therapy our borderline patients teach us how painful and anxiety-inducing, how shameful and escape-provoking the mere presence of the Other can be.

In more philosophical terms, the subjectivity of the Other entails a potential threat to my own. The threat lies in the fact that in the world of the Other I can become an object – with no life of my own, with no being for myself. In this form of anxiety any recognition of the subjectivity of the Other can be a self-destructive strategy. The joy and life-giving affirmation that characterizes a meeting with the gaze of the Other under normal conditions – and which is a prerequisite to the psychological survival of the infant – gives rise to persecutory anxiety for these patients, making it necessary for them to protect themselves by either shutting out the Other or shutting off themselves.

Franz Kafka depicted the vulnerability we all experience in consequence of the ubiquitous presence of the Other in several of his novels – particularly *The Trial* (1994 [1925]). The main character,

Joseph K – a respectable, conscientious citizen – as a consequence of legal prosecution, the grounds of which are never revealed, becomes entwined in hidden legal machinery, whose vast, branching network eventually encompasses his every move. In his blind, powerless struggle against what appears to be primitive, almost infantile logic, he capitulates – assuming the guilt he ultimately feels to be his own since he has simultaneously become estranged from himself.[4] From a psychoanalytical standpoint Kafka depicts the gaze of the Other, condensed into an alienating, primitive, sterile superego, knowing no way of escape. This is the internalization of the categorical moral imperative, described in Freud's terms as the turning of the drive against its own persona, so masterfully depicted in *The Trial*.

Kafka's literary world – like Sartre's philosophical reflections on being-for-Others – contains an uncanny (*unheimlich*) recognition of the ambivalence we see in borderline patients. As helpers we often experience ourselves as powerful tools in a reality that is unpredictable. One of my patients is extremely careful to ensure that we always understand things in exactly the same way. When her understanding coincides with mine, her world is secure, otherwise not only does the world become an unsafe place in which to exist, I become the frightening judge of both it and her.

It is the symbolic power of the gaze that launches many of these infinitely vulnerable people into their perpetual flight.

I have emphasized the fear of invasion as a distinctive trait of these patients. However, this is not as unambiguous as it might initially appear. For some, this fear masks its opposite; a wish to passively surrender completely to the Other, as if this capitulation could remove the anxiety of the threat that appears to be connected to insisting on one's own subjectivity: as if my subjectivity is the destruction of the Other, just as the subjectivity of the Other is the destruction of my own.

We also see this vulnerability of existence in a narcissistic effort to cancel the boundaries of the Other. This may happen through what Bion (1990a [1959]) called 'attacks on linking', which may assume a number of specific forms from absence and rejection of our interventions to misunderstandings and what are generally termed negative therapeutic reactions.

There is general agreement that borderline patients, like neurotics, retain an intact capacity for reality assessment, but they are no more neurotic than psychotic patients. They cannot choose to forsake the pleasure principle and immediate, absolute gratification. They live, as one of my patients expressed it, according to the principle: 'I only do what pleases me.' This is formulated either as a credo or as an emergency solution arising from impulsive and highly affective behaviour. Of course this does not mean that these patients lead lives of pleasure; quite the opposite, they are haunted by an inner pressure, constantly forcing them to act out tension-reducing behaviours. However, thanks to their intelligence, some of these patients are able to construct explanations that disarm the Other – in this case the analyst – and ultimately themselves. They live in a pattern of what Sartre (1995) termed bad faith, and which the patients often conceive of as the opposite, i.e. good faith. Winnicott (1990c) called this the false self and juxtaposed it with the true self. Winnicott's terms must not be misunderstood to the effect that the false self hides a core that we may term true. This falsity is more than an appearance – a veiling 'as-if' – which we should all strive to dispose of. Like Sartre he understands the false self or bad faith as a social necessity. However, when the distance between the unreflecting, spontaneous, and potentially creative self and learned 'as-if' behaviour grows too great and ultimately assumes the character of a sterile, stereotypical pattern, we may use the term 'as-if' personality (Deutsch 1986). We refer to these people as being ill at ease with themselves – simply because there is no ease to be found.

People with borderline structures are always in a state of flux. They lead a form of transitory existence (Kapadia 1998). They are always on their way to somewhere because they are always leaving. They flee contact as intensely as they seek it, because they are struck by a claustrophobic sense of being deprived of their freedom or feel annihilated by an evil inner image. As soon as they try to emancipate themselves, they are caught in an agoraphobic experience of disappearing into the void. Rey (1994) introduced the idea of a claustro-agoraphobic form of fear that becomes visible only in a phenomenological light.

To these patients, the gaze is a Medusa's head, to use Sartre's metaphor, whose petrifying effects impact either the self or the Other.

Borderline patients are in limbo – a suspended form of being – and because they do not accumulate experience in any actual sense, they are unable to learn from it. Bion (1988) emphasized the difference between evacuation, which consists of liberating oneself of tension and unpleasure and the modification of experience that requires tolerance as well as a certain degree of loss and discomfort as a prerequisite to the formation of thought and experience (Gammelgaard 1996).

Borderline patients are people who seek immediate gratification or better tension reduction. They cannot wait, have a hard time with silences and are generally trying to compress time and fill out any potential spaces. In short they have trouble being in and enjoying that condition of expectant waiting that enters into all transitions and intermediate spaces. Later I shall expand on the difficulties these people have in exploiting the creative possibilities of potential space. This does not mean that they lack creative ability. Quite the opposite, people with borderline personality structures count a considerable number of artists among their ranks, which indicates the necessity of distinguishing between the creative space in which they are able to function and the state of betweenity in which they find it difficult to thrive. Generally speaking, borderline patients rarely daydream, and when they do, their daydreams are characterized more by stereotypical, obsessive fantasies, than pleasure-seeking imaginings. They have a limited ability to use their imagination, or to use Winnicott's term, they are unable to make use of the transitional phenomena of potential space. This is also apparent in the fact that they cannot freely create and play with illusions in the space dividing one person from another, nor console themselves with illusions in times of absence, frustration and deferral of pleasure.

Another consequence of the sovereignty of the pleasure principle is the need to know that one is possessed of the good; or more precisely, to know with certainty that this is so by prerequisition (as opposed to by obtainment). These patients must reassure themselves that the good is already theirs, not merely present as an option, and they must do so at any price. For some this means that they prefer stealing to receiving, since receiving means acknowledging that the Other has something they want, which is far too risky an exposure of their own emptiness, arousing what Klein (1987a) and Rosenfeld (1990) term envy. Envy involves the desire to destroy the good insofar as it exists with the Other and not with oneself. Meanwhile, the problem is that the good in this magic or idealized meaning of the word is never good enough in the sense that it ensures permanent security. It is as though the good is never quite able to soften a dominating, useless, and destructively bad inner image. One of my patients expressed it quite specifically when she spontaneously and with great anxiety asked again and again how she could prevent the bad from gaining power, and whether I thought that the good was sufficiently strong to resist the force of all-overshadowing and all-dominating bad.

Feelings of gratitude do not arise. Gratitude is a result of being able to receive in the actual sense of the word, i.e. opening oneself to good coming from elsewhere. For some this is an unbearable exposure of their own powerlessness. The ability to receive and rejoice at gifts given by the Other requires a trust in good being given to one not by chance but by intent. As Balint expressed it, frustration is something to which these patients are intentionally subjected. 'Good things may happen by chance, but frustrations are unchallengeable proofs of evil and hostile sentiments in their environment' (Balint 1979: p. 19). This, he continues, is accepted at face value; such are the conditions of life and remarkably enough this is no cause for despair. I think this is also connected to the fact that despair presupposes a forward-oriented time perspective, which does not appear to exist in these patients, who live in the present, for better or for worse. A person dedicated to the pleasure principle can go to a great deal of trouble to achieve what from another perspective may appear to be nothing – and expend a great deal of energy on avoiding something that to us appears relatively less painful.

Absence

Living in the present may at first glance appear to be an existential enrichment. Being imprisoned in the temporal perspective of the moment may be the opposite. I think a highly significant explanation for the difficult lives led by borderline patients is that they cannot represent absence, but alternate between closeness and nothingness. In other words absence has no positive value but is entirely negative. This is specifically displayed in the fact that they have difficulty in being alone and in being alone with themselves, even in the presence of another person.

Absence, says Sartre (1995: p. 277), must – when we talk of being-for-Others – be distinguished from what we commonly understand by something simply not being present. If I cannot find my keys I will not term them absent, although I may say that they should be here or there. This is connected to the fact that material things are not attached to a locality as such. They are allotted a locality only through me. In human relations others are only absent in as much as they have to be defined as present in relation to me. I do not say of people who are distant and abstract to me that they are absent, rather I might say of my friend – who is usually present – that he is currently absent. Absence indicates a special bond between people – a bond for which closeness is a prerequisite. In a certain sense, absence specifies this closeness. For the same reason absence may feel like a particularly intense closeness, when we are able to fill the void of absence with sweet longing for a person who through his or her absence becomes close to us in a certain way, regardless of the actual distance dividing us. According to Sartre (1995: p. 279) this is because being-for-Others is not situated in relation to an empirically measurable locality. A literary expression hereof is found in 'Swann's Way' and the 'Guermantes Way' which in Proust's novel *Remembrance of Things Past* not only refer to the two paths the family took on their Saturday walks, but which to the narrator took on greater significance than mere geography. They became concepts with 'that cohesion, that unity which belong only to the figments of the mind' (Proust 1982: p. 147).

This is not the case for borderline patients. Winnicott has indicated that absence for these patients is often experienced as a regular void, a hole, a narcissistic wound from which they can only protect themselves by provoking desperation in the Other.

When Sartre so beautifully writes that '[t]he Other *looks* at me and as such he holds the secret of my being' and that 'the profound meaning of my being' must therefore be imprisoned in an absence, we as therapists must add that this life-affirming joy that lends the Other's gaze presence even in his or her absence is rarely felt by our borderline patients (Sartre 1995: p. 363). For them, absence is not a potentiality and a symbolized presence, but emptiness and death. In this kind of absence it becomes impossible to think of the Other. This is the picture in some cases. In others it appears that absence has become synonymous with the absence of an idealized Other. To use a Kleinian term the bad object permanently cathects psychological space, mobilizing permanent counter cathexis to prevent intrusion. The idealized good does not become available for symbolic representation but meets the person in what Lacan termed the real.

A female patient who continuously struggled with what she herself called 'the bad' and which I learned to understand as an experience of undifferentiated violence created through the mother's abuse as well as her own fight for survival, surprised me by recounting that her father, who had died many years ago, would collect her outside my door on a certain day (see page 81). This evasive, idealized, and only momentarily present good object had been unable to displace the bad object because this would mean the collapse of her psychological space. In other words, when the good object is not a stable inner figure, the bad may be preferable since it can after all function as a shield against total despair and emptiness.

Through our borderline patients we learn that absence is something other than emptiness or nothingness, and that conversely it may be associated with closeness. Under normal circumstances this is a potential creative opportunity, for only the absent can be reflected upon or symbolized. If, like this patient, one is not able to experience the absent as potential closeness, experiencing it instead purely as nothingness or as idealized absence created on the background of the diabolical presence of a continuously bad inner object, then thought is paralyzed. In this patient migraines and other pain symptoms localized to her head were presumably the specific physical expressions of her battles against a bad inner object that congested her psychological space.

In psychoanalytical thinking we have long been familiar with the significance of the object. Not until the work of Balint, Winnicott and Bion, however, did we acquire the concepts with which to reflect on the space and distance between subject and object. Balint has described different forms of relationships, which I will discuss shortly; Bion has elucidated relations; and Winnicott has shed light on the space between external and internal. In this connection I shall be particularly occupied with two of Winnicott's articles, where he deals with the significance of absence and the conditions for the subject's ability to acknowledge the Other as not-me. The first is about communicating and not communicating (Winnicott 1990b), the second about relating to and using an object (Winnicott 1971). Both are highly relevant for our theories on borderline and display a line of thinking that I find related to Sartre's thoughts on absence and the constitution of the Other.

Winnicott distinguishes between *relating to* the object, which he describes as a subjective object, and *using* the object, which presupposes that the object has become an objective object. The latter assumes that experiences of the absence of the object and of frustration have been of such a character as to have been thinkable, and that the absent has thus been symbolized. This experience creates the possibility of an ongoing, silent communication with a subjective object. Under normal circumstances, this silent communication is a significant part of our inner, strictly personal lives that we have no difficulty in upholding while carrying on an adapted (false) communication. Winnicott does not hesitate to call this silent communication sacred. It must be respected and often becomes evident in a therapeutic setting as a meaningful, creative silence. In the patients we are discussing here, protecting this silent communication may assume the shape of what Winnicott calls 'active non-communication' or 'negation of an active or reactive not-communicating' (Winnicott 1990b: p. 188). It is important to note that this negation of silence does not equal communication. Rather it is a veiling of the silence through a defensive form of communication. The patients are communicating but only to hide their true selves.

As I understand Winnicott, there is a precise connection between on the one hand the concepts of absence and active non-communication and on the other his idea of development from 'relating to' to 'utilizing' the object. In childhood development the child's negation – or in Winnicott's words, the destruction of the object – is requisite to its use. In order for the child to destroy the object, the object must be present and it must survive. What does this mean? Here, I think Sartre may be of assistance. It has been interesting for me to observe that Winnicott, in dealing with these difficult ideas concerning the necessity of destroying the object, carries on an indirect dialogue with philosophical thought.

> This change (from relating to usage) means that the subject destroys the object. From here it could be argued by an armchair philosopher that there is therefore no such thing in practice as the use of an object: if the object is external, then the object is destroyed by the subject. Should the philosopher come out of his chair and sit on the floor with his patient, however, he will find that there is an intermediate position.
>
> (Winnicott 1971: pp. 89–90)

Thus my reading of Winnicott is that the terms subject and object are insufficient. There is an area in-between, where this distinction is irrelevant. Secondly, Winnicott says that the child's use of the object involves its ability to move the object outside its own subjective control, and that this means destroying the object in fantasy. Sartre would not disagree, although he uses different terms. According to him, the Other is not significant to my being as an object. The Other is primarily significant to my being-for-myself. It is in being seen by an Other – and this of course can only emanate from another subjectivity – that my subjectivity is revealed. Sartre expresses this in the following paradoxical manner: 'the *Other's look* as the necessary condition of my objectivity is the destruction of all objectivity for me' (Sartre 1995: p. 269.) He continues in an argument that mirrors Winnicott's: for the Other to appear to me as otherness 'it is necessary above all that I be the one who is not the Other and it is in this very negation effected by me upon myself that I make myself be and that the Other arises as the Other' (Sartre 1995: p. 283).

In other words, according to Winnicott the creation of the Other and of being-for-Others requires the destruction of the object, and according to Sartre a negation of the me that is not the Other. I do not consider these statements contradictory. Like Winnicott, Sartre must mean that the object does not become objective until the separation between me and not-me can be accepted. According to Winnicott's line of thought this separation arises as a result of the imagined destruction of the object. This is precisely the process that appears to be incomplete in our borderline patients. Sartre writes:

> Consciousness must have to be itself and must spontaneously have to be this non-being, consciousness must freely disengage itself from the Other and wrench itself as a nothingness which is simply Other than the Other and thereby must be reunited in 'itself'. This very detachment which is the being of the For-itself, causes there to be an Other.
>
> (Sartre 1995: p. 283)

When we meet people through our psychoanalytical work to whom nothingness equals a threatening void or death, we may supplement the philosophical definition of being-for-Others with the experience that this presupposes the Other to be 'good-enough', to borrow an expression from Winnicott. Our borderline patients experience a particular difficulty in tolerating this negation that makes me something that is not another, and they frequently defend themselves by objectifying themselves or the Other.

As analysts we learn through these experiences how vulnerable is the process through which a child must pass; through which it experiences the necessary disillusionment or negation, as Sartre calls it, and gradually learns the joy of using other people in recognition of their difference from that which is me. We also experience the value of being able to enjoy the pleasure of silence – enclosed in one's own world – either in the company of another or alone.

This concludes my description of the specific ways in which borderline patients relate to others.

The logic of desperation and indifference

My experience in working with borderline patients has taught me to distinguish between two ways of creating relations. With terms borrowed from Green (1997b) I have previously referred to these as desperation and indifference, and distinguished them from the despair characteristic of neurotic patients (Gammelgaard 2000).

After working with these terms, I encountered in Michael Balint's book *The Basic Fault* (1979) a description of different ways of relating that I find reminiscent of what I had arrived at myself.[5] Balint's work constitutes one of the first attempts at describing analysands who function at what he termed the level of the basic fault. However, Balint was forced to discard the terminology of the classical neurotic model. His argument was that it turned out to be inapplicable to our understanding of the psychic problematic played out at the level of the basic fault. Like Winnicott, Balint combines a theoretical approach with a practical, unprejudiced attitude. Both manage to capture significant, distinct aspects concerning the functioning of these patients. Besides describing three psychological areas – equivalent to three levels of functioning which must be structurally distinguished: the level of creation, the level of the basic fault, and the Oedipal level – the book also contains a description of relational forms which Balint characterizes as different forms of cathexis. I recognize in these forms what I described as the logic of desperation and the logic of indifference. Balint distinguishes between the ocnophilic and philobatic structures of the world:

> In the ocnophilic world the primary cathexis, though mixed with a great deal of anxiety, seems to adhere to the emerging objects; these are felt to be safe and comforting while the spaces between them are threatening and horrid. In the philobatic world the objectless expanses retain the original primary cathexis and are experienced

> as safe and friendly, while the objects are felt as treacherous hazards.
>
> (Balint 1979: p. 68)

Both relational forms are an expression of a kind of basic fault and in short distinguish themselves in that the ocnophilic relation involves an over-cathexis of the object correspondent to my observation of the desperate clinging to the object. The philobatic patient, however, over-cathects his own self-function, which enables him to manage in a relatively self-sufficient world while protecting himself against what are perceived as dangerously deceitful objects.

Patients who live in the logic of desperation form very passionate and intense relations, but the object of their passion fills out the entire field, so that the space in-between disappears. The Other is entirely foregrounded and no actual interplay takes place. Rather, we are dealing with a parasitic clinging to the Other, who then assumes exaggerated proportions. All thought focuses on the doings of the Other and the individual is reduced in the shadow of this almighty, idealized inner image which then becomes vital to his or her life and well-being.

I have already referred several times to these tempestuous relations in the lives of borderline patients. In professional literature impulsive behaviour is referred to as one of the primary diagnostic signs of borderline pathology. The patients themselves often describe this as a tension-inducing strategy mounting to a kind of excess, where in an intense state of excitement they become angry and hateful and start shouting and criticizing. I understand this as a method of reducing anxiety but also as a way of feeling alive, although it is synonymous with losing oneself.

In some of these patients, who desperately seek dependence, transference has shown me how my presence becomes the guarantee that things exist and have value, i.e. that all is good. It may sound as though what remains is a relatively simple matter of affirming and supporting these patients in what is, and in what is good. But here we often encounter what I have termed a neither–nor logic, manifesting itself through the fact that affirmative interventions are not always experienced as supportive, but rather as the catastrophic consequences of an all-too-threatening unilateralism. One young female patient frequently reacts with horror at what is intended as a reality-affirming intervention, because she experiences my words as identical to things themselves, thus they turn into unshakeable realities. Words are no longer symbols that we can use as tools of thought; rather, according to Hanna Segal (1992), thinking takes on the character of 'symbolic equation', capable of actually calling forth the things it denotes. In order to understand why this is so anxiety provoking, it is important to add that only that which has already been written off or foreclosed by the psyche attains qualities characteristic of a reality beyond all control. Previously I mentioned an example of things that, once foreclosed, can return in the field of what Lacan termed the real. I will return to this in the following chapter, where I shall discuss Freud's concept of *Verwerfung* (foreclosure) and Lacan's interpretation of this defence mechanism. Hereby we may understand why evacuation becomes so necessary, and why processing or modification becomes something that requires the help of the analyst. For this particular female patient my help became a question – as she put it – of 'taking that away' which was characterized as unbearable. Anything may assume this character once it has been foreclosed from psychological reality and returns in the real, in the shape of book titles, statements on TV or radio, or newspaper headlines.

According to the logic of desperation a regressive dependence on an overly powerful inner object turns the relation to the Other into a question of either dominance or subjugation. The logic of indifference strives for the opposite: a de-cathexis of the object that henceforth appears of no value or significance. In this relational pattern the Other is the one left feeling desperate at his or her immutable insignificance. Sartre describes indifference as a defence against the look of the Other through choosing oneself as the one who is actively looking: 'This means that in my upsurge into the world, I can choose myself as looking at the Other's look and can build my subjectivity upon the collapse of the subjectivity of the Other' (Sartre 1995: p. 380).

In his discussion of bad faith, Sartre has shown that this may develop into actual cynicism. In my later discussion of Freud's concept of negation we shall see that this defence is linked to the death drive – hence its gruesome intentions in severely disturbed persons. In less serious cases, analytic sessions with such patients may involve the removal of our function as analysts: our own tools are turned against us and we are frequently rendered helpless.

Patients who live by the logic of indifference primarily have difficulty acknowledging feelings and recognizing significance. McDougall (1995) suggested the term 'disaffectation' as a denial of feelings as distinct from both neurotic and psychotic defence. The passions of hate and love stand on the same side of life, goes her argument. The true opposite of love is not hate, but indifference,[6] and such negation of one's own feelings results in a false self. McDougall terms these patients 'normopathic', which is to say that they display a form of pseudo-normality. Here relations are not desperately sought, but are used or exploited in order to prevent inner emptiness or bland sadness from becoming overwhelming. One young patient of mine apparently sought – with similar desperation – objects to fill the inner void. This search was not characterized, however, by a desire to merge with an idealized and overly powerful inner image; instead the object was reduced to a thing. In sadistic attacks the object was goaded and provoked into a form of excitement – which paradoxically enough served to calm him. In Winnicott's words he had developed an active non-communicative relation where his powerless self projected its narcissism onto an overly powerful object, which is then persecuted in endless, perverted, sexual provocations and teasing, taunting behaviours. His quest to protect his withdrawn self took place through these consistent attacks, especially against what felt like solicitude and offers of contact. Here we may observe a stereotypical objectification of that which is the most subjective in human relations: one person's attempt to understand the inner, subjective world of the Other.

The indifference we are dealing with here has nothing to do with the so-called *belle indifférence* we associate with hysterical patients. In the latter, indifference is a cover for the satisfaction of a secret wish through manipulation and seduction. Borderline patients, however, gain neither affirmation nor satisfaction, but are conversely further confirmed in their 'psychic retreat' (Steiner 1993). What is going on here is a tragic form of deception that reinforces itself in a vicious circle and which in its milder forms may be recognized as the narcissistic protective devices seen in ordinary life. It is a protective mechanism that presupposes a form of false omnipotence, but one so refined that it may deceive or even impress for a while. These are patients who are able to create relationships that require the active closeness of others and who have a sophisticated ability to copy the codes of respected and admirable social behaviour, but who adroitly manage to avoid any reciprocal involvement. They appear to be unassailably capable of being all and doing all for themselves, whereby they obtain the advantage of protecting their hidden selves. The deception may be carried through to such an extent that they expose their own faults in an appearance of self-examination and supreme honesty, merely to prevent others from doing so. This is the essence of Sartre's bad faith. Sartre illustrates this by referring to the person who deceptively terms himself a sincere person so brilliantly depicted in Camus' (1984 [1956]) *The Fall*: 'Who can not see that the sincere man constitutes himself as a thing in order to escape the condition of a thing by the same act of sincerity' (Sartre 1995: p. 65).

The patient I just mentioned may display a noticeable sincerity in describing his own behaviour as deceptive, lying, and deceitful, thus taking the sting out of what would be a harsh judgement were it formulated by another.

Sexuality and perversion

This description of borderline patients being-for-Others would be incomplete if we did not enter into their sexual problems. Sexual desire and its opposite, sexual repulsion, 'are fundamental structures of being-for-Others', writes Sartre (Sartre 1995: p. 383), thus repeating a fundamental thought already articulated by Freud. On this background it is strange that in today's clinical world we are presented with so few observations of sexual disturbance (Green 1995). Or perhaps we ought rather to say that sexual disturbances and perversions have been singled out as an area of specialization, receiving only peripheral attention in the work with, for example, personality disorders. In the case of both borderline and narcissistic disorders, descriptions have taken their point of departure in the ego – or rather the self –as well as in splitting, the dominant understanding of which has become a horizontal separation of self representations. The theory of drives has been toned down or disappeared entirely in favour of an object-relations and ego-psychological understanding of these personality disorders. One may, as I said, wonder at this, since sexuality is linked to being and thereby to the self that stands at the centre of many current theories on personality disorders. Sexuality and the classical theory of drives are absent from dominant views on personality disorders. I, however, am convinced that this aspect of personal life is just as important to borderline patients as it is to neurotics and normal people. In my experience the manifest sexuality of borderline patients veils secret imaginings which, like in other people, focus on questions concerning sexuality, and which in these patients – when we are permitted access – reveal a fantasy world reminiscent of the multitude of possible answers to these questions. Most people – including our patients – experience their sexual acts and choices of objects as ego-syntonic, even though others may consider them perverse. Of course, the fact that we no longer live with the sexual prohibitions of the prudish bourgeoisie from which Freud drew his clients has contributed to our acceptance of the manifold routes of sexuality. However, it would be misleading to think that our sexual lives have become more satisfying. Perhaps we are allowing ourselves to be deceived by a manifest form of sexual freedom and are overlooking that this may mask frustration and loneliness just as acute as that experienced by Freud's puritanically subjugated clients a century ago.

We have grown accustomed to thinking of psychoanalytic sexual theory as tantamount to the theory of phases, believing that satisfaction and pleasure can only take place when more primitive or fundamental needs have been met. Infant research and object-relations theory have underpinned this tendency to theoretically replace sexual instincts with a need for care and attachment. We forget that sexuality exists from the very beginning of life and that this was one of Freud's most radical realizations. Perhaps we have difficulty linking infantile modes of expression with sexuality (Zeuthen & Gammelgaard 2009). Borderline patients force us to assume that there is a phase where the id and the ego are still undifferentiated and where sexual and destructive impulses mix in the survival-oriented expressions of the early ego. Winnicott (1975b) aptly termed the love of the small child 'ruthless love'.

One of the psychoanalysts who has worked most systematically with the sexual functioning of borderline patients is Joyce McDougall (1995). Like Piera Aulagnier (2001), who worked with psychotic patients, McDougall has shown how the ego-functions of these patients become fragile because they are marked by attempts to solve the universal traumas of the soul: the existence of otherness, of gender difference, of generational differences, and of the ultimate loss, of death. Various perverse forms of eroticism may constitute attempts to seek the key to these great original mysteries.[7] For a number of years McDougall observed how archaic sexual theories and fantasies live underground in borderline patients and she emphasizes the innovative nature and colossal cathexes invested in what she calls neo-sexuality.[8] In order to distinguish between this and the reality distortion seen in psychotic patients McDougall speaks of a neo-reality (1995) which refers to the attempts of borderline patients to find solutions to their overwhelming frustrations by creating an illusory world based on their sexual constructions. This neo-sexuality often has a compulsive and pressing character which gives the impression that the sexual lives of these patients serve an addictive purpose. One of my patients is subject to a daily compulsion to seek and find release for sexual tensions; the sexual aim primarily consists in voyeuristically watching the sexual arousal he can induce in a preferably anonymous female partner. The ritualised compulsion and the ensuing emptiness or lack of actual satisfaction tells us something about how sexuality has become a potentially tension-reducing solution for people living with constant internal stress. These people do not have the option of satisfaction through daydreaming and have difficulty changing their ritualised scenarios, nor can they relate freely to their fantasies. Borderline patients force us to consider whether the concept of perverse fantasies is meaningful. Perversion is associated with action, not with fantasy, but does that mean that perversion is something that has avoided repression? Freud (1905) may have been of that opinion when he introduced the question of sexual deviations in *Three Essays on the Theory of Sexuality* and declared perversion to be the positive opposite of neurosis. In other words the pervert permits himself that which in normal and neurotic people only exists as repressed desire.

Perhaps it was the fact that perversion could not be entirely understood in light of the repressive mechanisms of neurosis that caused Freud to lose interest in the subject. At the time he was busy consolidating his theory of the apparatus of the psyche and understanding neurosis in this light.

Later in his work Freud resumed his interest in perversion, as he was obliged to examine neurosis and the entirely dominant role of repression in normal and pathological development. It was his study of fetishism (Freud 1927a) and psychosis that led to an examination of a form of defence that unlike repression targeted external reality rather than drives. In other words perversion and psychosis forced Freud to question his repressive model, acknowledging a mode of defence prior to repression.

In the following chapter I shall examine this development in psychoanalytic theory of a defence beyond neurosis, which I will follow up in Chapter 7 with a casuistic account underpinning the existence of a primitive defensive foreclosure in the particular workings of the special mechanisms of perversion and borderline pathology.

This concludes my discussion of McDougall's relevant contributions to an understanding of borderline and perversion.

McDougall appears to exploit an assumption of sexual development gleaned from Freud's *Three Essays on the Theory of Sexuality* (1905). Here we are presented with the important assumption that what we understand by psychosexuality is not a biological given but is developed. In other words, 'drive' is a concept located on the borderline between biology and psyche. Drives, Freud writes, arise in relation to (*Anlehnung an*) instincts. Independent sexual pleasure arises from the instinctual impulse for survival that attaches the child in complete dependency to the primary caregiver. This pleasure is underpinned by – yet at the same time distinct from – its instinctual foundations. The prototypical example is the baby nursing at its mother's breast, using its instinctual sucking reflex. From this manifestation of life we see the rise of an independent pleasure sucking, which does not have survival as its aim, but is instead auto-erotically centred on its own activity. It is important to note here that auto-eroticism is not a biologically original state. Rather we may say that it is psychologically original. In the displacement the child makes from the breast as a source of the satisfaction of hunger to a source of pleasure, the child creates a fantasy-image of the breast.[9] McDougall makes the point that borderline patients have been unable to make use of the fantasy object of the autoerotic phase. They are unable to connect agency and representation, or, in other words, to seek solace in autoerotic activity, since they lack an inner fantasy object. Where such an object ought to be, there is only emptiness or an absence of representation. Thus perversion becomes a substitute for autoeroticism and becomes a form of agency that presupposes an external Other since the Other is lacking as an internal representation.[10]

This clingy attachment prevents the individual from creating and possessing fantasy objects. The result is an inner absence of stable sexual relations and satisfactory loving relationships. This lack of inner objects leaves a void to be filled with sexually addictive solutions. We need to add the term 'neo-need' to the concept of neo-sexuality where the sexual object, partial object, or activity is used as a drug. The addictive object replaces the transitional object. Addictive objects are transitory rather than transitional. The sexual act is merely intended to discharge those affects that cannot be managed, repairing narcissistic affirmations of gender identity and deflecting infantile rage to prevent a backlash. It is a question of repairing the endangered or already-destroyed self, maintaining control at the cost of reciprocity and pleasure. I shall return later to McDougall and to a theory of perversion. First, as promised, I shall outline the basis of a theory beyond neurosis that may be derived from Freud's work.

Notes

1 See the preface for a discussion of the significance of the term I have coined in Danish, 'mellemværende', and the reasons for choosing 'betweenity' to translate it.
2 In my choice of the word betweenity I am also explicitly referring to Winnicott's intermediate and potential area as well as to the intermediate qualities of what continental philosophy has termed 'co-being' (Heidegger 2001 [1927]) and 'being-for-Others' (Sartre 1995 [1943]). German allows the possibility of distinguishing between the act of being and the entity that performs it (*Sein* and *Seiende*). This distinction is utilized by Heidegger, but is non-existent in English, which indiscriminately uses the term 'being'. My choice is not based on any philosophically founded standpoint vis-à-vis Heidegger's argument for *Mitsein* and *Mitdasein* as existentially constituting the act of being-in-the-world (Heidegger 2001: pp. 113–130) nor to Sartre's critique (Sartre 1995: pp. 244–254). Sartre's weighting of the conflictual aspects of relations and the ensuing consequences for the act of being do, however, appear to be closely related to a psychoanalytical line of thought. A psychoanalytic standpoint, which – like the one for which I am arguing – seeks to avoid polarization between self and object, sees the Other as a given prerequisite for my being, but my specific knowledge of the Other in me goes through a concrete other. This is the reasoning behind analytic relation.
3 This is a reference to Michael Balint's term 'the basic fault'. I shall try to account not for what these people lack, but for their manner of functioning.
4 Laplanche has introduced the thought-provoking idea that the superego is created in the same way as an internalized object, which is the result of perverse seduction. 'I have no doubt that a process related to intromission also has its role in the formation of the *superego*, a foreign body that cannot be metabolized' (Laplanche 1999: p.136).
5 In Chapter 10 I will be referring to the French analyst Jean-Bertrand

Pontalis and his description of two different types of borderline pathology; it could be inspired by Balint.

6 McDougall's 'disaffectation' is equivalent to what Green (1999) termed 'disobjectalisation'.

7 Stefano Bolognini (1994) drew attention to patients who eroticize transference through a form of perverted sexual defence, unlike the erotic transference described by Freud.

8 The prevalence of online chat is an illustration of the interdependence between the unfolding of this neo-sexuality and a virtual space – at once public and anonymous – that has become available as a screen on which to project sexual agency.

9 Theorists of object-relations and infancy researchers have critiqued Freud's idea of the infant as autoerotic and autistic. However, this criticism, as shown by Laplanche (1989), is based on a confusion of the primitive organism and the primitive psyche. The concept of *Anlehnung* – usually translated 'attachment' – is a significant factor in this misunderstanding. Freud uses this concept in two contexts: in his sexual theory – as previously mentioned – in relation to the rise of sexuality in *Anlehnung an* instinct, and in 'On Narcissism' (1914) in relation to an attachment pattern he called 'anaclitic'. The latter has meant that some have missed the important point inherent in the use of *Anlehnung* in *Three Essays on the Theory of Sexuality* (1905).

10 In recent years Botella & Botella (2005) have elaborated on the term autoerotic, distinguishing between primary and secondary autoeroticism (see Postscript).

6

Between neurosis and psychosis

Although Freud focused on neurosis through much of his literary and practical career, attempts at defining a non-neurotic form of pathology can be found scattered throughout his work.[1] He seems to be refraining, however, from unfolding the radical formulations he occasionally proposes about other ways of solving psychic conflicts than the one we know as the compromise formation of neurosis. It is almost as if he feared that pursuing a different track would lead him away from his work on neurosis, assigning it a peripheral position rather than letting it constitute the basis of psychoanalytic theory and technique. Presumably Freud had limited experience with psychotic patients, partly because he worked outside the psychiatric wards of the hospitals, and partly because – being in private practice – he gradually became able to select his patients in accordance with his interests and based on an assessment of which patient types would benefit from psychoanalytic treatment. He did not consider psychotic patients accessible to psychoanalysis. Yet Freud occasionally returned to considerations on the similarities and differences between neurosis and psychosis, and he devoted one of his five great case studies to the study of a paranoid psychotic based not on the treatment this patient received, but on the patient's autobiography. I shall return later to Freud's work on the autobiography of Senatspräsident Daniel Paul Schreber. Finally, it is also possible that Freud had a desire to wrest from psychiatry its monopoly on understanding psychosis.

Whatever the reason, Freud never developed a cohesive theory of psychosis and its adjacent pathological forms, instead merely leaving behind scattered fragments of an image of mechanisms and structures beyond neurosis. Thus an actual theory of psychosis must be extrapolated, which of course applies to an even greater extent to a theory of borderline pathology. Nevertheless I think it is possible to assemble a psychoanalytically based theory that may assist us in understanding borderline. This chapter will attempt to accomplish this.

Yet it is no easy task to put together a theory of non-neurotic pathology based on the writings of Freud. This is partly because, as previously mentioned, he was quite ambivalent in his understanding of psychosis, and partly because the development of his theory generally proceeds in leaps, frequently raising issues en route which remain uncorrected or are passed over in silence as he formulated new angles.

This means that there are choices to be made and coordinates to be plotted when interpreting Freud's writings, particularly when working on his sporadic and contradictory initial outlines of a theory of non-neurotic pathology. I have selected three areas of focus in my efforts to extract a theory of pathology positioned between neurosis and psychosis:

1 The first area of focus concerns different types of defences in neurosis and psychosis. I consistently indicate the existence of mechanisms besides repression which effectuate defences entirely different from those of neurosis.
2 The second concerns the relationship to reality. Freud's discourse on the difference between neurosis and psychosis concentrated chiefly on their different relationships to external reality. This is particularly evident in his two 1924 essays dealing explicitly with these two diagnostic groups. Thus he raised issues which still characterize the debate within the field of dynamic psychoanalysis. The chief distinction between these two types concerns precisely the relationship to external reality. Neurotic mechanisms are concentrated in the attempts of the ego to find solutions to opposing psychic impulses while paying due attention to external reality, whereas the suspension of regard for reality is emphasized as a characteristic trait of psychosis. As will become evident below, it is doubtful not only whether this is an adequate exposition of the difference between neurosis and psychosis, but also whether it is a correct rendition of Freud's view on the issue.
3 The final area of focus relates to the splitting mechanism of the

> ego. As previously mentioned, there has been a dominant tendency – particularly among those inspired by Kleinian or ego psychology – to consider splitting as the dominant defence mechanism of borderline pathology. However, a thorough examination of Freud's concept of a splitting of the ego (*Ichspaltung*) reveals that we are dealing with an entirely different mechanism than that of more recent psychoanalytic theory.

Naturally, there is an intimate connection between these three areas. The separate examinations of each area have served a purely heuristic purpose. It is my hope that they will permit me to bring together various threads and present a number of theoretical standpoints on a pathology we position between neurosis and psychosis.

The ego and its defences

In the early 1890s – prior to completing his work on the theory of repression – Freud proposed that different psychic illnesses were the expression of the inexpedient and morbid defences of the ego. He regrouped various clinical units such as hysterias, phobias, obsessive neuroses, and certain hallucinatory psychoses, which were all attributable to a particular form of failure in the defence functions of the ego. Thus, regardless of whether we are dealing with neurosis or psychosis, we face the inability of the ego to defend itself. Regarding neurosis, Freud was convinced even at this early stage that this failure derives from the fact that the danger is not exterior in character, but surprises the sufferer from within, thus rendering ordinary defence mechanisms useless. In the final analysis, this threat from within is constituted by sexuality and sexual impulses, which the defences tentatively target. Thus neurotic symptoms constitute a compromise that accommodates the defence mechanism even as it reveals its failure. On this basis, it is easy to imagine that certain forms of psychosis might also be understood as an expression of conflict as well as a defence against sexual impulses, and, as we shall see, Freud never entirely abandoned this viewpoint.

During this same period, however, Freud learned of an entirely different type of defence, aimed at the exterior world rather than against inner impulses, and that this type of defence had far more radical implications for psychic balance than those encountered in neurotic patients.

> There is, however, a much more energetic and successful kind of defence. Here, the ego rejects [*verwirft*] the incompatible idea together with its affect and behaves as if the idea had never occurred to the ego at all.
>
> (Freud 1894: p. 58)

A little further on in the same text, he adds:

> The ego breaks away from the incompatible idea; but the latter is inseparably connected with a piece of reality, so that, in so far as the ego achieves this result, it, too, has detached itself wholly or in part from reality.
>
> (Freud 1894: p. 59)

As described above, psychotic defence is not so much constituted by a weakening of unacceptable ideas, but in a radical and definitive separation of ego and idea. The ego forecloses the idea and with it that fragment of reality which is too threatening to be integrated. Psychotic defence lacks the supple character of neurosis. It is more promptly effectuated, with the result that the ego is thrown into a state of hallucinatory psychosis.

In this early text, Freud formulated the first inklings of a defence type which is quite radically different from repression. This defence targets external rather than internal reality, which has far more disturbing implications for the ego than those resulting from neurotic defence. Although Freud did not gather the threads in this manner, he considered these issues from various angles.

I believe, however, that we may observe this process in borderline patients without a concomitant fully developed hallucinatory psychosis. What constitutes a continuous anxiety-inducing problem for these patients may be simply described as a failure in the function of judgement. Not that they misjudge reality. We are not dealing with a failure to perceive reality, but with a failure in that function which permits us to distinguish internal impulses from the perception of external reality. The consequent unclear, anxiety-ridden experience of reality becomes threatening because – in a sense – it is infected with the anxious ideas of the sufferer, which cannot be repressed, and are thus foreclosed. At the same time normal judgement is impaired during this process. Thus these patients can be said to exist in the dreamland of nightmares.[2] I shall return later to the so-called failure of reality testing in borderline patients and proceed with my discourse on the defences of the ego.

We have already found that while neurosis is based on repression – regardless of the fact that Freud at this point has yet to introduce this term – psychotic defence consists of a type of defence which Freud early on termed foreclosure[3] (*Verwerfung*), where objectionable ideas are foreclosed together with a part of the reality to which they are linked. However, Freud has used the term foreclosure (*Verwerfung*) quite loosely and occasionally synonymously with the term suspension (*Aufhebung*) or disavowal (*Verleugnung*). Foreclosure gradually gained more defined and systematic meanings, and was used most explicitly in the case of the Wolf Man, while disavowal seems to take the foreground in that from 1924 onwards Freud associated this defence specifically with the fear of castration and in 1927 with fetishism. It is largely due to Lacan that the term foreclosure has become associated with the specific defences of psychosis. Lacan based his interpretation of repudiation on the story of the Wolf Man and Freud's little essay on negation. I shall return later to Lacan and foreclosure and in my concluding discussion I shall link it to the defence which Freud referred to as negation.

As early as his correspondence with Fliess and in the 1894 paper 'The Neuro-Psychoses of Defence', quoted above, Freud refers to psychotic defence as foreclosure (*Verwerfung*). However, once the term repression is introduced, foreclosure is, so to speak, absorbed by the concept of projection, which – not least in the study of Schreber – becomes the mechanism above all others to define psychotic defence. Therefore let us begin by examining projection and paranoia.

Projection and paranoia

Freud's use of the term projection, however, is not unambiguous. Firstly, he acknowledges that projection contains common psychological processes on which he does not wish to comment.

> Having thus been made aware that more general psychological problems are involved in the question of the nature of projection,

> let us make up our minds to postpone the investigation of it (and with it that of the mechanism of paranoic symptom-formation in general) until some other occasion.
>
> (Freud 1911a: p. 66)

However, Freud never published the promised study. Secondly, there is a certain ambiguity in Freud's use of the term projection since – as in the case of the Schreber analysis – he links the term to paranoid defence. Freud appears to meander between one point of view which links projection to paranoid psychotic defence, and another which organizes projection under the mechanisms we know from neurotic compromise formation.

Freud deals with paranoid defence as early as his correspondence with Fliess and even more explicitly in 'Further Remarks on the Neuro-Psychoses of Defence' (1896). In both cases he denotes projection as a primary defence whose nature may be comparable to repression, which is in play in the neurotic defence.

> For a considerable time I have harboured a suspicion that paranoia, too . . . is a psychosis of defence; that is to say, that, like hysteria and obsessions, it proceeds from the repression of distressing memories and that its symptoms are determined in their form by the content of what has been repressed.
>
> (Freud 1896: pp. 174–175)

Freud continues his investigation, specifying the mechanism by which repression takes place in the case of paranoia, analogous to the conversion mechanism of hysterical neurosis and the replacement mechanism of obsessional neurosis. In the latter the primary defence consists of a repression to the unconscious of the entire pathogenic memory and its displacement to a primary defensive symptom in the form of *self-doubt*. Paranoia works in principally the same manner: repression is being implemented, but here it takes on the form of projection and the defensive symptom in this case becomes the *mistrust of others*. Thus we are presented with an explanation of paranoid psychosis not unlike the one Freud had already developed on neurosis. While Freud studied projection during the early part of his career from the angle of paranoid defence, his later work links the concept of projection closely to neurotic symptom formation. The Rat Man is a clear example of this:

> In this disorder, as I have already explained . . . repression is effected not by means of amnesia but by a severance of causal connections brought about by withdrawal of affect. These repressed connections appear to persist in some kind of shadowy form (which I have elsewhere compared to an endopsychic perception) *and they are thus transferred, by a process of projection, into the external world, where they bear witness to what has been effaced from consciousness.*
>
> (Freud 1909: pp. 231–232; emphasis added)

There are three issues concerning the phenomenon of projection on which I cannot go into any detail, but on which I feel I must comment. Firstly, we may conclude that paranoia represents a particular form of repression. The question, however, is whether there is an identity between projection and repression. As we shall see in Freud's study of Schreber's paranoia, it became necessary in this case to distinguish explicitly between the process of repression and the process of symptom formation, and projection was henceforth associated with the latter.

Secondly, hallucinatory symptoms affect the ego in a more serious manner than do neurotic symptoms. This is because paranoid defences do not feature the subsequent, secondary defence characteristic of neurosis: 'no defence can avail against the returning symptoms [the symptoms of the return of the repressed] to which as we know, belief is attached' (Freud 1896: p. 185). This means that the ego is not subsequently obliged to modify its delusions, but must submit to them and thus alter itself. Here we see the first intimations of that encroachment on the organization of the ego entailed in psychotic defence which was later to become the subject of independent study by Freud.

Thirdly, it should be noted that projection is not merely constituted by the perceiving subject positioning something outside him- or herself. Projected delusions or hallucinations are additionally determined by structural factors originating in the context in which they were formed.[4] Even in these early works Freud ascribes a certain historical truth to hallucination and delusion. Both contain repressed childhood experiences and may thus be understood as symptoms of the return of the repressed. As late as 1937, Freud returned to the idea of the historical truth of delusions in the essay 'Constructions in Analysis' (1937b), claiming that they are of a similar character as the constructions we use to articulate themes in the psychic reality of the patient. Like all psychic realities, projections adhere to certain structures within external reality.[5] As we shall see, the Schreber thesis ascribed to projection a role quite different from the one we encounter in earlier writings. Projection was no longer considered from the angle of repression and thus was not attributed any primary defence characteristics.

In his interpretation of Schreber's paranoia, Freud emphasized his homosexual tendencies. The notion of homosexuality, however, was so repellent to Schreber that it was denied access to his consciousness. Yet we are not dealing with repression to the unconscious, but with a multifaceted process. Partly a reversal into the opposite is taking place, and partly the idea of an external reality is being displaced or projected. In the description of this process Freud was obliged to distinguish between the processes of repression and the formation of symptoms, placing the projective element within the latter. Internal perception is repressed and as a replacement its contents – having undergone some distortion – enter consciousness as external perception. In persecution mania the distortion consists of an affective transformation; that which should have been felt as love from within is perceived as hatred from without.

This is also the case study in which Freud revisited his previous formulation of the mechanism of foreclosure: 'It was incorrect to say that the perception which was suppressed internally is projected outwards, the truth is rather, as we now see, that what was abolished internally [*das innerlich Aufgehobene*] returns from without' (Freud 1911a: p. 71). Here there appears to be some ambiguity; in the psychotic form of projection we are not only dealing with – as previously suggested – something being displaced into external reality. Simultaneously an internal abolition is taking place which is so radical that it raises the question of whether it has ever been lived through.

This insight poses a serious challenge to the model of neurosis. We must henceforth ask ourselves how we are to understand this mechanism, which is thus not repression but actually an abolition or removal of something internal which we subsequently encounter as if it came from the outside. Are we dealing with an illusion and thus with a misrecognition, or is this an actual annihilation in the sense of negation or non-existence? This difference can also be expressed as the distinction between not wanting to know and not wanting to be (Laplanche & Pontalis 1988).

These doubts can only be addressed by drawing on Freud's later works. I refer specifically to the case study of the Wolf Man (1918) and the essay on negation (1925a). In the former Freud continues his work on the idea of foreclosure, and in the latter he connects foreclosure to repression.

Freud's case study of the Wolf Man provides us with the most convincing demonstration of that defence mechanism which Lacan termed foreclosure as a translation of Freud's term *Verwerfung*. It should be noted that while Freud refers more loosely to disavowal as well as foreclosure, Lacan's term is formed with a particular view to psychotic defence. Furthermore, in this context it is important to note that the Wolf Man is not Schreber; in other words, the Wolf Man is not psychotic but is presumably a unique example among Freud's case studies of what we would now term a borderline patient. Let us therefore examine what Freud thought of the little Wolf Man's attempts at resolving a particular psychic conflict. In his analysis of the Wolf Man's childhood phobia Freud suggests in quite unambiguous terms that it may be understood and interpreted as an expression of the Oedipal conflict at whose nucleus lies the fear of castration. The argument runs that in maintaining his original theory of the anal opening as the location of the sexual act, the boy has resisted the notion of castration.

> What he had learned in the meantime, the allusions which he had heard to castration, awoke and cast a doubt on the 'cloacal theory'; they brought to his notice the difference between the sexes and the sexual part played by women. In this contingency he behaved as children in general behave when they are give an unwished-for piece of information – whether sexual or of any other kind. He rejected [*verwarf*] what was new (in our case from motives connected with his fear of castration) and clung fast to what was old. [. . .] That it should have been possible from that time onwards for a fear of castration to exist side by side with an identification with women by means of the bowel admittedly involved a contradiction. But it was only a logical contradiction – which is not saying much. On the contrary the whole process is characteristic of the way in which the unconscious works.
>
> (Freud 1918: p. 79)

The reader may sense that Freud is not really able to decide whether to refer to foreclosure (*Verwerfung*) as radically different from repression. On the one hand, he hints that foreclosure is something other than repression. On the other, we see that the two opposing viewpoints or infantile sexual theories remain separated from one another through an act of repression.

Elsewhere, however, we are presented with a grave consequence of what Freud somewhat hesitatingly refers to as foreclosure:

> He rejected [*verwarf*] [castration], and held to his theory of intercourse by the anus. When I speak of his having rejected it [*das er sie verwarf*], the first meaning of the phrase is that he would have nothing to do with it, in the sense of having repressed it. This really involved no judgement upon the question of its existence, but it was the same as if it did not exist. Such an attitude, however, could not have been his final one, even at the time of his infantile neurosis.
>
> (Freud 1918: p. 84)

Freud subsequently reached the final conclusion as to the existence of:

> two contrary currents side by side, of which one abominated the idea of castration, while the other was prepared to accept it and console itself with femininity as a compensation. But beyond any doubt a third current, the oldest and deepest which did not as yet even raise the question of the reality of castration was still capable of coming into activity.
>
> (Freud 1918: p. 85)

Freud is clearly tracing a defence mechanism which is not identical to repression, characterized by the suspension of an idea in order to negate its value. It ceases to exist, so to speak. There is an idea of a form of suspension of something, in the sense of a judgement on the existence of reality of this something. This idea has guided my study of a particular defence mechanism in borderline patients.[6]

Lacan's argumentation for this type of defence mechanism – which he interprets as specifically psychotic – relates to an episode in the Wolf Man's past to which I have not yet referred. However, since it will be significant for later considerations, I shall here present Lacan's reasoning, thus adding his contribution to the understanding of negating defence mechanisms.

Foreclosure

Lacan's formulation of the mechanism of foreclosure centres on the negative hallucination of a severed finger. The Wolf Man told the story as follows:

> When I was five years old, I was playing in the garden near my nurse, and was carving with my pocket-knife in the bark of one of the walnut-trees that come into my dream as well. Suddenly to my unspeakable terror, I noticed that I had cut through the little finger of my (right or left?) hand, so that it was only hanging on by its skin. I felt no pain, but great fear. I did not venture to say anything to my nurse, who was only a few paces distant, but I sank down on the nearest seat and sat there incapable of casting another glance at my finger. At last I calmed down, took a look at the finger, and saw that it was entirely uninjured.
>
> (Freud 1918: p. 85)

In this case, says Lacan, it would be insufficient to refer to disavowal or negation. The latter presupposes previous affirmation, which exists neither in psychosis nor in this case of the severed finger.

Lacan (1988) suggests linking foreclosure to the two judgements which Freud (1925a) termed judgement of attribution and judgement of existence. For Lacan all later judgement is a tripartite distinction consisting of an original judgement of attribution, i.e. the universal assignment of a penis to all people; a subsequent judgement of existence, confirming particular absence, i.e. that there is at least one person – the mother – who does not have a penis; and finally the actual fact of lack. The symbolic dimension referred to by Lacan contains these three parts (Nasio 2001).

In the case of the Wolf Man, the argument runs that we must understand the foreclosure Freud refers to as 'non-confirmation'. This cannot be considered to equal negation, which always presupposes pre-existing affirmation, and it is precisely this primary affirmation which does not take place in psychosis.

> In a general way, in fact, the condition such that something exists for a subject is that there be *Bejahung* . . . What happens when this

> *Bejahung* doesn't happen, in such a way that nothing appears in the symbolic register?
>
> (Lacan 1988: p. 58)

In the case of the Wolf Man there was no such primary affirmation, i.e. no realization of the genital level; no trace of it in the symbolic register. The only trace we have is not presented as a historical phenomenon. Conversely it appears as a reality in the external world, a hallucination – in the form of the damaged finger. The existence of castration – which the Wolf Man has foreclosed – reappears in an imaginable form, creating such anxiety in him that he does not even dare mention it. The unmentionable becomes contemporary reality in that the nanny, who is nearby at the time, ceases to exist. The child is left terrified – without a voice – and the speech that has failed to surface within the symbolic register is transformed into hallucinatory reality (Nasio 2001).

Here we are dealing with a particular characteristic of psychosis, in the sense that clearly distinguishes it from neurosis. While in neurosis the repressed and its return are both symbolic in character, this cannot be said of that which is foreclosed in psychosis. Repression features the return of representation in a manner where its symbolic nature is retained and as such just as integrated within the ego as the representation that has been repressed. The return of what has been foreclosed is qualitatively marked in its difference by the mechanism of foreclosure. Not only do the sudden hallucinatory images of the severed little finger lack the symbolic properties of representation, but they are furthermore:

> seized by the I without affect and perceived with the clarity of an undeniable reality which would be foreign to it . . . in neurosis, the repressed and the return of the repressed are homogenous, whereas in psychosis, that which has been foreclosed and its return are heterogeneous.[7]
>
> (Nasio 2001: p. 261; translated from French by KM)

In other words foreclosure has severed the ties between the whole and the particular, or between the judgement of affirmation and the judgement of existence.

Laplanche and Pontalis (1988) formulate foreclosure as a non-symbolization of that which should be symbolized: castration.

In the Schreber case Freud corrected his ideas on the projective process and we understand that at the time, in speculating on the concept of projection, Freud was seeking to approach a defence that could not be compared to repression by considering the concept of projection. It was incorrect to say that perception – internally repressed – was externally projected. Instead, the truth, as we saw it, is 'that what was abolished internally returns from without' (Freud 1911a: p. 71). With Lacan's assistance we can reword this and say that what has been foreclosed from the symbolic reappears in the real.

In certain texts Lacan lets foreclosure be the suspension of the whole which he refers to as primary confirmation or the fundamental judgement of attribution defined by the myth of the universality of the penis. This means that the child is not even confronted with the Oedipal dilemma; as if the child has not had the opportunity to live though the myth's first illusion of the universality of the penis.

In one of his later works Lacan (2002) integrates foreclosure into his theory of language and claims that the name of the father is what is subjected to foreclosure. The result is a 'mere hole' in the Other, the symbolic order 'which, by the inadequacy of the metaphoric effect will provoke a corresponding hole at the place of the phallic signification' (Lacan 2002: p. 222). The result for such a person may be that he or she is capable of relating to certain others in spite of the fact that the relation to the Other or the symbolic order has been disturbed by a form of anomaly which has been termed 'partial delusion' (Lacan 2002: p. 237) for want of a better word. Thus I understand Lacan to indicate that when experiences cannot be fitted into the symbolic order, firstly a hole arises in this order. There is nothing where a symbol should be. Secondly, in order to suspend the effect of this hole, a linking occurs of signifier and signified, which manifests as delusions and linguistic disturbances.

> If the process of foreclusion is borne out, that is to say, if the Name of the Father does not appear where it was expected, the psychotic patient consequently experiences a series of modifications of the symbolic elements which disrupts their bearings in time and space and in particular affect representations of filiation.[8]
>
> (Nasio 2001: p. 270; translated from French by KM)

It is one of Lacan's great achievements to have developed Freud's concept of foreclosure and not least to have utilized it together with the judgement function. However, I believe it is wrong to limit foreclosure to psychoses and to interpret the Wolf Man and negative hallucinations as psychotic. We observe similar negative hallucinations in many of our borderline patients, and we encounter not least the mechanism of foreclosure as a form of rift which cuts deeply into the essence of the ego-functions of these patients. I shall attempt to demonstrate this in the following chapter. For now, however, we are attempting to develop a theoretical understanding of a type of defence which – unlike neurosis – relates to reality and the function of judgement, which makes it possible to determine the nature and existence of the external world. As part of such a theoretical explanation, we shall examine the relationship with reality more closely. Let me therefore turn to the next area of investigation, which deals precisely with the psychic apparatus and its relationship to external reality. Only then can we return to that splitting mechanism which Freud linked to negation and intellectual judgement.

The issue of reality stands at the centre of the two essays where Freud explicitly deals with the relationship between neurosis and psychosis and achieves a particular significance through the defence mechanism he termed negation, and which he links closely to the perception of phenomena within reality.

The ego and external reality

Throughout his career, Freud pondered the nature of the relation of the subject to external reality. In 1911 he formulated a metapsychological answer to this question, returning once again to the issue as late as 1938. Freud's answer to the question, however, is far more ambiguous than one might surmise from ensuing theories on psychosis that define psychosis as the loss of reality resulting from the ego's failing reality testing.[9]

Although Freud confirms this loss of reality in the two essays on neurosis and psychosis, it is generally overlooked that the problem does not lie in the reality that has been lost, but rather in the one created to replace it. In other words: a theory of psychosis must be able to explain the particular formation of hallucinations and delusion. I shall return to this later.

Freud's comparison of neurosis and psychosis took a decisive turn around 1920. At this point the idea of the ego and its unconscious functioning culminated and the previous topographic model was replaced by a structural one. In his treatise on narcissism, whose theme was foreshadowed as early as in the Schreber analysis, Freud realized that ego drives and sexual drives do not stand in opposition to one another. Similarly, clinical observations of the phenomenon of repetition obliged him to question the sovereign power of the pleasure principle. Freud took note of the oppositions inherent in the theory and tried to reshuffle the deck. This was significant not least for the idea of the ego on which Freud had theorized already in 'Project for a Scientific Psychology'; indeed in contemporary clinical writings he assigned it decisive importance vis-à-vis the development of psychopathology.

With his introduction of the theory of drive and fantasy, the ego was toned down and, as previously mentioned, the introduction of narcissism (Freud 1914) turned out to foreshadow a restructuring of the model of the psychic apparatus, which did not find its final form until the metapsychological writings of the 1920s, namely 'The Ego and the Id' (1923a), 'Beyond the Pleasure Principle' (1920) and *Inhibitions, Symptoms and Anxiety* (1926). The new theory of the psychic apparatus concentrated the neurosis–psychosis issue around the role of the ego vis-à-vis the id and reality. The argument runs that in neurosis, the ego-functions at a level close to reality, obeying the requirements of the superego, and abandoning the satisfaction of drive impulses, while psychosis leads to a break between the ego and reality, which the ego then leaves to the id. In a subsequent process the ego creates a new reality to match the wishes of the id.

Freud expresses elsewhere – namely in the essay 'Fetishism' (1927a) – that the model of psychosis which may be extrapolated from these two texts and which approaches psychosis to neurosis is in fact overly simple. In short, Freud's understanding can be summarized in the following brief passage: 'Transference neuroses correspond to a conflict between the ego and the id . . . and psychoses, to one between the ego and the external world' (Freud 1924b: p. 152). Freud's own comment to this assumption is that one must be suspicious of such a simple understanding, and that it presumably applies only as a rough approximation, although he does himself add that this would indeed be something.

I read Freud's attempts at returning to the question of diagnostic groupings in the 1920s after paying them little attention in the interim period as a desire once again to defend the neurotic model after the introduction of the structural model. Freud does not appear to have all that much to say. I shall adhere, however, to the concept of external reality to which Freud attributed a kind of agency in line with that of the psychic apparatus. What are we to think of such a reality, and its significance for the defences utilized within non-neurotic psychopathology?

In order to begin approaching a possible solution it should be noted that while Freud may have been busy defending his theory of neurosis vis-à-vis psychosis, there is another comparison with which he was equally preoccupied: the relationship between neurosis and perversion, which is where we find a closer specification of a defence mechanism – namely disavowal.

Neurosis and perversion

In his essay 'The Loss of Reality Involved in Neurosis and Psychosis' (1924a) Freud once again picks up the theme of defence beyond repression and suggests that the psychotic reaction consists in a disavowal of reality: 'Neurosis does not disavow [*verleugnet*] reality, it only ignores it; psychosis disavows [*verleugnet*] it and tries to replace it' (Freud 1924a: p. 185).

Unlike repression, the word disavowal does not designate an attempt to oppose something coming from within but refers to a desire to ignore information arising through perception, nor does Freud associate disavowal with just any observation. Where Freud speaks of either disavowal (*Verleugnung*) or foreclosure (*Verwerfung*), he is always referring to observation of gender differences. In his essays 'Fetishism' (1927a) and 'The Infantile Genital Organization' (1923b) it is apparent that it is the child's observation of gender differences which provoke this particular disavowal of reality:

> We know how children react to their first impressions of the absence of a penis. They disavow the fact and believe that they *do* see a penis, all the same. They gloss over the contradiction between observation and preconception by telling themselves that the penis is still small and will grow bigger presently; and they then slowly come to the

emotionally significant conclusion that after all the penis had at least been there before and had been taken away afterwards.

(Freud 1923b: pp. 143–144)

Freud resumed this argument in 'Some Psychical Consequences of the Anatomical Distinction between the Sexes' since he uses the term disavowal in this context also (Freud 1925b: p. 252) when talking about the little boy's first reaction to observing the girl's genitals.

In 'Fetishism' Freud introduced the concept of scotomization, gleaned from an idea originating from Laforgue: 'The boy "scotomizes" his perception of the woman's lack of a penis' (Freud 1927a: p. 153). However, he argues here that there is no need for a new term since nothing new is being said and concludes that repression is one of the oldest terms in psychoanalysis and that is all we are dealing with here. Yet as if this were not the whole truth after all, he adds that one might reserve the term repression for the affect and refer to disavowal when it comes to the idea. Thus Freud reasons that scotomization refers to an observation that is erased almost as if it fell on a blind spot. The observation itself, however, remains but an energetic reaction ensures that it is consistently disavowed. The child has at once preserved and abandoned the observation, and these conflicting tendencies are what give rise to the fetish symptom. This is beginning to sound like the model of conflict familiar from neurosis; a repetition of the argumentation from the story of the Wolf Man. It is as if Freud struggled to articulate something unfamiliar, and doubted whether he would be obliged to introduce new terminology or whether he would be able to organize perversion under the neurosis model just as he wished to arrange psychosis under psychosexual development centring on the pivotal Oedipal theme.

We might justify this reading of Freud on a strictly semantic level. From the first introduction of the term foreclosure (*Verwerfung*) in his 1894 essay 'The Neuro-Psychoses of Defence' to that of 'Fetishism' from 1927 we notice that the concept of disavowal has gradually replaced that of foreclosure, as if the latter were far too radical for a theory built in principle on the idea of the neurotic defence of repression.

Thus in 'Fetishism', Freud returns once more to the question of the difference between neurosis and psychosis, yet he pulls back, claiming that the difference may not, after all, be as radical as he had assumed in his two 1924 essays. Learning from the study of fetishism, he was able to conclude that it was apparently possible to disavow a segment of reality without becoming psychotic, and that in the case of fetishism it is possible for two oppositional tendencies to co-exist. 'Returning to my description of fetishism, I may say that there are many and weighty additional proofs of the divided attitude of fetishists to the question of castration of women' (Freud 1927a: p. 156).

In *An Outline of Psycho-Analysis* Freud (1938b) returned once again to a discussion of the splitting of the ego. He affirmed that 'it would be incorrect to describe the process when a fetish is constructed as a splitting of the ego; it is a compromise formed with the help of displacement, such that we have been familiar with in dreams' (Freud 1938b: p. 203). Once again the neurosis model is emphasized. Yet Freud does make an admission in that he refers to the fact that the fear of castration is not limited to fetishists, but plays the same role in those who have not developed fetishism. In order to explain the particular defence of fetishism Freud once again refers to a splitting between two tendencies, which he observed in the Wolf Man. On the one hand there is a disavowal of the fact of perception – that the female genitals have no penis. On the other hand the child recognizes that females do not have penises and draws the correct conclusions from the fact. The consequence is that two contrary attitudes exist throughout life without influencing one another. And this, Freud adds, constitutes what we may call a splitting of the ego. Fetishism is not the only case of such splitting; it merely provides a particularly suitable case study. On this basis Freud appears to be able to draw a number of general conclusions regarding the development of the childish psyche. The child will typically initiate repression in an attempt to liberate him- or herself from unpleasant impulses. However, when dealing with impressions from the real world, the child may attempt to defend itself against an unpleasant demand using disavowal. Thus we are definitely dealing with a mechanism of defence which targets the external world and one which always occurs next to a simultaneously existing correct attitude.

A few months before writing this work, Freud had written a little essay entitled 'Splitting of the Ego in the Process of Defence' (1938a). Here Freud once again circles the questions of the functioning of the ego as a result of defences, particularly those targeting the external world. Once again the concept of the threat of castration is used to refer to the reality being disavowed. Freud would have us assume that the child is under the influence of a sexual impulse which it has become accustomed to satisfying, and is suddenly rendered anxious by an experience which tells it that the continuation of this satisfaction may result in an almost intolerable danger. It can now choose to give up the satisfaction or disavow reality. However, the child chooses neither of the two, or rather, it chooses both. Freud refers once again to the fetishist. 'The boy did not simply contradict his perceptions and hallucinate a penis where there was none to be seen; he effected no more than a displacement of value' (Freud 1938a: p. 277).

From 1927 onwards disavowal is linked to fetishism and, as we have seen, this is an ambiguous term, since Freud refers both to the formation of a compromise between two opposing tendencies and to an opposition and an actual splitting. Not until the advent of the concept of ego splitting is it possible to reach a more consistent conclusion concerning disavowal.

However, there is one thing that must already be noted about this defence which targets external reality. As disavowal becomes more precise, this defence also becomes closely linked to the observation of gender difference and the idea of castration, but what is this reality Freud is referring to? Not even in the essay 'Formulations on the Two Principles of Mental Functioning' (1911b), where he comes the closest to attempting a metapsychological explanation of the relationships between the psychic apparatus and the external world, does he write much about the latter, and when dealing with the castration complex it is not so much the actual observation of gender differences, but the linking of the girl's lacking a penis and the threat of castration that are emphasized as the piece of reality being disavowed. However, here we must ask with Laplanche and Pontalis (1988) whether this disavowal – whose real consequences are in fact so obvious – is based on a reality that cannot be considered perceived fact, since it does not belong to external reality, constituting instead a base for specific subjective realities.[10]

Before I go into this and complete this discussion, I shall briefly elaborate on Freud's concept of ego splitting.

Splitting

The idea of splitting was not originally Freud's. It existed in psychiatry before Pierre Janet, Joseph Breuer and Freud introduced it in connection with their studies of hysteria. Splitting – in the broad sense referring to split, double, or multiple personalities – has been linked to the dissociation so characteristic of hysteria. In psychiatry, particularly in the work of Eugen Bleuler, the word splitting has been used to designate that mental functioning we see particularly in schizophrenic patients. Bleuler's use of the term is reminiscent of Janet's. Both understand splitting as a secondary phenomenon derived from a primary associative weakness, which results in a strict separation of mental groupings.

Freud criticized Bleuler's use of the term schizophrenia at an early stage in his work, and when he returned to the use of the word splitting late in his life, he did so in an attempt to approach psychotic defence from a different angle than Bleuler.

We have become accustomed to the concept of repression. The pre-psychoanalytic idea of splitting, however, presents us with something entirely different than the splitting so diligently employed by Kleinians, with reference to the split between self and object representations characteristic of borderline patients. Freud's concept of *Spaltung*, on the other hand, refers to a split in the ego itself and neither to a weakness in the mental apparatus nor to a division in self and object representations. Towards the end of his life, Freud expanded the concept from the limited use it had had in his essay on fetishism and extended it to psychosis. The theory of sexuality had focused on fixation and the return of the pathogenic, but Freud came to realize that infantile theories of sexuality have other effects on the ego. They produce ways of thinking – some of them prototypical, such as repression or disavowal, others more disturbed, such as foreclosure (Green 1999). There is no doubt that with these concepts Freud was obliged to reconsider some of his earlier and most solid theoretic gains. However, it seems that Freud hesitated to act on this new insight and only a few of his followers have taken over these terms and used them systematically.[11]

Introducing the term ego splitting late in his work, Freud (1938a) asked himself whether this idea 'should be regarded as something long familiar and obvious or as something entirely new and puzzling . . .' (Freud 1938a: p. 275). This statement is symptomatic. On the one hand Freud chooses to understand fetishism in light of the conflictual and compromise-seeking character of neurosis. On the other hand it is equally clear that when Freud refers to a splitting of the ego (intra-systemic) as opposed to a splitting between the psychic structures (inter-systemic) he is referring to a new insight and to a process that cannot be reduced to neurosis, repression and the return of the repressed.

In the essay 'Splitting of the Ego in the Process of Defence' (1938a) Freud writes that we have become so accustomed to observing the synthesizing functions of the ego that we take them for granted. Yet these functions may be affected by a series of disturbances.[12] Melanie Klein (1986 [1932]) demonstrated that the splitting mechanism is an important part of the normal development of the young child[13] and for the following generations of psychoanalysts splitting has become closely associated with the theory of the paranoid-schizoid splitting into good and bad object and self representations. The question, however, is whether this is sufficient to comprehend the extent of that splitting which is so dominant in the defence structures of borderline patients. Here I think we would do better to consider that splitting of the ego which Freud sporadically indicated in his later writings and which refers to a far more extensive rift in the structure of the ego, affecting all its functions and thus naturally also relations to other structures.

We illustrated the mechanism of repression as a horizontal barrier separating the repressed unconscious from consciousness. Yet this barrier is not absolute nor is it impermeable. Analytical interpretation presupposes that it is possible to build a bridge between the manifest and the latent, or to draw forth meaning from that which has been rendered unknowable to secondary logic through the condensation and displacement of primary processes. In the conflict-resolving and compromising characteristics of the symptoms we see the result of the association between the conscious and the unconscious, pleasure and unpleasure.

Repression is an inter-systemic mechanism utilized by the ego to mediate conflicts between the id, the superego, and reality. It operates according to the pleasure principle and attempts to separate that which from within would appear as pleasure and unpleasure in such a way that that which is consciously registered as unpleasure becomes connected to pleasure within the repressed. This corresponds to the assumption that the unconscious can only confirm; it does not know the word no.

In other words repression is a barrier primarily serving the ego in relation to impulses from within, while accommodating both reality and the superego. When we speak of splitting, however, we are primarily referring to the relationship between the inner and the outer world and thereby to the regulating mechanisms of projection and introjection associated with splitting. The assumption is that these mechanisms introject the pleasurable as part of the ego – in accordance with the mechanism of pleasure and unpleasure – and project that which is unpleasurable onto the exterior world.[14]

Unlike the Kleinian concept of splitting, Freud's ego splitting refers to an intra-systemic mechanism affecting the inner structure of the ego. Furthermore, this is a mechanism which – unlike repression – has to do with relations to the external world perceived with unpleasure. Thus it appears that Freud's definition of splitting is closely associated with cognitive processes that target the external world – with thought and perception.

As we have seen, Freud had two things in mind in working out his idea of the splitting of the ego. Firstly he wanted to explain the mechanisms at work in perversion – including fetishism – as stated in his 1927 essay, and secondly, he wanted to explain psychosis (Freud 1924a, 1924b, 1938a). Both disturbances affect the ego in its dealings with reality and the study of these disturbances forces us to acknowledge forms of defence quite radically different from repression. Freud termed these defences foreclosure and disavowal, with the prototype being the disavowal of castration. Through splitting and disavowal, however, we also become convinced that we are not dealing with the outright foreclosure of reality we usually encounter in the defence mechanisms of psychotic patients. In the case of the Wolf Man we see that the splitting mechanism consists of two opposing attitudes existing side by side: one acknowledges reality, while the other – influenced by drive – 'detaches the ego from reality' (Freud 1938b: p. 202). Unlike repression we are not dealing with any kind of conflict resolution and hence there is no compromise. Nor are we dealing with a form of primary process thinking, but rather a duality of thought or perception. In other words, this is not a logic of either-or but of neither-nor. How are we to utilize these assumptions in our study of the psychic structures and defences of borderline patients? I think it is necessary to continue Freud's line of thought and link his idea of the splitting of the ego to the relationship to reality and clarify the link between repression and reality-negating defence. To that end we shall make use of Freud's argument in his 1925 essay on negation.

Negation

I shall emphasize three things from the compact little essay 'Negation' (1925a) which I find particularly relevant to my topic: 1) the linguistic implications of negation, 2) the link between repression and negation, and 3) the link between negation and drive.

In the beginning of the essay Freud links negation closely to the semantic significance of affirmation and negation and more precisely to the two types of judgements that thought utilizes through linguistic logic. These are judgements of attribution, which distinguish the quality of things – good and bad; and judgements of existence, which determine whether something exists in the external world in spite of the tendency of the pleasure principle to distinguish between a pleasurable interior and the unpleasurable exterior. The resulting apparatus lets the equivalent of an unfettered principle of pleasure arise internally within the unconscious system – an apparatus which is able to let the reality principle apply purely in the conscious system, thanks to the barrier of repression. The judgement of attribution springs from the pleasure principle, which acknowledges only one distinction: either things are good and belong to the system, or they are bad and belong to the external world. Judgements of existence, on the other hand, work according to the reality principle and belong to the definitive reality ego which has developed from the pleasure ego.

I should add that a primitive form of judgement of existence is associated with what Freud (1923a) termed the original bodily ego. This bodily ego we must assume permits an initial reflective distinction between internal and external created by the boundary imposed by the skin, 'the skin ego' (Anzieu 1989).

This is one way to describe judgement within normal development, yet this is not the way things look for borderline or psychotic patients. We must assume that, besides repression, borderline patients feature within their psychic structures some kind of judgement characterized by both-and or neither-nor: neither pleasure nor unpleasure. Thus the splitting mechanism cannot be reduced to projective and introjective mechanisms that constitute the ego in the Kleinian sense, and which allow the distinctions between pleasure and unpleasure to coincide with the self and the object in the paranoid-schizoid position.

Freud lets the first ego formation coincide with the initial boundaries drawn by the bodily ego between interior and exterior. Only then does the pleasure principle lend projective and introjective mechanisms a helping hand; the system can then make the distinction, consigning the good to the system and the bad to the external world – in accordance with the pleasure principle. Using the definitive reality ego it is then possible to make the judgement of existence, which does not merely consist of judging something in the external world. The opposition between subject and object does not arise until thought possesses the capacity to reproduce a notion of something which was once perceived, even when it no longer exists in the world. 'The first and immediate aim, therefore, of reality testing is, not to *find* an object in real perception which corresponds to the one presented, but to *refind* such an object . . .' (Freud 1925a: p. 237).

Following this line of reasoning we must assume that splitting is not merely a question of projective and introjective mechanisms but actually utilizes what we, with Green (1999), may broadly term the work of the negative: foreclosure, disavowal and negation, which will affect not only judgements of attribution, but also judgements of existence. In other words this means that splitting must be presumed to take place at different mental levels prior to repression and followed by repression. Freud clearly lets the latter option shine through in his essay on negation:

> The performance of the function of judgement is not made possible until the creation of the symbol of negation has endowed thinking with a first measure of freedom from the consequences of repression and, with it, from the compulsion of the pleasure principle.
>
> (Freud 1925a: p. 239)

In our clinical work we encounter this form of negation in patients who consistently reject our intervention in such an extensive form of negation that we cannot help but ask: why must everything initially be countered by a 'no'? Freud writes that because the unconscious does not have negative symbolism at its disposal, the first insight into this fact can be the uttering of a no. I have learned to understand this paradoxical rebuff as a double affirmation: an inward acknowledgement and simultaneously an external negation of the addressee: 'I acknowledge what you are saying as belonging to me, but I do not acknowledge your access to it.' In this defence strategy the Other is objectified; a negation of being-for-Others functions as a means to maintain being for oneself, as described in Chapter 5. After receiving such rebuffs for months and years as an analyst, one is suddenly astounded when the analysand – having absorbed a great number of these interventions – has integrated them and reports them to others with no trace of negativity.

Another aspect of this combination of repression and negation is the apparent cynicism with which these patients appear able to treat their unconscious. They are capable of allowing some admissions as to their drives and desires, which more neurotic patients would clearly have subjected to repression and compromise. These patients are incapable of such compromises. Instead the split built into negation completes the task of isolating prohibition from the wish – which is clearly acknowledged – while the concomitant feelings of guilt and shame are negated yet acted out within another psychic domain. One analysand who lives a sexually promiscuous life admits to lying and cheating without appearing affected by it. Guilt is clearly present, but has been displaced and isolated and only appears in moments of great anxiety when his hypochondriac fantasies convince him that he is suffering from a deadly disease and he fears death, convinced that in death his sinful life will be punished. Here we see an expression of what Kernberg (1986) termed a non-integrated superego living its own infantile life in this otherwise irreligious man.

A third thing I wish to emphasize is that in the latter part of the essay Freud attributes a far more radical meaning to negation than the purely linguistic one. Linking it to his latest theory of drive dualism, he thus considers affirmation an expression of life and sexual drives and negation as an expression of the death drive. Thus the question is whether judgement can remain a purely intellectual exercise. Does it not in fact become a matter of life or death?

Drawing on these mechanisms of negation we may be able to find an explanation of what many have emphasized as characteristic of borderline patients. I am thinking for instance of Kernberg's (1986) well-known diagnostic criteria: 1) the degree of identity integration, 2) the defence mechanisms involved, and 3) the ability to adapt to reality as well as a non-specific weakness of the ego and a lack of integration of the superego. There can be no doubt as to the descriptive value of Kernberg's differential diagnostics, but I think we may enhance their explanatory value by drawing on Freud's ideas on splitting and negating defence mechanisms. Rather than relying on a differential diagnosis based on delimitation from neurosis and psychosis, and a claim that borderline patients retain their capacity for reality assessment, I think that the fluctuations in functioning these patients display, as well as the noticeable detachment and contradictions of their ideas, can best be explained by these negating principles, which may operate at different levels in the development of the ego. The question regarding the capacity to test reality cannot be answered without also reflecting on what is – from the psychoanalytic point of view – to be understood by reality. Borderline patients – unlike psychotic patients – do not create their own neo-reality. Yet their dealings with reality are coloured by numerous splitting mechanisms characteristic of their thinking. For as Freud writes:

> The reproduction of perception as a presentation is not always a faithful one; it may be modified by omissions, or changed by the merging of various elements.
>
> (Freud 1925a: p. 238)

Yet we must additionally consider that these judgements do in fact serve both the sexual and the death drives. Only then can we understand the passion with which they are upheld and the anxiety they provoke, as well as the emotional intensity associated with these judgements and experiences of the internal and external world in these patients, and which we encounter in condensed form through transference.

In the following chapter I shall extend my discussion of defence beyond repression and delve a little deeper into a psychic problematic which is played out at what we term the pre-Oedipal level. My point of departure will be my work with one of my own analysands and this shall serve to supplement Freud's speculations on the defences he termed foreclosure, negation and disavowal in order to examine which reality is in fact in one way or another being rejected.

Notes

1 When I use the term borderline, or refer to a non-neurotic pathological form as in this case, I do not intend to indicate a nosographic unit. What I am aiming for is a structural concept, which must be assumed to exist even in people who do not necessarily suffer from borderline personality disorder.

2 To contemporary readers, this may seem reminiscent of what Fonagy and his colleagues (2002) termed the equivalence mode; an experiential mode dominant in borderline patients which renders reality threatening because there is no distance between the external and the internal. In other words, things cannot exist with an as-if quality, and as such they cannot become the object of reflection.

3 As Laplanche and Pontalis (1988) point out in *Language of Psychoanalysis*, Freud is not consistent in his use of the various forms of defence beyond repression. I have chosen to follow Laplanche and Pontalis in translating *Verwerfung* as foreclosure, as Lacan suggests. In subsequent quotes from the English translation the original German term will also be indicated. In English *Verwerfung* is rendered sometimes as 'rejection' and sometimes as 'repudiation'. See also the preface to the English translation for a more detailed discussion of these different terms.

4 The idea of projection as anchored in an external context was systematized by Merleau-Ponty (2002 [1945]). Lacan (2002) has also made use of this idea in his discussion of foreclosure.

5 In this observation on projection we recognize the dilemma of the point of reference for historical reconstructions which Freud wrestled with throughout his career. I do not agree with the critique proffered by, for example, Spence (1982) against Freud's historical concept. Spence overlooks the fact that Freud has never worked with anything resembling a simple, material concept of history. I also disagree with the way Fonagy *et al.* (2002) define mental reality, disregarding the unconscious elements hereof. Conversely I find Morris's elegant formulation provides a more comprehensive expression of Freud's understanding of the relationship between external events and mental reality: 'As I read Freud, the historical and referential dilemma is instead persistently framed by a circular pair of questions: how does real experience become psychological trauma, how does real trauma become psychological experience?' (Morris 1993: p. 38).

6 Similarly, Adair (1993) has suggested that foreclosure is part of the defence mechanisms we may observe in perverts, who – like borderline patients – are situated between neurosis and psychosis. In Chapter 7 I shall go into Adair's viewpoint in greater detail.

7 '*saisie par le moi sans aucun affect et perçue avec la netteté d'une réalité indéniable qui lui serait étrangère . . . dans la névrose, le refoulé et le retour du refoulé sont homogènes, tandis que dans la psychose, le rejet et le retour du rejet sont hétérogènes.*'

8 '*Si l'opération de forclusion se vérifie, c'est-à-dire si le Nom-du-père ne surgit pas là où il était attendu, il s'ensuit chez le patient psychotique une serie de remaniements d'éléments symboliques bouleversant leur repères habituels de l'espace, du temps et surtout perturbant les représentations relatives à sa filiation.*'

9 Throughout his work Freud appears to attribute three functions to reality testing. The first, to which he devotes the greatest attention, consists in distinguishing between external and internal. As evidenced in Chapter 4, this primarily occurs by inhibiting the impulse to cathect an experience of satisfaction until the satisfying object exists in reality. The second function consists of correction of distortions of external reality, created by the subject through perception. Finally, the third function consists of distinguishing between unconscious fantasy and memories. Freud is mainly occupied, however, with the first function, and this is the one which we shall examine more closely.

10 For a further discussion of the problem of perception and representation, see the Postscript.

11 It is interesting that Anna Freud (1992 [1936]) refers only sporadically to negation in her book on the ego and defence mechanisms, and does not refer at all to the defences Freud termed foreclosure and disavowal.

12 Bion (1990b) and Green (1999) both demonstrated what seriously disturbing consequences this splitting mechanism may have on the ego.

13 Winnicott (1990d) has questioned Klein's claim that the small child always lives through a phase (paranoid-schizoid) of splitting the object into good and bad.

14 I shall return later to the question of whether the formation of the ego should be understood as a prerequisite for utilizing introjective and projective mechanisms or as a consequence thereof.

7

Splitting of the ego

It took many years of analysis for Finn to tell me about an idea which he had always had, and which had not actually worried him; yet now that he was telling me about it, it seemed peculiar.

As a child he had had his appendix removed. Naturally this had left a small but visible scar. It had, however, also left him with an idea which had never been corrected: Finn was convinced that everybody had had their appendix removed.

This little story sounds quite innocent in all its harmless simplicity. However, in my work with Finn, it was to become the grain of sand around which the threads of my understanding crystallized.

When Finn told me of this idea, he added that he was of course aware that this was not the case, but that somehow his observation of the intact belly skin of others failed to affect his conviction that everyone had had their appendix removed. The remarkable thing about this conviction is that it exists without any accompanying thoughts or affects, and unconnected to Finn's actual knowledge. He is unable to correct this idea. What we see here is a thought which Finn cannot possibly think and which does not lead to any other thought; in other words, this is a thought which refers only to itself. Finn does not think his thought and therefore my task becomes that of bringing this un-thought thought into Finn's psychic life and trying to imbue it with meaning.

Perhaps we might be satisfied with believing Finn's idea to merely be a harmless vestige of childishly naive and egocentric ideas as to the nature of the world, and we could allow ourselves to be convinced of this when we learn that many of Finn's other thoughts on external reality share the same egocentric point of departure. We might also – with Fonagy *et al.* (2002) – speak of Finn's experience of the world as dominated by an equivalence mode of experience, which features no distinction between subjective experience and objective reality. Finn believes – in a way that is apparently naive – that others think the same thoughts and experience the same emotions as he does. Or rather, he does not consider that things could be any different. This is not because Finn is unintelligent or lacks empathy, but simply because certain experiences apparently become universal truths prior to becoming concrete experiences that permit generalization.

It is no coincidence that I am particularly interested in this idea that everyone has had their appendix removed. Numerous children undergo appendectomies without the operation occasioning the universal conclusion we encounter in Finn's case. As I said earlier, I could have chosen to ascribe the phenomenon to Finn's generally solipsistic world-view. In so doing, however, I would be providing no explanation, simply claiming that Finn's thoughts feature naive traits characteristic of childhood and operate at a regressive level according to a logic that might be termed naive realism, universalism or the equivalence mode. I could also go further and suggest that Finn's statements are the expression of a significant experience he has not had and which has thus not served to free him from universally based thought nor helped him towards a mode of thinking which includes specificity or uniqueness, subsequently permitting generalization. In psychoanalytical terms this experience is referred to as the castration experience. Accordingly I might choose to consider Finn's universal statement about everybody having had their appendix removed as the expression of a castration fantasy, which has not acceded to the symbolic order, and hence investigate whether this might prove a productive clue to Finn's general way of relating to the world. Rather than discussing regressive thinking, however, and being left with the problem of explaining the regression, I have opted to take my cue from the assumption that Finn's statement is the expression of a painful experience of loss, whose only trace is a universal thought which appears as an isolated, pointless registration of a fact, quite devoid of affect.

Thus my starting point is the assumption that we are dealing with castration experience expressed through universality: it applies to everyone, yet we are immediately forced to admit that if this is the case, we are dealing with a particularly negative version of that experience. It appears that Finn is adhering to a different logic than the one with which we were presented in the previous chapter, featuring Freud's idea of the child's attempts at avoiding the threat of castration by clinging to the idea of the universality of the penis. Finn's idea does contain universality, but if we are to remain with the idea of castration, Finn is expressing the universality of castration through his idea that everybody has had an organ removed.

In order to investigate this apparent difference between Finn's universalism and the one suggested by Freud I shall once again return to the story of the Wolf Man.

The mechanism of foreclosure

It is possible to draw certain parallels between Finn's story and the one we know through Freud about the observations of gender difference made by the Wolf Man. This reference to Freud's case study is not only about finding parallels between the two stories, both of which feature the child's encounter with the reality of gender difference. It has been my intention to aim directly at the defensive mechanism implied here by Freud and which may turn out to explain how the ability to cogitate may be infiltrated by an experience which has never been registered in the symbolic order. I am once again referring to the defence which Freud termed *Verwerfung*, and about which Lacan went into greater detail using precisely the Wolf Man as a case study.

I shall let Finn's story begin where the child must resolve the implications of gender difference and let Freud's reasoning be my guide. Hopefully the grounds for my choice will become evident as this significant detail becomes woven into Finn's story.

In his attempts at avoiding the threat to which he was exposed by his observation of gender difference, the Wolf Man, according to Freud, upheld two contradictory ideas: 'He rejected [*verwarf*] castration, and held to his theory of intercourse by the anus . . . This really involved no judgement upon the question of its [castration's] existence, but it was the same as if it did not exist' (Freud 1918: p. 84).

Freud formulated the idea of foreclosure as a defensive mechanism which differs significantly from repression, and which leaves a splitting of the ego expressed in two equal ideas. Likewise we discover in Finn two ideas which clearly contradict one another without causing any form of correction, let alone concern. Here, however, it must be noted that one of the ideas – the idea of castration – appears negatively or, as Freud would put it, as if it did not exist. In Finn's case the negative principle is expressed in the fact that Finn does not acknowledge the existence of difference but simply ascribes a common attribute to everyone, which however – as an affectless trace – obliterates any connection to the process which preceded and created it. The result is that Finn is unable to make use of the existing fact that not everyone sports a visible surgical scar to make judgement and think thoughts, to use a term from Bion (1988). Similarly we must assume, with Freud, that with one part of his thought content the Wolf Man does not acknowledge the visible expression of gender difference. Instead of living through and integrating extant difference, the Wolf Man has destroyed this thought or this image, which then appears as a momentary, passing hallucination. The Wolf Man's tale of the severed finger and the memories associated with it presents us with the hallucinatory defence of a small boy against a horrific vision. What does all this mean?

As we have seen previously, Freud introduced a defence mechanism which, unlike repression, does not displace an idea to the unconscious, but destroys it. He linked this mechanism, which he termed *Verwerfung* (foreclosure) and *Verneinung* (disavowal), to the experience of castration. In other words Freud indicated that the foreclosure of the experience of castration is prototypical – and the source – of other forms of defence aimed at what seems to be a threat from without. However, Freud left us with a number of unanswered questions as to the nature of the reality whose destiny it was to be foreclosed as opposed to merely repressed. How, in other words, are we to understand the reality of castration or the perception of this reality? Is it the 'missing penis' of the woman that constitutes the content of that which is foreclosed? If so, it hardly seems reasonable to speak of such an idea as based on perceived fact. If, however, it is the idea of castration itself that is being foreclosed, then the object of foreclosure is not a perceived phenomenon, but the result of a theoretical construction carried out by the child in order to solve the riddle of gender difference.[1]

In attempting to resolve these ambiguities Lacan linked foreclosure to Freud's introduction of the term judgement from his essay 'Negation', thus contributing to a theory of a defence which differs from repression, and which Lacan linked closely to the mechanisms of psychosis and the consequences of the experience of castration. Only after Lacan did psychoanalysts come to view foreclosure as part of a more extensive principle, defined by Green (1999) as the work of the negative.

Let us now, however, pursue Lacan and examine how his ideas on foreclosure may assist us in our investigations of the defences we see in both Finn and the Wolf Man.

Lacan (1988) speaks of original affirmation or symbolization and believes that foreclosure happens when something that should be is not affirmed or symbolized; the consequence of which is a suspension of the symbolic order. Since Lacan refers to the hallucinatory finger in the story of the Wolf Man, he is able to expand on the diffuse thoughts on psychotic defence from Freud's early work, the most radical expressions of which were to be seen in his essay on Schreber: 'It was incorrect to say that the perception which was suppressed internally is projected outwards, the truth is rather . . . that what was abolished internally returns from without' (Freud 1911a: p. 71).

In accordance with Lacan and the theory of the judgement of attribution, Freud's claim that the child retains the idea that everyone has a penis until the Oedipal phase can be construed as a 'universal All' (*le Tout universel*) (Nasio 2001). The child's discovery of the existence of at least one castrated person, i.e. the mother, constitutes an exception from universal judgement and provokes a judgement of existence in the form of the 'existent particular'. The judgement of existence permits the unique or singular to always appear as a breach of the implied perfect whole. In other words, we are dealing with a dialectic of the particular and the universal, or of lack and completion. With Lacan, we can sum up the movement of symbolic life in a single formulation by saying that the symbolic is a constant production of an existence which positively insists on a becoming and which negatively creates a lack in the whole.

> The judgement of existence in attesting to a particular absence correlates to the judgement of attribution which attests to a universal presence.[2]
>
> (Nasio 2001: p. 255; translated from French by KM)

It sounds abstract, but means that the painful trial to which castration exposes us, and which is repeated throughout life, consists in the fact that we only succeed in confirming our existence as subjects in the moment we take action and make a judgement of existence in response to the demands of reality: 'Yes, that's how it is.' If this is to take place, we must first acknowledge the lack that marks our reality.

Lacan speaks of original affirmation as the ground on which lack is constituted as particular. His subsequent defence of the theory that this original affirmation is foreclosed implies that there is actually no belief in the universality of the penis. Thus if foreclosure includes the entire complex, including this original affirmation, it means that the child will not even be confronted with the dilemma of lack or castration – to either submit to the trial or retreat from it – as if the child has not even had the opportunity to experience the illusion of a penis ascribed to everybody. Since the illusion of the universality of the penis was not created by the child, it is subsequently unable to generate the thought of its absence in the mother. In this case we are dealing with such a fundamental infiltration of the symbolic order that to Lacan it becomes the prototype of psychosis.

Neither Finn nor the Wolf Man, however, is psychotic. In the latter case the castration experience has led to the hallucinatory image of a severed finger. Yet this is a passing hallucination with no ensuing psychotic development. In Finn's case the experience of gender difference is rendered harmless by a universal judgement which negates the previous one, and consequently the difference, thereby making it difficult for him to assume his gender and his subjectivity. Finn does not present us with a case of psychotic development either, but with a border problematic. Nonetheless I have found Lacan's assumption of a foreclosure of the original affirmation to be productive in my attempts to understand Finn. It has helped me to see his thoughts on the universal appendectomy as a failed attempt at living through the consequences of gender difference. Perhaps we should not limit foreclosure to psychosis but should try to see it as a typical form of defence in borderline pathology.

Finn is neither able to uphold the universal judgement of attribution nor to acknowledge the lack and make a final judgement of existence. On the contrary, he has negated the universal judgement or, rather, replaced the judgement of the universality of the penis with the judgement of the universality of castration. Why is this?

Let us take a close look at Finn's story and seek to link these theoretical considerations to specific facts from his life story that may help us approach a theory of rejection as part of borderline problematic.

Finn's story

Finn was born into a world already marked by the trauma of separation. His father had abandoned the family, leaving his mother to care for two children: one as yet unborn and a one-year-old sister. Furthermore the family included a grandmother and thus Finn spent his early years surrounded by women. Presumably his mother and grandmother were severely disturbed. When Finn was around eight years old his mother was admitted to a psychiatric ward and Finn's memories of the grandmother include both her bizarre traits and her behaviour, which was frightening and incomprehensible to the already stressed and neglected little boy. The burden of caring for two small children was too much for his mother, who saw no other option than to place Finn in an institution near their home. Finn spent the first year of his life here, receiving daily visits from his mother. His relationship to his sister was to become Finn's salvation – and his destiny. The two siblings compensated for the neglect and the unpredictable, incomprehensible behaviour they encountered in their mother and grandmother by entering into a symbiotic relationship, where the 'we' overshadowed the 'I and You'.

When I say that his relationship with his sister was to become Finn's destiny, I mean that his early relationship to her became the prototype of every later relationship, and his idealization of her became the hinge around which Finn's bisexuality turned, as well as the basis of identification with what we termed 'the dead princess'. I chose to let Finn's story of the universality of castration introduce his tale because gender difference stands as the greatest riddle of his life, and because sexuality was to be the Archimedean point or the site of trauma in Finn's development. However, unlike normal and neurotic solutions to the experience of gender difference, Finn's solution bears no trace of compromise to indicate repressed Oedipal content. Instead I was presented with a series of condensed images presenting an undifferentiated masculinity/femininity problematic. Like the appendectomy idea, they appear as isolated islands and Finn himself experiences them as peculiar and foreign, yet real. To put it simply, Finn's gender approaches him from the outside. For many years Finn has dreamed of a tower, and this tower figures in several of his fantasies and in his images of the dead princess who is frequently locked up in this tower. One day – a perfectly ordinary day – Finn was in the Swedish town of Helsingborg and he saw a tower. The sight aroused a strong desire in him. He needed to get into the tower, and when he gained permission to do so he felt a strong sense of joy – as if he had finally found his way home. My interpretation is that this is a confirmation of the fact that he had found part of his masculinity in this tower, which he at once absorbed and was surrounded by. At another point Finn tells me that he has imagined that by penetrating a man he would be able to penetrate through to the penis and thus experience what it is like to be a man.

Finn idealizes women; presumably the symbiotic and far too intimate relationship he had with his sister left him little choice. This process was boosted by the absence of the mother, whose memory – beautiful and desirable after she had prepared herself for a show – completes the idealized sister. Finn's mother was a ballet dancer and his sister was a model. Together they served as a backdrop for the condensed childhood image of the princess, who is either isolated from the surrounding world or murdered, but with no trace of brutality. She sleeps her dreamless sleep and Finn is obsessed with this image of undisturbed peace.

In this childhood world of feminine mystique Finn's difference became disoriented, diffuse and indecisive. He was clumsy and understood nothing. He often received comments like 'watch where you're going' and 'close your mouth' as messages from a world that chose this way to communicate his difficulties in finding a foothold in space, time and language. Finn's story has taught me how fatal the experience of gender difference can be to a child, and that Freud was right to specify the Oedipus complex as the hinge on which the psychosexual development of the child turns. This applies not only to normal and neurotic development, but also to the development of borderline patients. In the latter case we must simply supplement our knowledge of ordinary development with our insight into the problems posed by the Oedipal problematic for those who, like Finn, lack the psychological prerequisites of the previous phases. For obvious reasons the path to a normal Oedipal solution was highly complicated for Finn. He was abandoned in a place where the decisive gender difference was never integrated, and thus failed to become the necessary starting point for what Lacan termed the process between the particular and the universal. For Finn this meant an insecurity and a lack of clarity in his identification as a man, yet there is also an underlying insecurity of the entire symbolic order, which we may read in his use of language and in transference.

Finn was never integrated within the school system simply because he did not know the rules of the socially and linguistically regulated order. Since Finn had never experienced the give and take of basic communicative rhythms, he never became comfortable with the interchange characteristic of conversation. Naturally this was also evident in our analytic setting, where I frequently experienced that Finn had difficulty taking in my words. The messages failed to register at the symbolic level, and my words frequently reached him in such a way that he only perceived the tone and fell into a state of dreamlike unreality. With Finn I learned to speak in images and I experienced – quite literally – that Bion's concept of reverie is quite justified in my interactions with a patient such as he. Sometimes my words functioned much as a mother's lullaby: beyond semantic and symbolic content they were calming, like a maternal voice singing the child to sleep. In other – less poetic and more theoretic – words, in this case the symbolic order had not been based on the essential experience of lack as a figure against a backdrop of illusory universality, thus leading to the perception of all difference as a threat. This meant that when my words became distinct and appeared to him at the symbolic level, he often experienced an insurmountable chasm of difference between us. This was not the offence narcissistic patients may take at not being mirrored. Rather, Finn experienced any differences – including those verbally determined by the symbolic order – as falling into the abyss.

Finn was soon taken out of school and sent to full-time ballet school. This was the beginning of many years of experience within the world of paedophilia.

There can be no doubt that the paedophile assaults became a trauma that burned itself into Finn's soul as a sign of indelible impurity. Nor can there be any doubt that this cumulative trauma (Khan 1996a) is an important circumstance in the development of Finn's bisexuality as well as his borderline pathology. However, it would firstly be far too simple to understand this trauma as identical with the events in and of themselves. In Finn's case trauma was established retroactively (*nachträglich*) (see Chapter 4). Finn did not realize what had happened until he contracted a serious venereal disease as a teenager and underwent humiliating and stigmatizing treatment. Not only had he been branded by the violating humiliations; suddenly, *après coup*, the difference he had always felt was cemented, yet he felt and understood the consequences of this stigmatization with the senses of a half-grown boy. While the traumatic circumstances of his childhood made it difficult for him to find his way into the symbolic order, his encounter with adult sexuality had set him outside the social order.

The trauma must be understood in light of that which had gone before: in Finn's case, the decisive experience of gender was preceded by a development where it was mixed with the experience of more fundamentally existential questions. The idea that everyone has had their appendix removed – that all have been castrated – is a pre-Oedipal solution in a child on whom gender difference has been forced at a time at which the difference between the particular and the universal has not met the psychological requirements for resolution. I shall therefore return to Lacan's 'primary affirmation' but rather than linking this affirmation to the idea of castration, I shall indicate a form of original affirmation, not of gender but of existence, of being. Thus I am not referring to the judgement of existence of which Freud writes in his article on negation, where the question of existence is related to the acknowledgement of the reality of the external world, but to existence as a mode of being.

It turned out that Finn's statements on the universality of a physical procedure masked a universality of existence. Finn had never learned to consider his experience – such as subjective thoughts and emotions – as something that defines his existence. Well into the analytic process, he realized that others had their own thoughts and feelings, which were different from his. As previously mentioned I do not think it suffices to understand this as an expression of failure to differentiate between object and self, or as a regressive phenomenon, i.e. as some form of primitive thought structure. Finn's mental life affords only a very frail affirmation of what we might initially term existence or being. In other words, Finn does not have access to the space in which being unfolds, and where we may experience existential fullness. We could assume that Finn had not been familiar with the primary narcissistic experience of being, since its prerequisites – a supportive, containing environment – were not available. I think it is necessary to include this level of psychic life if we are to understand Finn's intersubjective world and the death wish, which has assumed the form of 'the dead princess'.

When I first met Finn, his vulnerability and fear of contact were so pronounced that he was unable to look at me, but shook with fear as he huddled on the couch, trying to protect himself from something that seemed colossally overwhelming. He asked for a glass of water, and when I gave it to him, there was panic in his voice as he said: 'Don't touch me'. Later he told me how anxious he had always been about being touched, because it produced a feeling of impurity – which for him was the same as indignity; even later I learned to understand that Finn's fear of touch was also connected to a deep insecurity about his own boundaries. Finn lacked the concrete experience of the physical delimitation of the body and the protective surface of the skin. Clearly this fundamental lack of delimitation was intensified by and also cleared the way for paedophile assaults and the masochistic patterns Finn went on to develop. Since he had failed to develop a clear distinction between the external and the internal in accordance with what Freud termed the original bodily ego, he never felt protected, as we normally do, by the delimitation of his body from the external world. This was specifically expressed in the fact that he never went barefoot, and even while dressed was unable to sit on the sand or the grass in summertime. Theoretically speaking this is an expression of the failure of the original reality ego to project onto the surface of the body or, to use Anzieu's (1989) apt term, to develop a 'skin ego'. However, this also means that Finn has not developed the 'holding function' that Winnicott has taught us to understand as a prerequisite for all later ego-functions.

The original ego

A number of terms have been suggested to cover the original ability of the psychic apparatus to contain and transform the child's very first impressions. Both Bion and Winnicott have drawn attention to a particular mental state which the mother enters with her very young child. Both have also indicated the holding and containing function she fulfils prior to assuming the character of an object. Furthermore, Bion (1988) has suggested the term alpha function to describe the mother's ability to transform the child's raw sensory impressions into processed mental elements. Others have used various terms to indicate this fundamental structure, which must be created within the childish psyche as a prerequisite to the various activities and processes of psychic life. In connection with his work on dreams Pontalis (1981) spoke of a dream screen, which Lehtonen (1997) developed further from an entirely different perspective. Salonen (1979, 1989) has suggested an original 'basic matrix' within the psychic apparatus, which he perceives to be the result of primary identification. Enckell (2002) recently suggested a metaphor he terms 'the warp' and 'the web', whereas Anzieu (1989) developed the concept of 'skin ego'.

All these concepts build on Freud's idea of the ability of the psychic apparatus to cathect a memory image of an experience of satisfaction, resulting in a so-called hallucinatory wish fulfilment. When the child learns that satisfaction does not occur unless the satisfying object is present in the external world, the apparatus is forced to form a conception of the real circumstances in the external world and develop a secondary, more secure method of satisfaction.

In the case of Finn and numerous other patients, however, we are forced to consider whether hallucinatory wish fulfilment has even been a possibility, and thus whether what we may term the original screen has been underpinned. Something would indicate that many borderline and psychotic patients have been exposed to a fear of destruction and death which has been so overpowering that the psychic apparatus has been unable to free itself from – never mind transform – these impressions. There is something in these patients that forces us to consider whether there is a form of negativity lurking behind the pleasure principle – a hole or a void far more devastating than what we understand by the unpleasurable accumulation of tension. In Finn's case this something beyond the pleasure principle has been expressed through self-destructive sexual acting-out and through obsessive autoerotic behaviour, such as rocking and the generation of excited emotional turbulence, in a desperate attempt to transform a feeling of death and inner void into a kind of life. In his work with psychotic patients Bion has made a significant contribution in suggesting a different starting point than the one suggested by Freud with his concept of hallucinatory wish fulfilment. Bion did not take for granted that this wish fulfilment would take place, and posed the question of how the original apparatus might rid itself of anxieties of existentially threatening dimensions. For Bion as well as for Winnicott these considerations led to the assumption that a holding and containing environment is a necessary prerequisite for what has been termed primary identification.

Adair (1993) has speculated as to the connection between hallucinatory wish fulfilment and perversion, and suggested that perverted acts are a way of using the body to replace the gratification that was originally expressed in hallucinatory form by the young child.

> The pervert cannot accept loss: not of mother nor of breast, nor of penis, nor of the object's love, nor of the superego's love. So he fills the vacuum with a mnemic image. He sexually uses his own body, or the body of the object with whom he is identified, to innervate a special type of hallucination.
>
> (Adair 1993: p. 88)

The hallucination we are dealing with here, however, is neither visual nor auditory in character. It is not through remote senses that the pervert expresses what Adair terms 'body hallucination' but 'through kinaesthetic, proprioceptive and enteroceptive pathways' (Adair 1993). It appears to me that this idea of a hallucination that circulates in the area for bodily processes may be supplemented with Anzieu's (1989) thoughts on the concept of skin ego.

Anzieu has developed further Freud's scattered sketches for a formulation of the original reality ego. We may use the concept of the skin ego to supplement Lacan's 'primary affirmation' with insights into the fact that this affirmation is located at the level of Freud's original body ego. Metaphorically speaking, this may not only be understood as a core, but as a delimiting space – a hollow. Anzieu's skin ego both confirms and expands Winnicott's concept of 'holding' and Bion's concept of 'containing'. Furthermore it adds a significant contribution to our understanding of borderline and to my own thoughts on betweenity – a bodily experienced form of being. Anzieu defines the skin ego as a double boundary. The most peripheral constitutes protection against the outside world and is hard. It protects or shields mainly against quantities from the external world. Anzieu refers to Freud's 'protective shield' (*fonction de pare-excitation*), meaning that it channels quantities of energy. The inner membrane is more permeable: it is thinner and more sensitive, being intended to receive and inscribe signifiers.[3] The totality of these two is what Anzieu calls the skin ego, which thus may be characterized as either a membrane or a cavity. The membrane is asymmetrical. Thus only the side facing the external world functions as a protective shield. This may explain why it is easier for us to protect ourselves against those quantities we encounter as external stimuli than against inner impulses. The two surfaces of the membrane are more or less separate and thus vary from one individual to another, or, more specifically, the particular pathology of a given individual is outlined by the structure of the envelope. The borderline patient, according to Anzieu, suffers from defective boundaries:

> uncertain of the frontiers between the psychological and bodily Egos, between the reality Ego and the ideal Ego, between what belongs to the Self and what to others. . . . The patient . . . experiences a diffuse sense of ill-being, a feeling of not being inside his life, of watching the functioning of his body and mind from outside, of being a spectator of something, which is and at the same time is not his own existence.
>
> (Anzieu 1989: p. 7)

In this light, Finn's conviction that all people have been exposed to bodily assault, which he concentrates on his appendectomy operation, can be considered the grain of sand around which his thoughts on a passive ego crystallize.

Thus Finn has not managed to establish a secure border between the internal and the external and has failed to establish a solid, original reality ego. This may explain why he feels himself to be exposed to destructive assaults from the external world, in the face of which he feels powerless yet paradoxically longs to surrender to completely. Finn's experiences of relations with others have been extreme, from the symbiotic relationship modelled on his relationship to his sister and the sexual assaults of his boyhood years to the non-existent father and the wildly fluctuating relation to his volatile mother. This means that Finn never experienced the ordinary interchange of give and take, of listening and responding. He belongs to that category of people who live according to what I previously termed the logic of desperation. Relations to others characteristically lack depth. The figure is entirely in the foreground, forcing Finn to continuously do battle with something which imposes itself relentlessly and unnervingly, and which seldom leaves him be. Nonetheless this is preferable to that which is significantly more frightening. The threat of the absence of the other sends Finn directly to a place beyond all life and straight into the abyss best described using Bion's (1988) term 'nameless dread' and Winnicott's (1992b) 'fear of breakdown'. Furthermore, as we have seen, this threat is not limited to any literal absence, but to difference, since difference, as we defined it, i.e. the relationship between the universal and the particular, is an experience Finn has not lived through. The idea of universal castration protects him from recognizing any particular existence, but thereby it also blocks his own subjective existence in finding affirmation. Finn flutters hither and yon in his quest for a place to belong, constantly fleeing contact with the void. His resort to masochistic activities is an expression of this attempt to avoiding empty space; they are intended to mask the 'deficient skin Ego' (Anzieu 1989: p. 107).

Anzieu claims that it is the membrane between the internal and the external that in the slightly older child provides the ego with the opportunity of hiding and choosing to non-communicate, as Winnicott (1990b) puts it. If the child fails to fully develop the membrane of the skin ego due to the insufficient holding function of the mother, the ego cannot unfold potentially, but only defensively. There are two ways to limit this potential space. The peripheral part may harden too early because an overly violent invasion results in a lack of distance to the inner membrane. If, on the other hand, the peripheral layer is too loose, the ego will display a flaw in consistency, in which the inner membrane attempts to replace the protective function against external stimulation, thereby developing what Anzieu terms structural inversion. Here the two surfaces of the skin ego do not merely coincide, but the other – inner – side turns around itself, inside out like a Moebius strip, which Lacan was the first to use as a metaphor for the ego. I believe this image may provide a more satisfactory answer to the consistent fear of invasion experienced by borderline patients, as well as their equally desperate need for contact, than the more pointillist ideas we associate with the defence of foreclosure. The image of the Moebius strip helps us to understand the alternating difficulties these patients experience in distinguishing what comes from inside with what comes from outside. Or put another way, the hard outer layer sometimes faces inwards, affording a certain ossified protection against impulses and fantasies, while the inner and more sensitive side faces outwards, thus rendering the world an inferno of impressions. This is how I interpret Finn's fantasies of disappearing into a tower or into another man's penis. They represent the attempt to find something to envelop the fragile ego which constantly risks having the sensitive interior turn inside out so that it offers no protection. On the other hand, this could explain why his fantasies often appear as unfamiliar, condensed configurations with no internal coherence. The image of the Moebius strip inverting itself, turning outside in, then again turning out and so on, is an apt illustration of the ego which in borderline patients is whirled into a movement which is sometimes centrifugal and at other times centripetal. In other words it is an image of the fact that these patients rarely experience a sense of belonging in their bodies; they quite literally lack grounding and ultimately fear being flung into empty space. Finn's masochistic acting-out, his autoerotic rocking, and his desperate attempts to make the other assume the empty position, are motivated by his fear of breakdown, as Winnicott aptly puts it.

I think we may understand Anzieu's skin ego as that which Bion termed the alpha function, and which is the apparatus for thinking thoughts. All the previously mentioned writers have wanted to indicate that the basis of psychic development is this container or membrane, which our borderline patients have brought to our attention, before focusing our attention on the psychic contents about which our neurotic patients have instructed us.

These patients have not only taught us the significance of this early container function, they have also forced us to conceptualize other ways of ridding oneself of unpleasurable ideas than what Freud collectively termed repression.

When considering our borderline patients' feelings of mental emptiness and their fear of nothingness, it is insufficient to understand this as the opposite of psychic fullness. I think it might help us if we consider Bion's differentiation between 'no thing' and 'nothing' and his idea of minus-K (see pages 166–167). The latter does not merely symbolize what might be termed a passive absence but rather a 'blank hole' (Green 1998), which attracts all psychic content and thoughts that are connected with the central theme of this empty space. A minus-K activity is a negative linking or negative attachment (Anzieu 1989). Presumably this corresponds to what Freud had in mind when he discussed Schreber's defence as an abolition rather than simply repression. It is insufficient to speak of evacuation. We must add that a primitive psychic apparatus may be forced to free itself from tension-ridden impressions by destroying them. This does not mean attacking the thoughts or images we perceive as the most primitive forms of representation, but dissolving them. This results in a void and a pain with no accompanying images of the wound created. We can term them the black holes of the psyche, capable of attracting these thoughts and images in order to destroy them. This may explain why these experiences first reach a person from the outside as what Lacan termed the real – what Bion (1990b) calls bizarre objects – and may also explain the peculiar phenomenon that borderline patients frequently resist our well-intentioned and affirmative positive interventions.

Finn was unable to create transitional objects, just as he was unable to self-soothe in a state where separation and emptiness take over. Yet he developed what McDougall (1995) has termed a transitory object. These are objects of an addictive nature, which, instead of symbolizing absence, are meant to soothe the consequences of that which cannot be symbolized. As a child Finn was fascinated with a comic which for him gained magical significance. He had to possess this comic; he had to find a certain figure, a woman, murdered but resting in tranquil beauty. What did this image mean, and how are we to understand it theoretically?

What initially caught my attention was Finn's desperate wish to gain possession of this comic and the image of the dead princess. This desperation gave rise to the idea that in this image Finn had found an expression of something which was an empty void within him, a framework for a state of nothingness. The image became the positive expression of a negative experience – the equivalent of a photographic negative.

This desperation is evident not only in Finn's strong impulse to seek and find this particular comic, however, but also in the fact that he cannot find within himself a positive image to correspond to the external image of the dead princess. This is the reason for the addictive nature of his obsession. We might say, with Winnicott (1971), that unlike a transitional object, this object not only has a soothing function, but a comforting one. We learned to understand the image of the tranquilly resting, beautiful princess as an expression of one of the few, isolated ideas Finn had preserved in his memory of his mother, when she was making herself beautiful in preparation for a show. Yet these solitary images were inanimate and therefore could not provide psychic nourishment for the boy, who for that same reason had so very few means at his disposal when trying to alleviate the inner feelings of emptiness and lifelessness.

In my analytical work with Finn I had the paradoxical experience that this man who was starving for contact was nevertheless unable to receive my well-intentioned interventions: instead of helping him, they provoked years of raging rejection. Thus I was reminded that the addictive or transitory objects Finn used to calm himself lacked any similarity to the soothing function that may be provided by another human being. It is as if Finn's desperate desire to possess his transitory objects stands in peculiar contrast to his rejection of 'good' offered to him from the outside. To Finn, the positive coming from without appears less real than the negative from within.

In the following chapter I shall use Winnicott to explore what may be termed negative experience.

Notes

1 See the Postscript for further discussion.
2 '*Le jugement d'existence attestant une absence particulière est le corrélat du jugement d'attribution attestant une présence universelle.*'
3 This reminds me of Freud's (1925c) little treatise on the magic block.

8

The psychopathology of the intermediate area

As indicated by the title of this chapter we are once again moving into Winnicott's universe in order to use his concepts to reconnoitre psychopathology on the border. Winnicott's name will always be linked to the concepts of the transitional object and of potential space. The concept of the transitional object has added a psychoanalytic term to the general experience of the very young child's particular use of teddy bears and 'blankies'. In adding the concept of potential space Winnicott has not only found a useful way to articulate a previously known phenomenon, he has created what may be one of the most important concepts in recent psychoanalytic literature. He termed this potential space a third area, thereby contributing to healing the split between the internal and the external, between subject and object, which has dogged western thought since Descartes (Turner 2002). However, Winnicott himself was not entirely satisfied with the way in which his contemporaries understood and used these concepts. As early as the time of the first publication of the concepts of the transitional object and transitional phenomena in his 1951 article of the same name, Winnicott specified in a footnote that he was not referring to specific objects, but to a quality inherent in the child's way of using them. In 1971, when he published *Playing and Reality*, he pursued this point with additional comments to what he must have perceived as misunderstandings of these popular concepts.

Winnicott commences his book with a reprint of his 1951 article, going on to add a few corrections and clinical material to clarify his points. These clarifications of the concepts and their clinical background constitute the framework for this chapter. Thorough reading has convinced me that Winnicott's ideas on what he terms the intermediate area provide an important contribution to our understanding of borderline pathology.

Winnicott introduced a concept which may not have had much standing in psychoanalysis, but which nevertheless had been known, acknowledged and used by others long before Winnicott suggested calling it a transitional object.

> I have introduced the terms 'transitional objects' and 'transitional phenomena' for designation of the intermediate area of experience, between the thumb and the teddy bear, between the oral eroticism and the true object-relationship . . .
>
> (Winnicott 1971: p. 2)

Winnicott's transitional object has gained almost mythological status as the loved teddy bears of childhood, immortalized by A. A. Milne (1954 [1926]) through the figure of Winnie-the-Pooh. Yet although part of the article is about this and similar transitional objects, Winnicott is more preoccupied with defining the place of its genesis. He indicated an intermediate or third area as the place to seek experiences with transitional phenomena, and indicates that this area is to be understood as a movement rather than a delimited locality. In other words we are dealing with a form of experience within boundaries in motion. The intermediate area, writes Winnicott, indicates a motion between what the child experiences as me and not-me, child and mother, separation and reunification.

That the concept of the transitional object has become connected to concrete things like blankets or teddy bears no doubt has to do with the fact that at the time when Winnicott introduced the concept, psychoanalytical thinking was dominated by object-relations theory. Since in his original article he had discussed the concept while drawing in the fetishistic object, it was easy to consider transitional objects as the natural precursor to the partial object and thence as the object of the child's autoerotic activities. According to Winnicott psychoanalysis focused either on the inner subjective world or on the external social world. This has hindered interest in the intermediate 'cultural' area and the particular forms of experience that are possible only there. It was difficult for his contemporaries as well as those who came after him to understand and maintain the paradox contained in the child's use of the transitional object. For

Winnicott it was essential to draw on a paradox in order to emphasize the evanescent nature of this phenomenon, as well as the contradictory character it would present to ordinary, logical reasoning.[1]

I have chosen to reproduce Winnicott's argument for the concepts of the transitional object and the intermediate and potential areas because it indicates the significance of the field in which borderline patients have such difficulties being.[2] In his revised article on transitional objects and phenomena Winnicott managed to indicate a psychopathology that becomes visible in the intermediate area, and which he links to separation, loss, and non-existence. Winnicott's ideas on transitional phenomena and the potential area have not only proven beneficial to the understanding of separation and non-existence, for conversely and positively Winnicott connects these phenomena to play, to illusion and to culture. In this chapter I shall take my cue from Winnicott's concept of the intermediate area to examine the way in which borderline patients use this area, and in Chapter 9 I shall discuss the field of play, dreams, and illusions.

The intermediate area

It was no coincidence that Winnicott used his 1951 article as a point of departure for *Playing and Reality* (1971). The latter shows that Winnicott is not interested in the object per se, but in that area that defines its creation and provides it with its particular experiential quality. Winnicott has chosen to omit the reference to the fetish object, as if seeking to clarify that we are not dealing with a partial object but are in fact in an area beyond psychosexuality. Other things have been added to inform the reader of the development of Winnicott's thinking and the experiences which paved the way.

Before going into the pathological phenomena that underpinned the idea of intermediate and potential areas, I am going to draw attention to some of the comments Winnicott added to his latest version of the article on transitional objects and phenomena. Winnicott writes of transitional objects that they are the first 'not-me' possession, thereby he consciously chooses a formulation in direct contradiction to object-relations terminology. This has to do with the fact that the object to which Winnicott is referring does not belong to the Kleinian school of inner objects; nor should it be misunderstood as an external object. Although this may not be how it appears to the casual observer, the child has a different experience. 'The transitional object is *not an internal object* (which is a mental concept) – it is a possession' (Winnicott 1971: p. 9). The transitional object, or – as Winnicott prefers to call it – the first 'not-me' phenomenon, can therefore not be understood as simply the mother's breast. The child's experience of not-me is localized in relation to the breast as two parts of two bodies: mouth and breast. In this intermediate area a third object is created, not only in the place separating the two parts of two bodies, but also as a potential area for their reunification. For instance we see the genesis of a transitional phenomenon when the child – while sucking the breast or the finger – uses the fingers of the other hand to perform a rhythmic caressing motion on the breast or its own nose or upper lip.

Psychoanalysis has largely focused on the development of partial objects: from the fingers in the mouth to the hand on the genitals, but few have focused on the movement that delineates the child's sucking on his or her fingers and which shows this to be an activity which cannot simply be understood in terms of drive impulses.[3] At some point the child will perhaps weave something extra into its sucking rhythm, something 'not-me'. Later the child's babbling and the way the older child sings itself to sleep represent other forms of transitional phenomena. Both the caressing movement and the material thing the child uses in executing its rhythmic movement may represent the breast. Yet Winnicott is not preoccupied with this representation. He assumes that there is a form of experience and a form of representation associated with the movements of the child as well as the material objects, and that these refer neither to something external nor to something internal.

These things do not represent anything; in other words, they have no symbolic value, they are concrete. 'The point of it is not its symbolic value as much as its actuality' (Winnicott 1971: p. 6). In emphasizing its character of reality, Winnicott seems to underline that for the child to create, it must assign the phenomenon in question the status of something real, an experience which is essential for the child's creativity. I shall have more to say about this later.

In normally developed children, these early transitional phenomena cease to have significance once the child learns to distinguish between fantasy and reality. They are not repressed, but simply lose their significance, or are relegated to a form of limbo. As I described in my discussion of Finn in Chapter 7, it is my experience that borderline patients utilize the same objects that would be termed transitional objects in a healthy child. However, it is precisely the child's use of this object that determines whether it deserves the term transitional object. Borderline patients frequently use both a blanket and a teddy bear as soothing objects, but in these cases they frequently function as stereotypical fetish objects whose use is linked to obsessive rituals which do not dissolve as in the healthy child.

In his 1951 article Winnicott refers to two brothers. The older brother had an early, enduring attachment to the mother and did not develop a transitional object. Although he derived pleasure from a toy rabbit, it never had the character of a transitional object. It is not the existence of an object that resembles a transitional object so much as the presence or absence of signs that indicate the quality of the object that justifies use of the term transitional object. As a child, my patient Finn had a number of different objects that could be termed transitional objects. Thus the corner of his duvet became what accompanied his thumb sucking; however, this was not a question of the boy creatively combining his autoerotic activity with a transitional phenomenon with a view towards freeing himself from his dependence on the concrete mother. He was unable to free himself since he could not retrieve the mother as an imaginary inner figure. In Winnicott's terms he could not use the object to soothe himself. Instead it assumed the character of a 'comforter' to which he was able to resort at any time.[4] These addictive objects do not have the liberating potential of the transitional object. 'Unlike transitional objects, however, addictive objects necessarily fail because they are *somatic* rather than *psychological* attempts to deal with absence and therefore provide only temporary relief' (McDougall 1995: p. 187).

Using Adair's reasoning, as quoted above (see page 150), we might suggest that some children use these objects not as the first hint of not-me, but rather as a substitute for hallucinated wish fulfilment. In Winnicott's words, the fetishistic object detains the child in a defensive use of the hallucinatory illusion, whereas the transitional object has a potential function which consists in using the illusion in a creative and developing manner. I shall return later to Winnicott's controversial use of the term illusion and for now merely mention that while in his early work – including the article from 1951 – the concept figures prominently, it appears that in his later work Winnicott preferred the terms fantasy and imagination. This latter conceptual opposition permitted him to capture the difference between the fetishist or 'transitory' use of the object and the healthy use of the transitional objet. While imagination denotes a free, spontaneous, creative activity, fantasy refers to a stereotypical and pathological use of the transitional object.

My patient, Finn, replaced the corner of the duvet with other objects, such as comics and magazines, and continued to suck his thumb until puberty. This autoerotic activity was later replaced by sexual acting-out and rocking back and forth, which instead of having a soothing effect actually provoked a short-lived yet intense state of excitement followed by brief relief. Rather than limbo, what we see here is an inferno; a sexual or autoerotic experience which imprisons, rather than providing release.[5] 'In favourable circumstances', explains Winnicott, 'the potential space becomes filled with the products of the baby's own creative imagination. In unfavourable circumstances, the creative use of objects is missing or relatively uncertain' (Winnicott 1971: p. 102). Furthermore, we might add that while the healthy child detaches itself from its childish transitional objects to replace them with various activities from the cultural domain, the not-so-healthy child will retain the object which has become fetishistic. Transitional objects leave room for understanding similarities and differences, helping the child to perform judgements of both attribution and existence. It 'describes the infant's journey from the purely subjective to objectivity; and it seems to me that the transitional object . . . is what we see of this journey of progress towards experiencing' (Winnicott 1971: p. 6). Once again this formulation highlights the intermediate area not so much as a place but as a movement, in time as well as space; it cannot merely be described as something delimited. Thus Winnicott's area is not a framed space, but a space with mobile borders – a potential space. '[I]t is a space where the future subject is *in transit*, a transit in which he takes possession of a created object in the vicinity of a real external one, before he has reached it' (Green 1997a: p. 1073). I shall return to this notion of frames and space at the end of this chapter in connection with my discussion of therapeutic space.

The last aspect of the transitional object which I shall discuss is its illusory character. This is the property that connects the child's experience of phenomena of a not-me nature with the adult pleasure in art and other phenomena that are located in the intermediate and potential area we term culture. Winnicott's use of the term illusion becomes apparent in his explanation of the relationship between the infant and the 'ordinary devoted mother'.

In order to take pleasure in this illusion, what Winnicott would term a 'good-enough mother' is required, i.e. a mother who actively adapts to the needs of the child and who is able to regulate this adaptation in accordance with the child's growing ability to tolerate flawed adaptation and the inevitable accompanying frustration. Under such circumstances a mother will provide the child with the opportunity of experiencing the illusion that the mother's breast is part of the child itself. 'In another language, the breast is created by the infant over and over again . . . [when t]he mother places the actual breast just there where the infant is ready to create, and at the right moment' (Winnicott 1971: p. 11). This means that the mother's adaptation to the needs of her child provides the child with the illusion that there is an external reality that corresponds to the child's ability to create. The creative ability of the child is confirmed through the illusion that what the child creates exists in reality, and presupposes an intermediate area in which the creative illusion can come into being.

There is an intimate connection between Winnicott's use of the concepts of illusion and the intermediate and potential areas. As I wrote in the introduction to this chapter, Winnicott uses these concepts to indicate a form of experience which is difficult for us to comprehend through words because we have become so used to thinking in internal/external and subject/object dichotomies. Winnicott is convinced, however, that we have access to a form of experience which can be usefully described as neither upholding these conceptual opposites, nor attempting to build a bridge between them. There simply exists an experiential area where these concepts have no relevance. Winnicott has expressed this most precisely in his commentary on Milner's (1950) book *On Not Being Able to Paint*:

> What is illusion when seen from outside is not best described as illusion when seen from inside; for that fusion which occurs when the object is felt to be one with the dream, as in falling in love with someone or something, is, when seen from inside, a psychic reality for which the word illusion is inappropriate. For this is the process by which the inner becomes actualised in external form and as such becomes the basis, not only of internal perception but also of all true perception of environment. Thus perception itself is seen as a creative process.
>
> (Winnicott 1992a: pp. 391–392)

Such formulations are a rarity in psychoanalytic literature, yet we find them in the work of those artists who – besides creating art – have reflected on the creative process. We find it in the work of Marcel Proust whose *À la Recherche du Temps Perdu* rests on the observation of the phenomenon he has called involuntary memory. Their property is that they bring together past and present through random meetings with trivial contemporary objects such as a madeleine biscuit dipped into a cup of tea or the sound of a spoon against a plate. However, these experiences are of such a nature that reality fades and we are seized by an experience of bliss which can only be understood as those moments of eternity where time ceases and past and present, imagination and thought merge. Danish poet Inger Christensen termed this form of experience the 'condition of secrecy', borrowing from Novalis the saying 'The external is an inner world raised to the condition of secrecy' (Christensen 2000: p. 40; translated by KM).[6] Here I see a connection to Winnicott's potential area and the experiences of the intermediate area in that external things cease to be objectively characterized when creative and spontaneous urges connect them to subjective experience, whereby the latter assumes the form and character of reality.[7]

In his postscript to *Playing and Reality* Winnicott expressed the paradoxical prerequisites of creation as follows:

> I am proposing that there is a stage in the development of human beings that comes before objectivity and perceptibility . . . This conception–perception gap provides rich material for study. I postulate an essential paradox, one that we must accept and that is not for resolution. This paradox, which is central to the concept, needs to be allowed and allowed for over a period of time in the care of each baby.
>
> (Winnicott 1971: p. 151)

Spontaneity and primary creativity spring from experiences in this intermediate area between what can objectively be observed and that which may be subjectively imagined.

Winnicott is aware that illusory or imaginary space may have both progressive and regressive functions, and may be both potentially creative and serve as a defence against reality. We may read the following as an expression of the latter:

> It is assumed here that the task of reality-acceptance is never completed, that no human being is free from the strain of relating inner and outer reality, and that relief from this strain is provided by an intermediate area of experience . . . which is not challenged (arts, religion, etc.). This intermediate area is in direct continuity with the play area of the small child who is 'lost' in play.
>
> (Winnicott 1971: p. 13)

Here it appears as if Winnicott perceives the intermediate area as a protection against a reality with which we never really come to terms. A few pages earlier in *Playing and Reality*, yet written 20 years before in his article on transitional objects and phenomena at a time when Winnicott was grappling with the concept of illusion, he writes:

> The mother, at the beginning, by an almost 100 per cent adaptation affords the infant the opportunity for the *illusion* that her breast is part of the infant. It is, as it were, under the baby's magical control . . . Omnipotence is nearly a fact of experience.
>
> (Winnicott 1971: p. 11)

We might read this 'nearly' as a special trait ascribed by Winnicott to illusion. It is not an actual delusion but a potential for the child to encounter reality in full confidence that it too has something valuable to offer and thus is also able to appreciate that which is not-me.[8]

In Chapter 9 I shall return to Winnicott and discuss the potential area of play. Here I shall pursue the question of how we may understand the form of pathology that plays out in the intermediate area.

Negative experience

Winnicott did not arrive at his final formulations on play and its potential for growth and creativity until late in his life. Furthermore, he did so by a detour, which we shall now study, and which he refers to in several places as negative experience. This idea was introduced in his 1963 article 'Fear of Breakdown' (1992b [1963]) and was discussed again in the case report with which he finished his revised article on transitional objects and phenomena. Both articles deal with the form taken by psychopathology of the intermediate area, which Winnicott links to the traumatic separation experiences of his patients.

Winnicott (1971) refers to a certain session with a female patient who he describes as intelligent and as in some respects well-functioning, although her personal relations are seriously disturbed and marked by a schizoid personality structure. The session in question begins with the patient narrating a dream which in the clear language of transference displays her present analyst as an 'avaricious dominating woman', who makes her long for the previous analyst, an unambiguously male figure. From here she delves into a number of repetitive frightening fantasies concerning travel and accidents and some deeply worrying thoughts about how her children and her analyst will be informed. She imagines crying and adds that the mother does not hear her. This makes her think of 'a most awful experience'. She had abandoned a little cat, which she later learned had cried for hours. She links this with the numerous separation experiences of her childhood which exceeded what it was possible to represent and therefore became traumatic. Winnicott now links the following significant remarks to the patient's associations:

> Much of the material in this analysis has to do with coming to the negative side of relationships; that is to say, with the gradual failure that has to be experienced by the child when the parents are not available.
>
> (Winnicott 1971: p. 21)

She transfers this failure to her own children and is racked with guilt at having abandoned her first child to give birth to the second, a guilt which was powerfully emphasized when she learned that the child had cried for hours.

These fantasies all concern the negative experiences of the small child when the absence of the mother exceeds the child's ability to comprehend. The child does of course register the separation and may maintain the mother in living memory for a while. After this point the mother is non-existent from the child's point of view and Winnicott concludes: 'This is what dead means' (Winnicott 1971: p. 22). From here, two extremes become apparent: a mother who is dead when she is present, and a mother who is dead when the child cannot recall her and thereby bring her back to life. I shall return later to the psychological significance we may attribute to these two different experiences but presently merely remark that we are touching upon the important difference between symbolized absence, and absence which cannot be symbolized.

The life of the patient in question had been one long experience of these extremes. When she was 11 she had been evacuated because of the war. She forgot her childhood and her parents, but consistently refused to call the people who looked after her 'uncle' and 'auntie', which was the common mode of address in such cases. As Winnicott writes, '[s]he managed *never to call them anything*' and he considers this 'the negative of remembering her mother and father' (Winnicott 1971: p. 22). To Winnicott this patient becomes an example of the negative character which may be assumed by even the most real. Separation, emptiness and death can be more real than proximity, fullness, and life. During the session in question she experienced a certain amnesia, and Winnicott learned that '[t]he amnesia is real, whereas what is forgotten has lost its reality' (Winnicott 1971: p. 22). The only real thing is the void that arises where something has been erased.

He provides us with another example that illustrates how the patient actively creates a situation where non-existence becomes more real than existence. At a certain point the patient refuses to use the blanket in which she has often previously wrapped herself. The reason for this is that the blanket, which is not there – specifically because she is not using it – is more real than the blanket the analyst is prepared to bring her. This once again makes the patient remember her previous analyst. He 'will always be more important to me than my present analyst . . . You may do more good, but I like him better' (Winnicott 1971: pp. 22–23). The non-present is the most real for this patient as well as for others.

We cannot grasp this negative phenomenon using common terms for the good and bad object. The bad expressed by the patient is negative in two respects: it is bad and it has non-existence. Bion (1992) understood this and added a dimension to the Kleinian polarization of good and bad. He suggested a distinction between nothing and no thing, introducing the thought that all affective dimensions may be negative in character. The antithesis of love is not hatred but absence of love.[9] It is, however, Bion's idea of thinking as an independent affective category that comes closest to what Winnicott termed a negative experience. The antithesis of knowledge – which Bion terms minus-K – is not merely ignorance, but eradication or non-existence. Like Winnicott, Bion (1988) is preoccupied with the question of how the primitive psyche rids itself of painful experiences, and while Bion refers to evacuation as opposed to modification as a way of rejecting these experiences, Winnicott appears to go one step further, approaching what we have previously discussed as foreclosure. They do appear to be united, however, in the idea that this form of negativization results in a void in the psyche, a destruction of representation, a hole where there are no representations. Bion speaks of the black holes of the psyche that attract and destroy thoughts.

Inspired by the work of Winnicott and Bion, André Green elaborated on the idea of the negative work of the psyche, prototypically expressed by negative hallucinations (Green 1997a, 1998, 1999, 2000d). While repression keeps the repressed away from the conscious mind by displacing it to the unconscious, the implication of the negative hallucination is that representations are lost because they are eradicated and leave no visible traces, as we learned from our re-examination of Freud's ideas of foreclosure (*Verwerfung*) and negation (*Verneinung*).

What Winnicott and Green after him add to Freud's concept is the use of the negative principle in our understanding of borderline pathology.

Through a memory, Winnicott's patient is approaching that trauma against which she has been defending herself using a form of negation that we may, with Green, term a negative hallucination. The family album features a picture of her toy dog Toby, which calls forth a memory of her mother at one point saying to her, '[b]ut we "heard" you cry all the time we were away'. The parents were in fact too far away to have been able to hear the child, and although she was only two years old, she knew it. This gave rise to the thought: 'Could it possibly be that my mother told me a lie' (Winnicott 1971: p. 24). But that thought was too unbearable for the two-year-old and she consequently tried to deny what she otherwise knew was true, that her mother had lied to her.

> Here was the picture of a child and the child had transitional objects, and there were transitional phenomena that were evident, and all of these were symbolical of something and were real for the child; but gradually, or perhaps frequently for a little while she had to *doubt the reality of the thing that they were* symbolizing. That is to say, if they were symbolical of her mother's devotion and reliability

> they remained real in themselves but what they stood for was not real.
>
> (Winnicott 1971: p. 24)

This little story becomes the grain of sand around which the other material crystallizes. Throughout her life this woman has been haunted by a negative hallucination arising from an attack on the connection between the symbol and that which it symbolizes; an eradication of the most painful experience of all, that the symbol of motherly care hides the experience of her non-presence and lack of devotion. 'All I have got is what I have not got' (Winnicott 1971: p. 24). Her analyst adds that this remark is the expression of 'a last-ditch defence against the end of everything. The negative is the only positive' (Winnicott 1971: p. 24).

Green (1997a, 1997b) has further developed Winnicott's observations of absence as an axis of borderline pathology. In the concepts of the dead mother and 'white' psychosis he has shown how the negative works towards a form of representation where emptiness and nothingness are the most realistic. I shall return to this later after expanding a little on Winnicott's experiences.

As previously mentioned, the case to which we have been introduced has been added to the original article from 1951. Apparently Winnicott wanted to enrich the ideas of transitional phenomena and the intermediate area with an experience which, although not new, is nevertheless an important element of his thought, at least during the last decades of his life.

In the 1963 article 'Fear of Breakdown', Winnicott introduced his idea of the pathogenic significance of separation for the borderline problematic. The argument runs that we cannot understand psychosis merely as a breakdown; it is also a defence organization vis-à-vis a primitive terror, which, to paraphrase Bion (1988), is nameless. Phenomenologically speaking, we may approach the quality of this terror though descriptions such as loss of a sense of reality, loss of bodily anchoring, and depersonalization. Winnicott introduced the theory that imminent breakdown is feared because it has already taken place at some point in the past. Yet – and this is a paradox – it has been unable to find a psychic place. It was never deposited, thus this is no hidden or buried trauma. Nor has it been repressed, just as it would be insufficient to speak of splitting, which does after all presuppose the presence of the elements thus separated. It is as though

Winnicott cannot bring himself to use the term unconscious, but continues to circle around a nothingness which appears as a phenomenological void within the subject. Something has taken place which has no place. However, that which it has not been possible to experience, and which escapes all recollection, is connected to the existential dimension of being, a term which Winnicott has contributed to psychoanalysis. The void is not a delimited space, nor a gap in speech. It cannot be understood as something latent behind something manifest. It is an experience that has not actually been had, deposited within being as non-existence, yet accompanied by a desperate demand for expression and meaning.

The dead mother

A person's ability to symbolize absence and live through grief forms the experiential basis of Winnicott's speculations on what he termed negative experience.

Alternatively – in accordance with Green (1999) – this could be termed experiences concerning the work of the negative. Rather than emphasizing the element of drive as we do in speaking of the death drive, this can be conceptualized as a working process that can only be described as anti-life, or, in other words, as negative. Specifically we are dealing with the small child's experiences of separation and absence that exceed the child's ability to uphold and process them. The result is a negative experience, i.e. one that, since it cannot take place, leaves behind only the contours of something negative.

Winnicott expresses this as follows: 'The feeling of the mother's existence lasts x minutes. If the mother is away more than x minutes, then the imago fades, and along with this the baby's capacity to use the symbol of the union ceases' (Winnicott 1971: p. 97). Such experiences do not create traumas in and of themselves. The child will repair its despair when the mother returns within 'x+y' minutes. After 'x+y+z' minutes, however, the child has become traumatized and the degree of deprivation will henceforth depend on the mother's ability to remedy the traumatic separation. Some children will desperately carry the experience of having been 'mad' insofar that 'mad' in this case simply refers to a '*break-up . . . of a personal continuity of existence*' (Winnicott 1971: p. 97).

It appears to me that Winnicott hints at two psychologically distinct traumatizing separation experiences. Previously I referred to the two extreme forms in which psychic death may appear to the child. 'From here we come to the two extremes, so different from each other. The death of the mother when she is present, and her death when she is not able to reappear and therefore to come alive again' (Winnicott 1971: p. 22). In both cases we are dealing with an experience of psychic death – of non-existence. Winnicott indicates that we are in fact dealing with two, psychologically speaking, quite different phenomena – in spite of the shared negative experience. He does not elucidate this difference, for which reason the differentiation made here is based on my experiences. In the latter case the reference is to a physical separation exceeding the child's threshold for maintaining a living image of the mother. Once this limit is surpassed, the mother is dead, i.e. her absence cannot be presented within the psyche of the child as a symbolized absence and the child becomes unable to grieve. In other words the child can no longer uphold the symbol of their union. The result is a void in the psyche corresponding to what Bion termed nothing. However, if we are dealing with a mother who is physically present but mentally inaccessible, the results are presumably different. This may be a depressed mother, or a mother whose attention is consistently elsewhere for other reasons. This does not necessarily give rise to an inner void, but to a contour of a dead inner image – which Green (1997b) termed the dead mother. In this case we are not dealing with an experience of separation or loss, but with an experience of an object whose absent presence has become cathected and inscribed within the psyche as a negative hallucination. The result, as formulated by Anzieu (1989), is that the life of the psyche unfolds with no affective resonance, and we experience a form of communication that somehow lacks life. I think there is a difference of degree between nothing and no thing, to use Bion's terms. The complex which Green termed the dead mother is a depressive state, though not necessarily an obvious one, nor is it the primary reason for a person to seek treatment. Nevertheless this is the result of the unperformed work of mourning for a mother who, while not physically dead, has been engrossed in her own despair. Through her absence the not-present mother has transformed 'a living object which was a source of vitality for the child into a distant figure, toneless, practically inanimate' (Green 1997b: p. 142).

Green also refers to this as 'blankness', a category he links to a series of concepts under the heading of the negative: negative hallucination, blank psychosis and blank mourning. Meta-psychologically speaking this is an element of primal repression in the form of a massive decathexis of the primary maternal object, leaving a psychic void in the unconscious, as well as identification with the dead mother. For the child this means not only the loss of love, but the loss of meaning.

Compensation for this loss of meaning is sought either through the early development of a capacity for compulsive fantasizing (unlike what Winnicott terms the capacity for imagination) or through a compulsive form of intellectualization, which Fonagy *et al.* (2002) refer to as 'hyperactive mentalization'. All this must be understood as an attempt to veil the gap left by the massive decathexis. In his article 'Communicating and Not Communicating Leading to a Study of Certain Opposites' (1990c [1963]), Winnicott hints at another dimension that may underpin the notion of two different consequences of negative experience. He distinguishes between simple non-communication and active non-communication, going on to say that communication may arise from non-communication either as a quite natural need or as a negation of silence. The latter does not necessarily equal communication, but rather an active non-communication through which one may attempt to defend one's inner silence, which we must imagine is meant to protect a hidden and highly vulnerable ego. This defensive use of communication may for instance be seen in the lifelessness hiding behind manic defence, but it is also evident in what Winnicott termed anti-life. Ogden (1999) used a series of clinical vignettes to illustrate the breadth of variety of this anti-life factor as evidenced in counter-transference phenomena. When the child must attempt to handle and adapt to the dead mother, the result can be a compensatory form of liveliness. Here we find a parallel to Balint's ocnophilic object-relations (see page 100), expressed in a desperate search for a highly idealized object. However, this may also be expressed in a form of non-communication aimed at defending against the revelation of the negative hallucination assumed by the figure of the 'dead mother'. Presumably individual circumstances in a child's development decide whether an unsuccessful mourning process results in subsequent emptiness or is internally maintained in the form of a negative hallucination.

Winnicott's indication of the psychological difference between the child's experiences of death, which he has associated with both physical separation from the mother and with her psychic absence, inspired the connection to Green's concept of the dead mother and Bion's distinction between no thing and nothing. Despite these differences at the levels of both symptomatology and aetiology, a very large part of treatment to help borderline patients consists in providing symbolic expression of these early experiences of loss of both love and meaning. However, unlike our work with neurotic patients, which may simplistically be said to consist of revealing meaning, this work involves the opposite: the creation of meaning (Killingmo 1989, 1995).

Frames and spaces

Winnicott felt it was necessary to break with parts of classical psychoanalytical terminology in order to indicate the limitations not only of our psychoanalytic technique but of any form of psychic organization. He had become aware of something which Freud had in fact already observed – although he had not pursued it – the fact that some patients develop a defence to protect against an internal breakdown of the organization of the ego. The fear of this possible future breakdown was so terrible because the breakdown had already taken place – in the past – without having found a psychic place. In these cases we are not dealing with reminiscences and are not required – metaphorically speaking – to perform archaeological excavations. What we are dealing with is not deposited anywhere. These are not traumas in the sense of buried or isolated remnants of memory. No repression has taken place, nor are there any traces that point back, nor would it be sufficient to speak of splitting. Although Winnicott uses these classical terms, he does not find them adequate to what he wishes to communicate. The actual idea of the repressed unconscious does not correspond to Winnicott's experiences of a dimension of absence, emptiness, or nothingness. Something has taken place which cannot be located.[10] Thus we are forced to consider whether the model of the psychic apparatus which we have inherited from Freud allows room to explain these experiences with the work of the negative. I think we must read *Playing and Reality* as the fruit of Winnicott's labours to delineate these experiences. His experiences with the negative allow him to pose the simple question: what makes us feel alive?

It is difficult to describe Winnicott's intermediate and potential spaces and even more so to find words to describe the form of being unfolding here. We can only delimit space using those spaces that are already familiar to us, and which we try to control: external and internal space. Here, however, we are only indicating its place as something absent, something which exists only potentially.

Nonetheless the form of being potentially showing itself here is what creates and confirms our existence. It is a playground, as Freud expressed it, between illness and life, a '*Zwischenreich*' (Freud 1954, letter dated 16 April 1896) with mobile borders. The potential space discussed by Winnicott in *Playing and Reality* is characterized by the possibility of confirming our existence. What does this mean? Winnicott is in no doubt. It is about the feeling of being alive, that something is of deep personal significance, arising as the few moments Proust described with his concept of involuntary memory (see page 163). Often it does not require much at the external level; something trivial or a sudden meeting between two people. It may not seem like much, but it gives us the feeling of being alive. There are experiences which appear certain and convincing even though they are not realized through forward actions. These are, to paraphrase Sartre, experiences which are expressed as potential possibilities, before they become reality (Sartre 1962).[11]

We frequently become aware of the framework of these experiences only when they are breached.

Psychoanalysts and therapists are increasingly aware of the therapeutic frame, and not least the disruption of this frame, which appears to have become an unambiguous call for therapeutic intervention. There is no doubt that borderline patients and others with a fragile personality structure have shifted attention from content to frame. In our encounters with these patients, psychoanalytic theory and theory in general – i.e. ways of listening, answering, and being with these patients – are challenged. In other words, they have taught us that in a given analytical situation, the frame consists of more than the physical surroundings and specific analytic rules. Indeed, it frequently comprises the silent background or – to use Winnicott's term – the holding function which is so especially important to borderline patients.

As Bleger (1967) and others have observed, we become aware of this frame, which may also be defined as the silent element of therapy, when it is broken.[12] To use Winnicott's term, the frame constitutes the therapeutic element of 'not-me' which reveals its existence in its absence (Milner 1996). With this in mind it seems logical to compare the silent background of therapy to the *holding* function of the mother, as long as we do not reduce or identify the therapeutic relationship with the mother–child relationship. This understanding of the importance of frame has been significantly enriched by working with borderline patients, not least because they have difficulty in making use of it, as in the case of Winnicott's patient for whom the proffered blanket became significant precisely through her refusal to make use of it. This provides us with a significant message, namely that what we may be inclined to interpret as the patient's attack on the frame should perhaps rather be considered an expression of non-use (Bleger 1967). Our patients bring whatever they have into therapy (Klauber 1987) and that which we may interpret as an attack may be an expression of the personality organization of the patient. Thus the transference we observe in these patients is not about affect or object-relations but the entire personality structure, which repeats itself in its relationship to the frame. In other words, the frame represents the very basis of the patient's mental organization in that it is the foundation for the creation of self and object as well as the relation between them. If the frame cannot be said merely to represent, but actually to function as the basis of the psyche, it becomes easier to understand why a breakdown of frame can become as disastrous as what we see in these patients. One particular analysand underwent years of therapy during which the breakdown of frame was kept at a minimum. One day another analysand arrived far too early for the next session thus breaking the frame for the first patient. This breakdown became the topic of the next session and my analysand had become almost shockingly aware that what he had taken for granted and given no thought to had revealed itself to be fragile and destabilizing. He had thought of previous sessions I had been obliged to cancel and had realized that not only could I disappear, but this breakdown of frame had apparently opened an abyss within him.

As long as the frame functions as a silent background, the analysand has the illusion of the permanent presence of a primary caregiver. Breakdown of frame, however, opens a 'crack' into the reality associated with the original caregiving function. Thus the disruption may be understood to open an abyss formerly kept at bay by the frame, but now suddenly appearing before the analysand with the catastrophic character of sudden delusion. Thereby we understand why object-relations terminology is insufficient. Maternal care or holding do not signify objects, but rather the function or properties of an object. By these terms we are to understand not the specific mother, but what she gives her child through empathic presence and continuity. Mothering is not attached to any specific object, but, as Gantheret (1983) aptly put it, is 'a substantivization', as described in Chapter 3.

The analytical situation consists of a process and a frame which is a non-process in the sense that it functions as the constant element that ensures that the process can proceed.

When working with neurotic patients we rarely worry about the frame. Once these patients have grown accustomed to the slightly unusual arrangement, they normally forget fixed parameters such as the length and frequency of the session, its limitation to linguistic statements, and the encouragement to associate freely. They delve into their internal processes and have no difficulty letting the external arrangements fade into the background as a necessary but unnoticed constant. Thus as therapists we do not have to pay attention to the frame.

This is not so with borderline patients. Since they either attack the frame, or – as I have suggested – seem unable to make use of it, part of the therapeutic process ends up focusing directly on the frame. This movement from content to frame is distinct not only to the analysand, but above all to the analyst, who feels a great deal of pressure to take action in order to maintain the therapeutic frame and ultimately the therapeutic situation. However, this inner pressure not only concerns ensuring consistency of frame: sooner or later it also becomes the therapist's experience of having to maintain the patient's own internal frame and structure. Bion's (1988) suggestion of distinguishing between thoughts and an apparatus with which to think becomes relevant in this context. As a therapist one may feel subjected to significant pressure to function as the thinking apparatus for holding and processing the patient's thoughts.

What Winnicott may add to our understanding of this psychotherapeutic work is that it takes place in the intermediate area. Thus we are dealing neither with subjective processes on the part of the therapist nor with intersubjective processes, but with the overlapping field in which this particular form of experience may come into existence. In consequence, what is at stake is not deciphering a latent meaning behind a manifest significance, but rather constructing a meaning that has hitherto been absent; not only a meaning, but an experience of lived life.

Thus several analysts (Ogden 1994b, Green 2000a, Britton 1989, Gammelgaard 2001) have spoken of the analytic object as a third object, perceiving it as something which is constituted as a combined result of intra- and interpsychic processes. We have become aware of this analytic 'third' because these patients experience difficulty in creating it for themselves. One consequence of the principle of the negative is that they have a hard time creating links between different psychic representations. Rather than being symbolic in nature, the character of these representations is – as Freud (1915) expressed it – that of things. For these patients dreams do not become meaningful as significant expressions of a psychic reality but function as specific references to an external or even a bodily reality. Fantasies either become compulsive activities to fill out a void, are experienced as facts (Bion 1990b), or appear as what Segal (1992) termed 'concrete symbolic equations'. All of these refer to a form of psychic representation devoid of the connecting option characteristic of symbolization and situated at the level of concrete thought. Since the work of mourning has not been able to take place and it has not been possible to symbolize absence, thinking has lost what Freud (1911b) called its 'experimental kind of acting'. Thinking becomes dangerous or, in other words, it becomes impossible to separate thought and action. Thought is action or actualization. Another way to express this is that for these patients the intermediate area is filled with the threatening reality of concrete ideas rather than representing the potential for creating analytic objects. It is impossible for them to think and create symbols because the space in which thought is to take place is already populated with frightening fantasies which – having been foreclosed – have assumed a factual reality.

Evidently the creation of a frame to make thought possible is an essential prerequisite to helping these patients. More specifically this means establishing a frame in which spontaneous gesture, living experience, and the free unfolding of thoughts or notions may meet a form of reflective resonance, which confirms a basic experience of life and existence. We may say – with Winnicott – that we must retrieve the breakdown that took place but never found a place to stay.

This is the place we strive to find because it is the only thing that can create life and existence where formerly there was non-existence. However, this is also the place from which existence unfolds creatively in a space that only now assumes the possibility of suggestion.

Notes

1 The highly personal style of writing that characterizes Winnicott's literary work and which emphasizes the paradox as well as other rhetorical figures no doubt derives from the fact that this was a way in which he could preserve his own creativity, keeping a safe distance to those who would threaten it (see Turner 1993 and 2002).

2 Ronald Britton (1998), who takes a Kleinian stance, has put this slightly differently, believing that borderline patients actually seek to remain in what Winnicott termed the intermediate area. He refers to the need of these patients for an either/or state, in that they use ambiguity as a defence against ambivalence. It is this sought either-or state which Britton believes corresponds to Winnicott's intermediate area. In my opinion Britton is referring only to the defensive use of the space of illusion and intermediarity, which does not capture the full complexity of Winnicott's concept. It should be added that Britton, Henri Rey (1994) and John Steiner (1993) have all contributed significant views on borderline pathology. However, they are also strongly influenced by Kleinian thinking which lacks the openness of Winnicott's concepts and paradoxes and therefore does not open up to dialogue and reflection. It appears to me that the Kleinian universe tends to close in on itself, which makes it less open to dialogue.

3 Although Winnicott is right that this form of activity can hardly be understood purely in terms of drive, I would add that it cannot be understood without. In this context I would like to refer to Laplanche's (1976) reading of Freud's *Three Essays on the Theory of Sexuality* (1905) and suggest that through this autoerotic caressing activity the child is showing the first signs that the other as a fantasy functions as an element of this autoeroticism. See also Note 9 on page 109.

4 Soothing refers to the function of the transitional object, whereas comforting refers to the function of the fetish object. I have previously utilized McDougall's term transitory or addictive object (see page 107).

5 In this context it might be useful to refer to Anzieu (1989) who in an examination of Bion's concept of 'containing' distinguishes two aspects of this function and thus succeeds in incorporating Winnicott's concept of 'holding' in Bion's 'containing'. The container (*contenant*) is still, stable, and forms a passive receptacle where the baby may store its sensations, images and affects, which in this way are neutralized and preserved. The second aspect of the container (*conteneur*) is active; in Bion's words it is maternal reverie, projective identification and the use of alpha function which elaborate, transform and restore to the child its sensations, images and affects in a representable form (Anzieu 1989: p. 101). According to Anzieu, disharmonies between these two functions may

explain the fluctuating functional level of borderline patients. Anzieu indicates a form of parenting which is quite common today, and which may result in such disharmonies, where children are subjected to almost traumatizing concentrations of attention and communication, interspersed with periods of the opposite. This takes place within boundaries that become continuously narrower and more insecure, since they feature so few participants, who while taking care of the child must simultaneously further their own ambitions. Phenomena such as acting-out and autoerotic and obsessive stimulation may in extension hereof be perceived as attempts to stem the fear of a diffuse and non-directional flow of energy against which there is no protection. According to Anzieu, borderline pathology is played out between the double wall of the two barriers: the protecting shield and the shield of signification. Because these two functions have never been balanced, the child has been unable to establish the envelope in which fantasy and representation may grow (see also page 152).

6 '*Das Äussere ist ein in einen Geheimniszustand aufgehobenes Innere.*'

7 In his examination of the historical background of Winnicott's use of the term illusion, Turner (2002) indicates the legacy of the British post-Romantic literary tradition as well as the difficult position Winnicott and the so-called 'independent group analysts' occupied in the controversy between Melanie Klein and Anna Freud and their respective followers. He believes that the concept of illusion and some of Winnicott's other concepts have been both a weapon and a refuge for the development of Winnicott's own creativity.

8 We usually understand illusion to be a deception of our sense of reality. However, Winnicott and Milner wished to let the term denote a significant form of experience which precedes the separation of subject and object. Rycroft (1968) has defended this use of the term in a series of essays.

9 Hence he refers to minus-L (love) and minus-K (knowledge).

10 See Postscript for further discussion.

11 I find it important to refer to this form of certain experience and juxtapose it with the demands for evidentially based knowledge which currently appear to be spreading like wildfire in large parts of scientific thought. In other words we must insist that beside so-called evidence-based knowledge we have what Britton (2003) termed 'experience-based knowledge'.

12 Bleger, however, is not as interested in the frame when it is broken as when it is maintained. In a clinical example, he demonstrates how precisely because the frame was held constant, non-representation brought to light the patient's most permanent structures of personality, his 'ghost world' (Bleger 1967: p. 421).

9

On the prerequisites for playing and dreaming

In this chapter I shall once again take my cue from Winnicott's *Playing and Reality*, this time exploring the explicitly positive theme of children's play.

Most of us have caught ourselves – fascinated and not without regret – observing children completely absorbed in play, forgetting themselves as well as time. Children play and appear to have entirely natural access to the illusory space of playing. As observers we must ask ourselves what happens to this ability once we cease playing. Play is characterized by two things; its function and the place in which it unfolds. Playing is spontaneous, unplanned, and unwilled; the result of an immediate urge with no other purpose than creating a space for the child's unfolding of its self and its capacity for imagination. It is only later that children begin to partake in games that follow rules, and later still, that they learn to enjoy following the rules associated with play and games. The other characteristic trait of playing is its location in what Winnicott calls intermediate or potential space. 'I call this a playground because play starts here. The playground is a potential space between the mother and the baby or joining mother and baby' (Winnicott 1971: p. 47).

In playing the child moves on the border of the two spaces we know and try to control: internal and external space. In this potential space things can come into existence, objects come alive and are positioned here between me and not-me.

Winnicott's last work is paradoxical in content as well as form. Entirely in keeping with the phenomenon being examined, the main point of Winnicott's perception of play can be summarized in the following statement: 'The baby creates the object, but the object was there waiting to be created and to become a cathected object' (Winnicott 1971: p. 89). The child at play must never be challenged with that most demoralizing of inquiries: 'Did you make that up, or did you get it from somewhere?' Because Winnicott points to the area between subject and object, between imagination and reality, between presence and absence, an area for which we have no language, he has attempted to articulate it in an almost poetic form of prose.

I have mentioned previously that borderline patients lack precisely the ability to uphold the paradox of potential space and are hence in the Winnicottian sense incapable of playing.

To me, the psychological significance and consequences of this claim have been highlighted by understanding what play is to the healthy child. This insight could not have arisen purely through the observation of children playing. I came to understand the paradoxical nature of playing and the influence of the environment on children's ability to exploit play for their own development only through reading *Playing and Reality*.[1] This has to do with the fact that it reads as more than simply a scientific work. Winnicott completed his writings with a work in which his ideas had not only gained their final form, but where his writing style has come to fruition in such a way that the reader is presented with the author's lifelong project: demonstrating how the ordinarily devoted mother helps the expression and development of the child's true self. In other words, *Playing and Reality* is a demonstration – rather than a purely theoretical account – of the care provided by the good-enough mother for those parts of her child that require a certain amount of gentleness and protection in order to develop and thrive.

I wish to initiate this discussion of the uses made by the healthy child of potential space and of playing by characterizing Winnicott's own investigation in its almost poetically creative form.

The paradox

The paradox has been a favourite rhetorical figure throughout Winnicott's work, which culminates in *Playing and Reality*. Here his experiences seem to have found their final form, including a style of writing which turns out to make a significant contribution to the communication of this experience. The theme of the book appears at once a challenge and a protection. Readers are challenged in the sense that reading this book is at once frustrating and stimulating to read. When do we get to the heart of the matter? Why must we take so many detours in order to answer the reasonably simple question of what playing is to the young child? My own answer – after numerous readings of this fascinating work – is that the reader gradually, with Winnicott, works through the process that led him to this perception of children playing. Playing features a certain element of suspense which is also to be found in the book. Playing is exciting because we move into the 'precariousness of the interplay of personal psychic reality and the experience of control of actual objects' (Winnicott 1971: p. 47).[2] Winnicott's message is that what he terms 'the self' comes into being neither in the subjective inner world nor in the objective world of facts. Just as spontaneous playing provides children with the time and space to unfold their selves, we as readers are guided into encountering this special experiential space by an author who has laid out his material in such a way as to create an illusion.

Naturally Winnicott's many observations of young children and their mothers – first as a paediatrician and later as an analyst – constitute both his starting point and the experience behind this work. However, his analytical work with adult patients who had not received this form of protection and had therefore been unable to uphold the illusion of the intermediate space and its potentially creative function serves as the main underlying body of experience of the book.

Thus *Playing and Reality* opens with the story of a boy whose fetishistic relationship to a piece of string discloses his failing relations to the important people around him. Even in the introductory story, Winnicott uses a poetic tone. Instead of opting to tell this and other cases in the prosaic style of scientific casuistry, he has chosen an entirely different style of writing in order to communicate an experiential mode that may be difficult to tune in to, but in which the adult must nevertheless enable the child to rest safely and securely until it is ready to experience itself and the world as separate entities.

In many of his writings Winnicott has exploited the expressive force of the paradox, seizing the reader by surprise and inspiring thought. Here I shall restrict myself to mentioning two other texts: 'The Capacity to be Alone' (1990a) and 'Communicating and Not Communicating Leading to a Study of Certain Opposites' (1990b).

On one of the first pages of the former, Winnicott says of this capacity to be alone that it arises through the experience of being alone in the presence of another. In the latter he mentions that the joy of hiding may turn into the disaster of not being found and adds to this another paradox, that alternatively it may be a disaster to actually be found. This is because of the 'incommunicado element' that constitutes the centre of each person, which Winnicott does not hesitate to call holy: 'Rape and being eaten by cannibals, these are mere bagatelles as compared with the violation of the self's core, the alteration of the self's central elements by communication seeping through the defences' (Winnicott 1990b: p. 187).

Winnicott uses paradox in the same way as the mother, whose holding and devotion permit the child to maintain the illusion of its omnipotent creative ability. Thus his style of writing protects the fragile form of becoming made possible by that intermediate area where the self may drown itself in the world and feel at home because it is a product of that space. The child needs a kind of moratorium to move from the merely hallucinatory wish-fulfilling activity of the internal world towards adaptation to and mastery of the external world. This is where it experiences that hallucinatory productions correspond to a piece of reality. It is the mother's task to bring in reality at the right time, i.e. when the child is able to have the experience of having created it. Perhaps this could be expressed as follows: the mother entices the child's psyche out of the hallucinatory state using the reward of the pleasure we connect with creative activity. This makes the child want to live.

Winnicott connects creative impulses to this illusory and potential space and is thereby able to link the child's playing with creative activities such as art and other cultural activities in adulthood.

> This intermediate area of experience, unchallenged in respect of its belonging to inner or external (shared) reality, constitutes the greater part of the infant's experience. And throughout life is retained in the intense experiencing that belongs to the arts and to religion and to imaginative living, and to creative and scientific work.
>
> (Winnicott 1971: p. 14)

A simple question that presents itself when reading *Playing and Reality* is this: What is it that makes us feel alive apart from that moment of necessary adjustment to reality? This is a question which we as therapists may be inclined to overlook insofar as we are busy uncovering meaning behind the statements of our analysands. However, our work with borderline patients confronts us with such existential questions and one of the merits of *Playing and Reality* is that it not only answers this question but does so in existential terms. Winnicott brings the concepts of existential philosophy into psychoanalytical terminology in order to indicate what is going on with these patients who have such difficulty finding a place to be.

The paradox serves other functions, stimulating curiosity in the reader by not leading us directly to the heart of the matter. We must travel detours and negotiate paradoxical terms in order to stimulate our own ability to create images, linked precisely to the feeling that life is worth living. These feelings are created in spite of the difficulties of comprehension and the many indirect statements – or perhaps precisely because of them.

The paradox insists on the importance of that difficulty which is linked to understanding. Here it is important to draw attention to the connotations of the word experience. Khan (1996e) made an important contribution to the differentiation and specification of the difference between 'experiencing', 'knowing' and 'being', which I shall not go into here. I shall limit myself to pointing out that knowledge and realization never entirely match our experiences, and that besides knowledge and insight there is the basic question of what gives our lives meaning and value. For Winnicott the field of play and illusion does not stand in opposition to the world of reality, rather it is a necessary bridge to reach it. With his sharp eye for the healthy function of playing, Winnicott convinces us that the goal of normal development in the child as well as in the patient in a therapeutic situation is not only a question of acknowledging internal and external reality, but of developing the capacity to play and thereby find joy and value in what we do.

The paradoxical statement concerning the capacity to be alone should not be cancelled out by being reduced to the act of being alone or to what we normally understand by loneliness. Within the paradox resides the insight that we are dealing with a capacity developed through an illusion, on condition that the mother leaves her child be – in its own world – while creating a necessary safe setting for her child by remaining present. These are the prerequisites for a child to develop the ability to enjoy aloneness.

One of my patients was clearly relieved that I seemed to have understood the nature of this particular feeling of loneliness which he had had his whole life, and which was neither related to the act of being alone nor to the negative value we associate with being lonely. However, he had no other words for this melancholy mood attached to an absent object – the mother – as he remembered her from before she became depressed. After that point she had no longer been able to let him be alone in her presence because her own need for his presence overshadowed her respect for his need to be alone in hers.

Paradox, like metaphor, teaches us that understanding is not only based on dissection or analysis, but also on connection. These two rhetorical figures – like poetry and other cultural activity – refer to a state we have all experienced before we learned the necessary distinction between internal and external, for instance by being alone in the presence of others.

Winnicott's poetic writing style has contributed lived experience to theoretical understanding. In this way he addresses the child in us, which shelters an important form of experience. According to Winnicott it is important that all children have time and space to explore this place.

My reading of *Playing and Reality* has honed my understanding of the difficulty of borderline patients. They do not possess this shelter for eternal moments. They have no access to an experiential space to which they can withdraw; a place dating back to before time and space became the parameters that subdivide our world.

Playing and necessary illusion

After the following account of the connection between form and content in *Playing and Reality* I shall delve into the prerequisites for children's play.

Winnicott learned to understand the child's use of play through spontaneous ideas that came to him during his work with young children and their mothers. He had made a habit of leaving out the spatula he used for examinations, so the child could reach for and play with it. This prompted a number of observations concerning the child's approach to this foreign object. Winnicott (1975a [1941]) has summarized this in the concept of the 'period of hesitation'. He is referring to the particular behaviour pattern exhibited by a child aged between five and 13 months in its relation to and use of the spatula. This pattern falls into three distinct stages.

Stage 1: The child reaches for the spatula – but arrests its movement as if to reconsider. The child appears frozen; the body is entirely immobile while it looks at Winnicott and its mother respectively. In some cases, the child becomes overwhelmed, gives up, and buries its face in its mother's blouse. However, the child's interest in the spatula always returns.

Stage 2: After the period of hesitation the child gradually becomes more comfortable with the situation and is therefore able to give free rein to its curiosity. A distinct change is observable at this stage, in that the child's desire for the spatula becomes evident: the oral cavity fills with saliva, the tongue grows large and soft, and the child starts drooling. Before long it will put the spatula into its mouth and chew on it – clearly satisfied. If, however, an attempt is made to offer the spatula to the child during what Winnicott termed the period of hesitation, the result will be the opposite of what was intended: the child will refuse, start to cry, and become deeply unhappy if one insists, for instance by putting the spatula into its mouth.

Conversely, if the child is allowed the time it needs, it will soon express that it is now in possession of the spatula, and that it is controlling the object, and is capable of putting it to its own uses. This is expressed by the child beginning to bang the spatula on various objects, clearly enjoying the loud noise. Alternatively it will put the spatula in its mouth or in the mother's mouth, and pretend to be feeding the mother. According to Winnicott the child is clearly playing a game called feeding and will grow frustrated if the adult puts the object into their mouth, thus ruining the game.

Stage 3: Subsequently, a sequel plays out in which the child drops the spatula, as if by accident. If the spatula is then returned to the child it becomes clearly pleased, plays with it a little and then lets it drop once again. This time there is no doubt that interest has been lost, and the child is especially pleased if the spatula hits the floor with a loud bang. There can be no doubt as to the child's ability to indicate that its interest in this object has now come to an end, and it will subsequently look around for other things.

I have reproduced this excellent observation, which will be recognizable to all who occupy themselves with young children, because it demonstrates the first intimation of that illusory space which is the prerequisite for playing. What Winnicott terms the period of hesitation in his 1941 article is the first indication of potential or illusory space, which is necessary for the child to unfold itself in an investigative relationship to the objects around it.

The mother's ability to adapt to the needs of the child in a way that is appropriate to its development is necessary for the child to make use of this space. What may be the ideal at one point is not necessarily so at a later stage. Whereas the mother, as Winnicott expresses it, adapts almost one hundred percent at the start of the infant's life, her empathy must take into account the growing independence of the child and the abilities it develops. During the first phase of the child's playing its perception of the object is subjective and 'the mother is oriented towards the making actual of what the baby is ready to find' (Winnicott 1971: p. 47). Later on,

> [t]he object is repudiated, re-accepted, and perceived objectively. . . . This means that the mother (or part of mother) is in a 'to and fro' between being that which the baby has capacity to find and (alternatively) being herself waiting to be found.
>
> (Winnicott 1971: p. 47)

During the next phase the child is playing alone in the presence of the other and only thereafter can the child begin experimenting by letting the two areas of playing overlap, where mother and child each bring their suggestions for playing into the relationship.

The child's period of hesitation is the time it needs to take possession of things for itself, and the time the surroundings must respect if the spontaneity and creativity of the child is not to be stifled or repressed. 'Playing is doing' says Winnicott. 'To control what is outside one has to *do* things, not simply to think or to wish, and *doing things takes time*' (Winnicott 1971: p. 41).

Thus the child's hesitation is an illustration of the meeting between the objective facts of the external world and the child's ability to cathect them with the enchantment associated with creation. More specifically I imagine the child hesitates to take possession of the object because it does not immediately want to let go of the urge to independently attribute value to the object. This is the hesitation we all know from creative moments where random things in the world suddenly come together with experiences from our personal lives. Inger Christensen has written about these creative moments and says 'in our heart of hearts we know that beginning is a bridge, built ahead of time, but it is not until we set foot in empty space that we feel the bridge beneath our feet' (Christensen 2000: p.41; translated from Danish by KM). Before taking this step and starting to write, she continues, we have been sitting for hours with a feeling of 'having lost our way' (ibid.).

With the concept of the period of hesitation Winnicott has indicated an important psychic ability; that of suspending an experience while it is at hand. Not only does this serve the purpose of investigating what is going on, i.e. moving from experience to observation, but it also closes off awareness of the experience, with a view towards recreating it at a later stage within one's own self. Another way to put this might be that we should distinguish between the time of the experience and the time at which this experience becomes meaningful to us. Milner (1996 [1952]) has described her therapeutic work with an 11-year-old boy, which illustrates the importance of the surroundings meeting the needs of the child at the right time. Despite being intelligent and having a great deal of creative resources at his disposal, this boy had developed an apathetic and disinclined relation to all schoolwork and was clearly dealing with significant psychic problems. This was during the war and the father had been drafted right when his little brother had been born.

The boy had arranged a game in which two villages – both populated with animals and people – were to go to war. The boy's comments made Milner curious. He said that 'there was to be a war, "but not yet"' (Milner 1996: p. 101). Why this qualification? The boy's comments forced Milner's attention away from the mental content of the boy's conflicts to the space that must be present if these conflicts are to play out. The boy's comments correspond to Winnicott's period of hesitation. At a symbolic level this boy is explaining that he is not yet ready to enter into the mutual and creative battle with existence which is a prerequisite for healthy development.

For many people large areas of their psychic lives have not been met by a forthcoming environment and have therefore not been able to take root as an experience with mutuality. As always, when dialogue fails, the results, according to Milner, are the dictatorial exertion of one side in a relationship, i.e. dominance or submission. Once hope of finding a response in the external world fails, the person may withdraw into himself and deny his dependence on others. Alternatively it may lead to an attempt to control the object with a view towards making up for a disillusionment that has been too intense.

This is the seed of the development of a logic of indifference and desperation.

In one of his most significant contributions to the discussion of the concept of illusion, Rycroft (1968) introduced the idea of pathological illusion, which takes the form of a defensive idealization accompanied by withdrawal from the world. The intention behind such withdrawal is protection against one's own ambivalence, while the idealization is understood as a defence against emptiness and a general lack of interest and involvement.

In Milner's work with the 11-year-old boy – who knew there would be war, just not right now – we find another example of how important it is that the child should be met by reality at the right time. The school had made numerous attempts to motivate the boy to take an interest in his schoolwork. The situation was turned around only when he was offered the option of working with photographs, making the boy feel that reality was meeting him in relation to an interest that he himself had spontaneously developed. This example shows how necessary it is for both young and older children to experience a world that offers itself in response to the desires with which they encounter the world. In this perspective, the development we associate with youth and adulthood consists in finding a place where we may experience that what we have to offer corresponds to a reality that wishes to accept what we may give.

Through his observation of the child's period of hesitation, Winnicott experienced the nuances and attuned interplay that take place between the healthy mother and her child. Nevertheless, frustration is not only inevitable, but also necessary for the child's development. Evidently it is impossible to adapt to the child's spontaneous actions to such a degree as to avoid frustrating it. The mere fact that it takes time for the child's needs and desires to find their way into the adult–child dialogue bears witness to a certain amount of unavoidable frustration. Not only the time but also the difficulties inherent in interpreting the child's non-verbal communication must of necessity lead to certain oversights and misinterpretations.

The following example illustrates how easy it is to miscommunicate with children who, although pre-verbal, have a rich body language with which spontaneously to express both joy and frustration. Five-month-old Emilie was visiting with her parents. She sat happily in her father's lap while playing a game with me that appeared to involve lifting her arms above her head. I repeated the movement, believing I was following a spontaneous utterance on her part. I was wrong, however, and although she tried to imitate the movement I had introduced, it was clearly too difficult, and she finally unleashed her frustration and cried. Her father, who had not participated in our game, must have registered the whole incident and was therefore able to console his daughter with the words: 'And that's the end of that.' A week later, Emilie's mother called and told me that Emilie had suddenly demonstrated that she was now able to lift both arms above her head, and was proudly showing off her new-found skill to all around her.

Frustration is inevitable, and may in ideal doses also spur development: '*If all goes well* the infant can actually come to gain from the experience of frustration, since incomplete adaptation to need makes objects real . . .' (Winnicott 1971: p. 11).

Yet it would be incorrect to interpret Winnicott's words to mean that frustration helps the child adapt to reality and acknowledge its objective existence outside the omnipotent fantasies of illusion. Winnicott upholds the paradox that frustration and disillusionment are inevitable, although illusion continues to play a role in our acknowledgement of reality, and that it is through the creative element of illusion that reality awakens joy and interest in us. Winnicott formulated the point of the paradox of illusion as follows: 'The mother's adaptation to the infant's need, when good enough, gives the infant the *illusion* that there is an external reality that corresponds to the infant's own capacity to create' (Winnicott 1971: p. 12). Thus although it is the mother's task to gradually frustrate the child, 'she has no hope of success unless at first she has been able to give sufficient opportunity for illusion' (Winnicott 1971: p.11).

I have mentioned several times that illusion and disillusionment have been important concepts in Winnicott's view of early mother–child relationships. The concept of illusion became a tool for Winnicott in his quest to acknowledge the gap between linguistic categories and our experience. Thus Winnicott upheld the paradox inherent in the term illusion in that it does refer to reality. 'There is no such thing as an infant' (Winnicott 1990f: p. 39) is one of many expressions of the role that illusion plays in every self–other relation. The child's first illusion is the germ of its belief in its own omnipotence; the breast exists but the child creates it. However, as emphasized by Khan (1996c), we should not mistake experiences of omnipotence for its defensive use. The latter belongs to a magical form of control, while the healthy experience of powerfulness is a spontaneous and natural expression of the child's joy in its own creative activity. Disillusionment is necessary and healthy so long as it takes place in accordance with the child's ability to wait and to tolerate a certain amount of frustration. Yet disillusionment also becomes acceptable because it is followed by new, age-appropriate illusions. This illusion is not only on the part of the child. After the illusion of the breast we have transitional objects, play, and adult cultural activity.

We generally understand illusion as a fraudulent desire to improve reality. Freud (1927b) was among the first to define illusion in accordance with this general understanding and specify that in illusion the wish-fulfilling aspect of our relationship with reality plays a dominant role. Winnicott and those around him – not least Milner – reacted against a too-negative interpretation of the function of illusion. Their work rediscovered the term with the 'countercultural significance' it has historically had in western thought (Turner 2002), and they wielded it as a weapon against what they perceived to be a unilateral practice of scientism and the function of intellect.

Winnicott and Milner introduced the idea that illusion is a means whereby we may cathect or enchant things in the world around us, providing us with pleasure and joy in our undertakings. Milner expressed her homage to illusion as follows:

> Moments when the original 'poet' in each of us created the outside world for us, by finding the familiar in the unfamiliar, are perhaps forgotten by most people; or else they are guarded in some secret place of memory because they were too much like visitations of the gods to be mixed with everyday thinking.
>
> (Milner 1996: p. 88)

It was the observation of the small child's hesitation prior to making use of objects in external reality that led to the idea of necessary illusion and potential space, and which made Winnicott postulate the paradox of an insurmountable gap between imagination and perception. One might claim that Winnicott carried on Freud's idea of the child's hallucinatory production of the breast by adding the illusory experience the child gets of its own creative power when the mother places the breast exactly where the child is ready to create it. While Winnicott was convinced of the creative element of illusion, in Freud's case dreams were what opened this secret space where 'the original "poet" in each of us' unfolds under the protection of sleep. We close our eyes and hallucinate, as Freud said in connection with his study of dreams. In the following I shall supplement Winnicott's thoughts on the potential spaces of play and illusion with a few thoughts on the space of dreams.

Dream space

Although dreams belong to the inner world, we position them in relational space by narrating them. Therefore, to use a term from Winnicott, we may designate the narrated dreams as a transitional phenomenon. Note that we are dealing with dreams once they have 'left the dream machine' (Pontalis 1981: p. 25), described so clearly by Freud (1900b) in his monumental work, *The Interpretation of Dreams*. When an analysand brings a dream into therapeutic space, it is generally associated with a certain expectation. Without knowing precisely where it will take us, the analysand has an experience of a living, creatively formed material that corresponds to a piece of lived life. Telling a dream is connected to an excitement similar to that associated with playing. In both instances we are entering into a space where subjective experience encounters a form of external reality, which in the case of dreams may be their connection to our personal lives. Dreaming and living belong to the same category, according to Winnicott, while daydreaming and fantasizing are something entirely different. 'Dreams fit into object-relating in the real world, and living in the real world fits into the dream-world . . . By contrast, however, fantasying remains an isolated phenomenon, absorbing energy but not contributing – either to dreaming or to living' (Winnicott 1971: p. 26). In other words, we may juxtapose daydreaming and fantasizing with the fetish while the dream as a product of symbolization shows us layer upon layer of significances intimately connected to our personal lives.

According to Milner, the limitation of daydreaming is that it has severed the link to action. Here thought plays with itself in ontological freewheeling. Dreams, however, like all other creative activities, uphold their connection to some fragment of lived life. In telling a dream we behave like a child playing. We allow our internal mental world to meet a piece of reality and this meeting forms something to connect the two. Creativity, then, supposedly stems from allowing the two worlds we have been obliged to isolate from one another to meet again and in doing so, to provide them with form. There is a particular experiential quality attached to this creative moment where things come together or overlap. Inger Christensen called it 'the condition of secrecy' (see Chapter 8). This state is dependent on a particular relationship between internal and external, in other words a creative relationship. 'To raise up the internal to the external we must begin with the external, begin in all that is visible, which – through life lived – has been saved and forgotten in its corresponding forms of visibility' (Christensen 2000: p. 40; translated from Danish by KM).

Winnicott arrived at his distinction between dream and fantasy by working with a patient who had sought refuge in daydreams her entire life. Instead of living life, she had broken with it and in her dissociated state of consciousness had shut off her own creative impulses. The result was that her daydreams had no symbolic value. '*It had no poetic value*' (Winnicott 1971: p. 35). Her dreams, however, were the result of symbolic activity and for this reason did contain certain poetic moments. The key to understanding why this woman had isolated herself in her daydreaming routine turned out to be the word formlessness, the code word for the creative possibilities of dreaming as well as playing. Fabric is formless before it is cut and shaped. 'Both prior to sitting down to paper in order to perhaps, perhaps not, write a poem, and later, when we sit there for hours, it is like this: as if we have lost our way' (Christensen 2000: p. 41; by KM). Winnicott believed that both playing and dreaming have this formless or unfocused character. The patient in question gradually acknowledged that no-one in her childhood had understood that she had to begin in formlessness. Thus we have introduced another word for the hesitation described above; the state of the child when spontaneously playing, and which Winnicott also termed 'a non-purposive state, as one might say a sort of ticking over of the unintegrated personality' (Winnicott 1971: p. 55).

Just as the young child requires the environment to facilitate its exploitation of the illusory space of play, there also appear to be certain things which need to be present if unfocused dream activity is to create a dream of symbolic or poetic value. Once again experiences from working with borderline patients have made it necessary to distinguish between dreams of symbolic value and dreams that are narrated without a narrative form. These experiences have made significant contributions to classical dream theory and emphasized the importance of the holding function of the mother.

On being unable to dream

One of my first borderline analysands surprised me by showing up for her sessions with long, dramatic, image-laden dreams. She often had to spend the entire session telling such a dream, which was all but impossible to comment on. In the beginning I was enthusiastic about this opportunity to work through what classical psychoanalytic technique had taught me was the privileged route to the unconscious. However, it soon turned out that these dreams could not be interpreted using the technique described by Freud in *The Interpretation of Dreams*. There was no gap between the latent and the manifest, nor was there any structuring of unconscious material in accordance with the mechanisms of condensation and displacement. It appeared that my patient's dreams had not been through the process of dream work and therefore failed to present themselves according to the logic of secondary processes. Rather, the primary processes were mingling directly with the narrative and structuring function of the ego.

Numerous analysts have had this experience, which has led to a different understanding and handling of dreams than that classically prescribed in the literature. Upon reading *The Interpretation of Dreams* it becomes clear that for Freud this work consisted in uncovering the meaning of latent dreams. The title of Freud's book seduces us into combining dreams and interpretation and into believing that the primary significance of dreams is always to be found through interpretation, and is not immediately apparent. Freud's achievement consisted in documenting that dreams can be understood and that they have a meaning and a purpose, which he determined to be wish fulfilment. The dreams of our non-neurotic patients have made it necessary to modify both these assumptions.

However, Freud did realize that some dreams appear to contradict the purpose of wish fulfilment. Traumatic dreams were one of the examples he referred to in speculating on the necessity of a principle beyond pleasure. In this context he admits that there appear to be certain preconditions for dreams to establish themselves with the function of wish fulfilment. Freud was not satisfied with common-sense explanations that would claim it natural to return to painful memories, nor was he ready to give up on the theory of the wish-fulfilling function of dreams and thus ended up suggesting: 'that the function of dreaming, like so much else, is upset in this condition and diverted from its purposes' (Freud 1920: p. 13). Elsewhere in the same text he says of traumatic dreams that they

> are here helping to carry out another task, which must be accomplished before the dominance of the pleasure principle can ever begin . . . it is only consistent to grant that there was also a time before the purpose of dreams was the fulfilment of wishes.
>
> (Freud 1920: pp. 32–33)

It was only his successors, however, who continued to work along the lines indicated here, based on their experiences with other types of patients. They have contributed various suggestions as to the preconditions necessary for the wish-fulfilling function of dreams.

Lewin (1946) introduced the concept of the dream screen and thereby the idea that dreams require a screen on which to be projected. Just as we need a canvas on which to paint a picture, a stage on which to perform a play and a screen on which to show a film, dreams too require their framework.[3] Winnicott distinguishes between the dream that accompanies sleep, where the mind is unfocused, and the dream that can be shaped and told. In other words we must distinguish between dream experiences and the shaped dream. Khan (1996d) expanded Lewin's idea and suggested a distinction between the dream screen and the space of dreams. 'The dream screen is something *on to* which the dream imagery is projected. Whereas the dream-space is a psychic area *in* which the dream-process is actualized into experiential reality' (Khan 1996d: p. 314). Furthermore, he suggests distinguishing between the dream process, which is a biological phenomenon, and the acquired space of dreams, which depends on an ability developed by the child analogous to the creation of intermediate space. Through experiences with patients like mine, Khan was led to the insight that what some patients believed to be a dream might be better described as an 'absurd *mélange* of images' (Khan 1996d: p. 309) which leaves the patient depersonalized and exhausted. In consequence he introduced the concept of the good dream (Khan 1996b) and argued that dreams do not necessarily serve the wish-fulfilling purpose defined by Freud. Good dreams require certain preconditions that may all be described as ego capacities. Thus Khan refers to, 'the ego's capacity to sustain the sleep-wish, controlling excessive influx of the primary process and appropriate dosage of "day residues" to structuralize the latent "dream wish" into a contained dream text' (Khan 1989: p. 42).

Pontalis (1981) suggested that dreams can only achieve their 'binding' function when some form of 'pre-binding' has taken place. In accordance with Lewin and Khan he believes that '[t]he dream process cannot function along the lines of its own logic until the dream-space – the "psychic system" – has been constituted as such' (Pontalis 1981: pp. 31–32).

Pontalis supplemented Lewin's idea of the dream screen with the assumption that the interface of dreams not only serves as a protective shield against the outside world, but also serves to protect against the internal world. This corresponds to the barrier described by Bion (1988) which on the one hand protects us from becoming overwhelmed by unconscious material while on the other permits psychic material to reach consciousness through some form of processing. I take this to mean that we are dealing with the earliest ego-functions, which Freud claimed were binding in character.

The above researchers all postulate a space, a framework or a screen as a necessary structural precondition for the symbolizing and wish-fulfilling purpose of dreams to be established. They arrive at this assumption through their experiences with patients who do not appear to have established this space for dreams, and whose dreams therefore do not acquire the character of dream text. In attempting to address the questions of how we imagine this space for dreams to have arisen and under what necessary conditions, I would like to quote Milner's poetic description of this psychic space:

> It is one's own inner body awareness that takes over the role of the external mother; not just in the sense that one learns to do for oneself the external acts of bodily care that one's mother once did, but in this sense of fashioning a kind of psychic or new womb out of one's own body image, as being the only secure place to inhabit, from which to put one's feelers to the world.
>
> (Milner 1969: p. 273)

Milner is not referring to the mother as the good and bad object, but to her function, which the child internalizes or identifies with. The child creates the mother's containing function within itself on condition that her absence and necessary frustrations have not been too overwhelming, but have been able to serve as a driving force behind the establishment of thought and symbolization.

When this screen fails to function, the dream is not able to function in accordance with the purpose of wish fulfilment defined by Freud. Quite the opposite, dreams appear to serve the purpose of evacuating painful experiences rather than processing them in the service of the principle of pleasure. Just as the small child needs the mother's holding function and the patient requires the analytic setting, we may add that dreams also need a framework in order to manifest themselves as dreams. The actual formation of dreams as perceived by Freud confirms the assumptions of the mother's holding function as a prerequisite for the establishment of psychic structure in the young child, as claimed by Winnicott, Bion, and others.

Dreaming, said Freud, is hallucinatory wish fulfilment. In Chapter 4 I laid out the model of the psychic apparatus first formulated by Freud in 'Project for a Scientific Psychology' (1895a), where he defined hallucinatory wish fulfilment as the recathecting of a memory trace associated with an experience of satisfaction. The prerequisite for that hallucinatory wish fulfilment and later for the pleasure ego is the existence of previous experiences of optimal satisfaction. The relationship between experiences of satisfaction and experiences of pain firstly indicates the environment with which the child's needs are met as a prerequisite for what will later instigate wish fulfilment and uphold the mechanism of pleasure/unpleasure. Secondly, it indicates that in lieu of the psychically binding function attached to hallucinatory wish fulfilment there may be an unbinding function, which derives from the child's inability to master excessive experiences of pain.

Here we begin to discern a connection between hallucinatory experiences of satisfaction, dreams, and Winnicott's idea of the necessity of illusion. The reason for this necessity is that it is linked to a hope and belief in the possibility of shared experiences. Associating oneself with an object creates freedom and pleasure. In this context, pleasure may be defined by the binding of the ego to an object that functions as an optimum object, i.e. as an object that ensures optimal satisfaction. In other words, hallucinatory satisfaction requires an optimally good object. If the difference between hallucination and perception is too great and the projection onto the object cannot be confirmed by the real object, a chasm opens between the wished-for object and the perceived object. The result may be that the child fails to make use of illusory images of satisfactory situations and, as Winnicott (1975c) says, does not undergo 'satisfactory personalization'. Later in life this may result in magical attempts to compensate this fundamental lack of experiences of satisfaction or, as described by Rycroft (1968), withdrawal from the world and the creation of a defensively idealized inner object. Borderline patients, according to Khan (1996b), are as a result unable to make use of the illusory character of transferential space. They either deny their dependence or compulsively act out in a concrete way their needs, thus transcending the 'transference limits'.

To paraphrase Milner, we meet people who shut off their creative urges and who fear dreaming and playing or who shut out reality and magically try to cling to the primary object. I have referred to several of my own experiences with these patients in light of two very different ways of using therapeutic space, which in many ways correspond to what Milner, Khan, and Rycroft have described. In one case we are dealing with patients who appear to have shut off all connection to the inner experiences of their lives and seek refuge in what Khan aptly terms mentalization. Alternatively the patients cling desperately to a magical and omnipotent form of control over the primary object, from which they fear invasion even as they wish to fuse with it.

After having read *Playing and Reality* I wish to suggest what I consider an important difference between the playfulness of the healthy child and borderline patients' enclosure within a magical and stereotypical fantasy universe.

Assuming the availability of the ordinary devoted mother's holding function, the child will be able to internalize this function and form the first, delicate beginnings of its own inner space and the accompanying earliest ego function of binding. The term 'ordinary devoted mother' signifies a mother who is capable of meeting the child's needs in such a way as to give the child the experience that they match reality. Part of the concept, however, is the – to the child – vitally important fact that the mother can never adapt perfectly. The child will be unable to develop thinking and symbolization if it does not encounter a certain measure of frustration and absence. Once this space has been created and the child has found confidence in its own creative ability under protective illusion, it will be able to use its transitional objects and populate potential space. By moving out into the world and back into an inner state, the child will learn to be alone in the presence of another, i.e. it will learn to be alone with itself. This will allow it to experience a place where it feels at home, the nascent ego will be able to make use of creative spaces to unfold symbolizing activity, and the child will then be able to both play and dream.

If the preconditions are not met, or are met incompletely, i.e. if absence and frustrations shake the child's confidence, it will fail to develop a solidly anchored inner space – a place to belong. Instead of transitional objects it will resort to fetishistic objects and rather than being able to be alone, it will desperately seek in others that primary figure who answered its needs incompletely. A fossilized space arises in lieu of potential space, where fantasy takes the place of imagination and symbolization frequently tends to become concrete due to the flawed binding function of the ego. These people do not feel at home in themselves but are restlessly chasing an external object to serve these functions. Instead of the psychically binding function we see various expressions of the work of the negative, and a form of mental pseudo reality takes the place of normal psychic reality.

Notes

1 Milner's books *On Not Being Able to Paint* (1950) and *The Hands of the Living God* (1969) have the same character as Winnicott's work. She too is able to lay out her material in such a way that content and narrative style harmonize. Both Milner's books supplement Winnicott's ideas on play as a creative process.

2 Winnicott perceives games and their organization as a way of attempting to avoid the frightening aspect of play. One might say that organized games feature a form of suspended suspense, attached to the act of following the rules of the game, with which most children are intensely preoccupied and which a lot of adults are more interested in than the game itself.

3 Henrik Enckell (2002) has suggested a metaphor for the matrix that precedes the symbolizing function of the psyche, namely the warp. The psychic material which is produced in this invisible warp he calls the web, with deliberate reference to the work of weaving.

10

The borderline concept

Although observations of patients with pathologies located in the border zone between neurosis and psychosis date back to the birth of modern psychiatry, the concept of borderline was not used until the mid 1900s.

As previously mentioned, it was Adolph Stern who introduced the term 'borderline group of neuroses' to denote patients who could not be understood based on traditional diagnostic terms. The great interest in the borderline concept and the colossal amount of literature later written on the subject reflects the fact that borderline pathologies must be considered the dominant psychopathology of our time. I myself have used the term borderline in a broad, structural sense. I have sought to delimit the key problematic of what we understand by schizoid and borderline personality structure, both in those patients who develop psychosis and those who present with either hysterical or obsessive neurotic personality structures.

As described in the historical account outlined in Chapter 2, the word borderline not only denotes a border area between psychosis and neurosis; it also reflects a border problematic between psychiatry and psychoanalysis. Thus it is no coincidence that it was primarily psychoanalysts working in psychiatry up through the 1900s who described these patients. The current agreement between clinicians and researchers in the field of psychiatry when it comes to the description and treatment of these patients is largely due to their efforts.

There are still great theoretical divergences, however, when it comes to understanding the aetiology of borderline patients, particularly their personality structure and its mode of functioning. These theoretical differences become evident when studying borderline phenomena with clinicians who work with other, broader concepts than the one known from descriptive psychiatry and diagnostic categorization.

As representatives of such a broader view on the subject of borderline I have included British object-relational theorists such as Balint, Winnicott, and Bion, as well as French analysts among whom Laplanche, Aulagnier, Green and Pontalis are the most prominent.

These different understandings are not just of theoretical interest; naturally they have certain implications for treatment. This becomes particularly evident when comparing the treatment studies featured in the works of Kernberg, Masterson and Gabbard with descriptions found in the work of Balint, Winnicott and others from the British school.

One of the underlying intentions behind this present work has been to debate these very different theoretical approaches to a pathological form beyond neurosis. In this final chapter I shall gather the threads and try to retrace the different steps on the road to the concept of borderline pathology which I have indicated throughout the previous chapters.

Theoretical views on borderline pathology

In spite of differences in their explanations, most theories on borderline pathology take their cue from a psychological developmental perspective. This also applies to the two explanatory models described as the mother–child interaction model and the trauma model. Kernberg (1972, 1985, 1986), Masterson (1972, 1973, 2000), and Masterson and Rinsley (1975) have been highlighted as representatives of the viewpoint that the aetiological origins of borderline pathology must be sought in the earliest mother–child relationships. Yet there is one important difference, since Kernberg – in accordance with his ego-psychological, Kleinian starting point – has formulated a complex theory of internalized object-relations and emphasized the tendency of borderline patients to split positive and negative self and object representations. Conversely, Masterson emphasizes the rewarding or punishing behaviour of the empirical mother vis-à-vis the child in what Mahler termed the rapprochement phase. Masterson's approach to understanding the aetiology of borderline pathology follows the same explanatory tradition as the trauma model, where external phenomena are emphasized as important aetiological factors.

Together these theories give the impression of a broad and complex psychopathological phenomenon, and all indicate the necessity of a multifactorial explanation. Each of these theories has contributed significant clinical observations. Masterson (1972, 1973, 1990) suggested the apt phrase 'abandonment depression', and indicated a particularly vulnerable stage in the rapprochement phase. Adler (1975) and Adler and Buie (1979) indicated patients' lacking the capacity for evocative memory and self-soothing. In spite of the numerous important clinical observations, I should like to emphasize the two main problems limiting the theoretical value of these explanations: 1) The distinction between the phenomenological clinical level and the abstract theoretical level is insufficient. Among other things this is apparent in the difficulties in explaining how certain external factors become internal mental processes; 2) Normal psychological developmental phenomena are used to explain a particular psychopathological phenomenon. In the following, I shall briefly explain what I mean.

It is important to distinguish between the level of clinical description where we may, for instance, examine psychic states and mental configurations. This is how I understand Masterson's concept of abandonment depression; it makes sense because it sums up an emotional register which is highly evident in clinical practice. We could also say that Masterson addresses the clinician in each of us. Yet Masterson leaves us with some confusion at the theoretical level, simply because he treats theoretical explanations as though they were phenomenological descriptions. When Masterson explains the development of the disturbed ego-functions of borderline patients he typically formulates it as follows: 'Certain functions of the ego – reality perception, impulse control, frustration tolerance and stable ego boundaries – can only develop through successful separation and individuation' (Masterson 1990: p. 75). However, this is not a theoretical explanation. We are brought no closer to understanding how these ego-functions might be linked to the development of separation and individuation. They belong to a fairly abstract metapsychological level, yet they are referred to as though they pertain to the same clinical, descriptive level as processes of individuation and separation. Masterson owes us an explanation of how the child's specific separation and independence affects such complex ego-functions.

Here we touch upon a problem of a more general nature: how may we explain the processes by which mother–child interplay becomes internal structures within the child? Introjection, internalization, and identification are merely descriptive reformulations that offer no actual explanation to the problem (see Note 5 on page 136). The clinical world does not always distinguish clearly between this basic descriptive level and the abstract level at which theories are generated. In other words, we need such a level of abstraction in order to create models capable of capturing the difference and complexity of the fundamental structures that we assume lie behind manifest clinical phenomena.

Masterson's emphasis on separation and individuation as the psychological developmental explanation of the weak ego-functions of borderline patients will serve to illustrate the other pitfall that springs to mind when explaining borderline pathology. This is particularly evident within the psychological developmental research tradition of which Masterson is also a part. The problem lies in making a normal psychological developmental phenomenon the explanation of psychopathological development.[1] There can be no doubt as to the value, for instance, of Mahler's concept of the rapprochement phase or Adler's concept of evocative memory in aiding our understanding of both normal and pathological development. Problems and the limitations arise only when we make specific developmental psychological phases and phenomena the final explanations of a phenomenon as complex as what we may observe in borderline patients. One of Winnicott's great achievements was the emphasizing of the good-enough mother as a mother who, although she is capable of adapting to her child's needs, never does so perfectly. Frustrations and disappointment are equally important parts of the normal mother's care as her own unconscious fantasies and desires, which reveal the existence of quite contradictory impulses and fantasies even in the most devoted of mothers. Thus when we in our explanations take our cues from mother–child interaction, it is important that we specify the disturbances in this interaction instead of resorting to general statements that all too easily veil the difference between normal and pathological development. For instance, when Masterson says that some of the functioning of the ego can only develop under the conditions of successful processes of individuation and separation, it constitutes an untimely generalization that leaves an open question as to the exact difference between normal and pathological separation and individuation, and how the latter may result in disturbances in ego functioning.

I think these are the kinds of difficulties that have caused many clinicians and researchers to suggest adopting a multifactorial explanation for borderline pathology. However, such a multifactorial explanation does not solve the two problems I have indicated here, which consist in distinguishing between descriptive and abstract levels as well as between specific and generalized explanations. Multifactorial solutions may in fact obscure these problems even further.

The above critique cannot be addressed to Kernberg. He formulated a complex theory comprising a genetic–dynamic as well as a structural point of view. Thereby Kernberg's theory lives up to the requirement for metapyschological complexity, yet it still lacks connection to the world of clinical practice. When Kernberg speaks as a clinician and draws on cases and vignettes, he does so with the voice of the psychiatrist. When he expresses himself as a researcher or theorist he does so using his metapsychological overview. Thus Kernberg's theories move between the discourses of psychiatry and metapsychology. One might even, with Green (1997b) – and perhaps a little polemically – term his theory borderline, since it exists on the border between ego psychology and Kleinian theory, between psychiatry and classical metapsychology. However, Kernberg did contribute a theoretical overview, and it is not unjustified to highlight him as the bridge-builder between the worlds of psychiatry and psychoanalysis. Kernberg is convinced that borderline patients are not a colourful multitude of various psychopathologies along a continuum between neurosis and psychosis. Rather, we are dealing with a certain form of pathology organized within a personality structure to which he attributed three characteristics: a) non-specific manifestations of ego weakness, b) identity diffusion, and c) specific defensive mechanisms, including especially splitting, which he views in light of internalized object-relations.

Kernberg believes that the fundamental defect in borderline pathology is related to the capacity of the individual to synthesize positive and negative self and object representations. Quite in keeping with a Kleinian interpretation of drive theory, Kernberg emphasizes an innate potential for aggression which in these patients is particularly fixed within the oral phase. Thus for Kernberg, as for most clinicians, the concept of splitting plays a central role in a dynamic understanding of borderline pathology. However, as we saw in Chapter 6, Klein's (1987b) concept of splitting found quite other implications than those of the concept of splitting introduced by Freud in his attempts to understand psychotic defence.

From the earliest attempts at a descriptive delimitation of borderline phenomena, dominant theoretic developments have moved along two tracks. The mainly psychiatric one emphasized external conditions: focus was either on early mother–child interaction or early trauma. The more psychodynamically oriented school of thought, however, combined dynamic and structural explanations with particular emphasis on the defensive splitting tendencies of the ego, in keeping with the dominant tradition of ego psychology.

We have the work of Winnicott and Bion to thank for the existence of an alternative to empirical approaches focusing on the responses of the specific mother to her child, and the traumatological explanations of borderline pathology. Both have contributed to nuancing the concept of the object, introduced the idea of the relation between self and object, and indicated a concept of the object freed from the notion of objectivity (see Note 10 on page 59). Winnicott never developed a cohesive theory of borderline pathology, but in many ways his work has turned out to be rich in observations and concepts relating to the structural problematic of borderline patients. This applies to his article on communication and non-communication, his ideas on the true and the false self, and not least on the psychopathology of the intermediate area and the idea of negative experience. Green (1997b, 1999) pointed out the significance of the negative through the concepts of blank psychosis and the dead mother. Green (1997a, 1998) also demonstrated that the idea of negative experience was latent in both Winnicott's and Bion's work.

Although Winnicott repeatedly underlined the significance of the mother's capacity for empathy and presence, he distinguishes himself from the more Kleinian analysts through his concept of the object. He emphasizes that the significance of the mother in her early relations with the child is not to do with her being an object, but rather a function or a functional entity (Gantheret 1983). Before the child internalizes an introject or identifies with an object it creates within itself a holding function. Bion (1988) pointed out the mother's ability for reverie as a prerequisite for the child to develop an apparatus with which to think thoughts. Winnicott (1971) expresses this in the concept of being and claims that the mother's ability to offer a breast which *is* – rather than one which *does* – is required if the young child is to experience confirmation of its existence. This corresponds to what he elsewhere terms the difference between responding to the child's spontaneous gesture and reacting to the child. I shall return to this later, since it has played an important part in my attempts to elucidate the fundamental problematic of borderline patients. Winnicott's work has been highly influential in understanding this problematic, which is created through an overwhelming reaction or intrusion.

It has appeared necessary, however, to supplement Winnicott's charming descriptions of the good-enough mother with a dimension which seems absent in his terminology. In Winnicott's universe the primary caregiver is depicted purely through its maternal functions with no trace of the mother's desire for the child. The entire field of object-relational understanding of early mother–child relations, from Klein to Winnicott, appears to miss what Scarfone (2002–03) termed 'the exciting mother' in an extension of Laplanche's terminology. He refers to an '*exciting* mother, endowed with a repressed sexuality, who contrasts with Winnicott's *good enough* mother, whose importance we would not otherwise doubt' (Scarfone 2002–2003: p. 72). In Winnicott's description of mother–child interaction only the child demands recognition – first of being and then of the satisfaction of its drive impulses. Winnicott appears to have no eye for the communication from mother to child, which contains enigmatic signifiers – to quote Laplanche – nor for what Aulagnier described as the prerequisite status of the mother's ability to repress her unconscious wishes and transform them into motherly tenderness and love.

This assumption is strictly necessary, however, if we wish to understand the difference between normal motherly care and the form of failure or assault we often sum up in the concept of trauma. There is inevitable seduction in every mother's interplay with her very young child. There are two reasons behind this: 1) The mother must of necessity interpret the needs of her child and she must satisfy these needs in accordance with her understanding and interpretation. In this respect seduction means leading the child's libidinous impulses into forms that accord with culturally prescribed norms of loving interaction between mother and child; 2) Since the mother is driven by libidinous impulses we must assume that there is an inherent repression barrier in the care of the ordinarily devoted mother ensuring against unveiled libidinous, narcissistic or destructive impulses.

Traumatic seduction, however, arises when the mother or another adult is unable to distinguish between normal caregiving and the satisfaction of her own primitive drives. Aulagnier (2001) distinguishes between necessary and abusive violence, while Laplanche speaks of general and perverse seduction.[2] However, we only understand the implications of traumatic seduction when we associate it with infantile ego development and examine how the primitive ego becomes able to handle such early trauma. When all goes well the child will be able to repress the pain at the time and later – when the repressed material returns – after-pressure can take place. In this case we are dealing with the complex phenomenon which is repression and which consists of primal repression followed by after-pressure. The latter derives from signal anxiety, which in normal development both signals and inhibits destructive traumatic anxiety.

In less fortunate cases the pain is so overwhelming and the child's ego so undeveloped that this process is not possible. The child will then be forced to use more primitive defence mechanisms. This is where concepts such as foreclosure, negation and disavowal have been introduced. I shall expand on this later, restrict myself now to mentioning that while the return of repressed material creates anxiety, the return of the foreclosed to consciousness will trigger helplessness (Freud 1926), nameless terror (Bion 1988), or fear of breakdown (Winnicott 1992b).

It is not merely in descriptions of mother–child interaction, however, that object-relations theory excludes the aspect of Freudian drive. Borderline symptomatologies are notably silent on the subject of sexual difficulties. McDougall (1995), Aulagnier (2001) and Green (2000b) have described in different ways how these patients construct their own primitive sexual theories in a form of secret life. Furthermore, the object-relations of these patients is subject to obsessive and ritualized forms of sexuality, frequently of an addictive nature and bearing witness to the use of sexual activity to reduce tension, rather than for satisfaction.

Betweenity

The fact that borderline patients' difficulties play out in their intimate relations has been emphasized numerous times, both in this present work and in the general literature. The typical ambivalent behaviour pattern is either clingy or rejecting, revealing that these people not only fear abandonment as well as invasion, but also long for both. This is the dilemma at the heart of their lacking capacity to symbolize absence, which is experienced as loss and nothingness.

Their difficulties become apparent in interactions both in a therapeutic setting and in their outside lives. I have introduced the word betweenity and referred to Winnicott's concept of the intermediate area as the place where these patients' difficulties play out. They are fundamentally unable to enter into normal give and take and are therefore incapable of expressing themselves creatively in human relationships. They fear closeness as much as they long for it in an almost fusionary sense.

Closer examinations of these patients' ways of relating reveal great differences, indicative of fundamentally different defence strategies as well as variations in personality structure and functioning. Balint (1979) was among the first to draw attention to such different modes of relationality, which he termed ocnophilic and philobatic. Pontalis (1981) and Laing (1990) both confirmed and expanded on these relational modes. I have used the terms the logic of desperation and the logic of indifference to indicate these two very different experiences in the field of transference and counter-transference as they appear in working with borderline patients.

The most evident experience we encounter in working with borderline patients is one of overwhelming invasion. Space as well as thought is invaded. Psychic distances are impossible to uphold, because the patient fills out space with what is experienced as a bombardment of fantasies, memories and acting-out. The as-if nature of therapeutic space no longer exists. Once again we are reminded of Winnicott's distinction between imagination and fantasy; in this context adding the temporal dimension he attributes to the latter. Everything that happens takes place in the now, except that it does not take place at all. Conversely, imagination has the future as its temporal perspective. In this group of patients separation anxiety is dominant. The analytical situation is marked by acting-out. Thinking and symbolization are blocked, and instead we find what Segal (1992) called symbolic equation. It is as though psychic thought activity had been transferred to the body from which experiences are evacuated in what Green (1999) termed excorporation. Neither the relation nor the narration displays any mental distance. Fantasies and memories are presented as endless thoughts devoid of pause or reason: like figures in a puppet show. Space is entirely filled and the analyst experiences an overriding sense of exhaustion and a claustrophobic feeling of suffocating in a space that allows no room for movement.

I understand all these activities as desperate attempts to cover up an inner void: to fill it up and fill it out in order to make it appear less, and to avoid feeling it.

In contrast to this group we have patients who are difficult to reach. Joseph (1994) and McDougall (1992) have called them anti-analysands. I myself have grouped them under the term indifference.

With this group of patients the analyst may – for a while – feel that things are progressing as they should, but soon we are obliged to realize that no change is taking place, and that we are in fact moving in circles. We are dealing with people who are subjected to a consistent compulsion to produce thoughts and create meaning in order to avoid connecting with their bodies and emotions. This is what Winnicott means by the false self, where a closed system is created in order to avoid formlessness and encapsulate the void, to prevent it breaking though. As analysts we have a clear impression that helping these patients means evoking life and finding the self, in contrast to the former group where the most important task seems to be rendering existence visible. In both cases we are dealing with a borderline problematic. Within the transference area this may be experienced as an opposition between being included vis-à-vis excluded. In the first case we experience alternating sensations of closeness and emptiness while at the same time feeling invaded. In the second, splitting is experienced firstly as a splitting within the patient; a dissociation of thought and affect and of body and intellect. In these cases the therapist's experience may perhaps best be described as aimless wandering in a lifeless landscape. Both groups of patients require the creation of connection. But where the former group is in need of a connection to the object in terms of both relation and distance because of dominant separation anxiety, the second group requires the creation of new connections since the established ones are frozen and serve only defensive purposes, hence the extensive use of negation and 'attacks on linking', to use Bion's (1990a) phrase. In the former case, it could be said that our work consists of elaboration and symbolization; while in the latter it is a question of re-establishing broken connections to bodies and emotions. Both require the creation of an overlapping area, a field that may be traversed and which, metaphorically speaking, permits an experience of being touched.

Splitting and other primitive defence mechanisms

The idea of the defensive splitting of the ego may be encountered in several places in Freud's writings and is most often associated with attempts at understanding psychotic defence. While splitting has been widely used after Klein's introduction of split ego and object representations, Freud speaks of a split in the functions of the ego, which are of critical importance to patients' ability to relate to reality.

Freud writes in his 1924 article on neurosis and psychosis:

> In conclusion, there remains to be considered the question of what mechanism, analogous to repression, can be the means of which the ego detaches itself from the external world. This cannot, I think, be answered without fresh investigations; but such a mechanism, it would seem, must like repression comprise a withdrawal of the cathexis sent out by the ego.
>
> (Freud 1924b: p. 153)

This idea is followed up by notions of the ego's attempts to avoid a rupture in any direction by deforming itself. This means that the ego will subject itself to assault and even in the worst case to a splitting of its own core. Attempting to specify the difference between neurosis and psychosis, Freud claimed that while neurosis ignores reality, psychosis disavows (*verleugnet*) and attempts to replace it.[3] Disavowal is clearly different from repression, for it targets the external world, while repression targets internal impulses. Freud further developed this line of thought. In psychosis a transformation of external reality takes place on the psychic sedimentations of previous relations, i.e. on memory traces, ideas, and judgements which have previously arisen through encounters with reality and which later come to represent reality within the psyche. This viewpoint was presented by Federn, who claimed in 1953 that the first step of psychosis consists not in the loss of reality, but in thoughts becoming reality. We may sum up these two intimations in a couple of significant observations. While neurosis refers to a horizontal separation between consciousness and the repressed, more primitive defences must also feature a vertical split between consciousness and reality. Such a split has a double effect of the ego losing a piece of reality as well as part of its own functioning. These are the disturbances we may observe as 'the inconsistencies, eccentricities and follies of men' (Freud 1924b: p. 153) and are as such a form of perversion of the functions of the ego corresponding to the sexual disturbances observable in neurotics. Federn (1977) discussed decathexis of the ego and Pontalis (1981) believed that these patients display significant destructive powers, seeking to exterminate psychic reality.

Freud linked the splitting of the ego to reality testing or what he termed the function of judgement. These two mechanisms, vertical splitting and the function of judgement, became the ingredients in the defence mechanisms which Freud referred to variously as foreclosure, disavowal and negation.

In a 1925 article on negation Freud describes a relatively sophisticated defence mechanism which both presupposes repression and in a way cancels it out. The starting point was the clinical observation of patients' negative statements, such as 'that person is *not* my mother', which lead to the certain affirmation that this is in fact the case. This type of observation, summed up in the term negation, constitutes a statement about unconscious ideas. These are in fact able to escape repression on condition that they are negated. Thus negation turns out to be double; as it always contains a simultaneous affirmation. In this way ideas are only allowed access to consciousness on the condition that they are negated. Affects associated with these ideas remain unconscious. Thus we are dealing with a purely intellectual function of judgement, as Freud calls it, or a merely intellectual appropriation of the unconscious. In negation, defence targets associated affects, which are thus isolated from intellectual appropriation. Negation is not quite the same as what we generally understand by intellectualization. Freud linked negation to his theory of drive and believed that negation serves the death drive. The dissolution of drives is what makes negativism so serious. I believe this mechanism of negation constitutes a very large part of the defence described above as the logic of indifference. Patients who utilize this form of logic frequently make admissions of a nature that others normally seek to hide and repress. These admissions are surprising in their lack of affect and regret. In Chapter 5 I referred to Sartre's introduction of the term bad faith. The link to affect and the body is severed and patients frequently resist any attempt to connect thought and emotion. In one of my patients, permanent hypochondriac ideas were the only remnant affectively linking body and thought. However, these ideas lived a life of their own. They appropriated consciousness accompanied by severe anxiety, but there was absolutely no connection between this man's intellectual acuity and the bodily sensations that resulted in a number of entirely foreign symptoms.

Intellectual negation is an expression of the general function of intellectual judgement which, according to Freud, is concerned in the main with two sorts of decisions. It can affirm or disaffirm the possession by an object of a particular attribute, in what is called a judgement of attribution; or it asserts whether an idea exists in reality, termed the judgement of existence.

Freud's discussion of the judgement of existence deals purely with differentiating between the internal and the external. Thus the existence of something means that it exists in reality and not purely as a subjective matter. However, when it comes to negation as it appears in clinical work, we must add that existence is not only about the external world, but in a very real way is also about the internal world. I realize that I am using the word existence in a somewhat different sense than the intellectual judgement discussed by Freud in his article on negation. Hopefully the following will clarify my argument.

If we are to follow Freud's idea of negation, we are dealing with a relatively advanced defence mechanism, which not only presupposes repression but is also capable – in accordance with the definitive reality ego – of determining whether something exists as an objective phenomenon or merely subjectively. In this case negation consists in the rejection of the subjective validity of an objectively existent phenomenon. These are the negating processes I believe to be present in one type of borderline patients, those I described under the heading of the logic of indifference. They are at the most mature and socially integrated end of the spectrum and approach narcissistic personality structures.

One might say that negation affects the ideas that might have been subjected to after-pressure, but which are accepted into consciousness under the symbol of negation. In other words, this mechanism of negation presupposes that a primal repression has taken place. This might also be expressed in such a way that negation steps in as a replacement for after-pressure. I believe something else is going on in foreclosure. I assume that it *replaces* primal repression and thus has other implications for reality testing.[4]

Freud intimated at an early stage that another defence mechanism exists besides repression, one which is more 'energetic and successful' and which consists in 'the ego reject[ing] the incompatible idea together with its affect and behav[ing] as if the idea had never occurred to the ego at all' (Freud 1894: p. 58). As we have seen, Freud returned several times to the mechanism of foreclosure. In his essay on Schreber he discussed it in relation to the mechanism of projection, and stated that ideas may be destined to be internally abolished only to thence return from the outside. With Lacan we may speak of an idea being foreclosed and returning in the real. In the story of the Wolf Man and in the writings where Freud explicitly deals with the difference between neurosis and psychosis, the mechanism of foreclosure is linked to the idea of castration. To Freud the idea of castration is subjected to foreclosure and linked to the function of judgement he discusses in his essay on negation. Furthermore he links foreclosure to castration more broadly understood as the fact of lack in the symbolic order. Lacan says of the Wolf Man that there can be no question of the boy negating castration, since this mechanism presupposes an affirmation and, he adds, this previous affirmation is what has not taken place in this case. Lacan introduces the idea of an original affirmation and asks what happens when this affirmation does not take place, i.e. when something which should have been symbolized fails to be so and therefore does not exist within the symbolic register.

In my discussion of Finn's story (see Chapter 7) I followed Freud and Lacan's idea of foreclosure as a suspension of primary affirmation or the fundamental judgement of attribution, which both Freud and Lacan define through the myth of the universality of the penis. In Finn's case I illustrated this by a form of hallucination: Finn sees something which is not there, and is therefore able to live in the conviction that everybody has had their appendix removed.

However, Finn's story can not be understood purely through an interpretation linking foreclosure to the idea of castration. Although Finn's problematic is played out within an Oedipal theme, his key conflict was not of an Oedipal nature. Nor was it sufficient to understand it in terms of separation. The mechanism of foreclosure appears to run deeper, based on a form of disaffirmation of existence itself. The question is no longer one of objective versus subjective existence, but of a form of acknowledgement related to existence in and of itself. Therefore we must add a dimension to Freud's function of judgement if we are to understand foreclosure and make it a significant part of a concept of borderline dynamics.

In the article 'Beyond the Pleasure Principle: The Affirmation of Existence' Karlsson (1998) – as indicated by the title – suggests supplementing Freud's theory of drives with the addition of some form of original affirmation of existence. The argument runs that existence is not only a question of the nature of the external world; 'the concept also entails an experience of inner constancy, endurance and gestalt' (Karlsson 1998: p. 46). Karlsson wishes to add an existential, phenomenological dimension to the psychoanalytic theory of drives. He thus approaches Winnicott's universe, where we are repeatedly confronted with the concepts of existential philosophy. At this point I shall not delve into a discussion on intimations of an existentialist dimension in Freud's conceptual world but merely content myself with stating that experiences with patients beyond a neurotic personality structure indicate that we must supplement Freud's function of judgement with a form of judgement of existence, confirming the subjective experience of continuity over time.

We might, however, express the same idea in the terminology of psychoanalysis and suggest that concepts such as being and existence refer to cathexes of the ego. This would not be far removed from Karlsson's thinking since he also states in the same text that the affirmation of existence can also be expressed as the binding of energy, which is one of the earliest and most important functions of the ego.[5]

As we saw in Chapter 4, the primary task of the ego is not in relation to reality, it is to function as an internal inhibition. In the 'Project for a Scientific Psychology', Freud (1895a) illustrated this inhibitive process through the so-called 'side cathexes', which are another expression of counter cathexis and thus of what we understand by primal repression (as mentioned previously we may understand this line of thought by transferring what is described here to the familiar phenomenon of thinking of something else in order to avoid thinking of something unpleasant).

In order for the ego to perform this inhibitive task, it must already be equipped with bound energy. Following Winnicott, we must assume that continuous experiences of satisfaction are a prerequisite for this. These satisfactions over time are what create the original reality ego, which is a narcissistically cathected ego, which might also be termed the bodily ego. At this point it might be appropriate to recall Anzieu's (1989) skin ego.

Transferring this to the psychic problematic of borderline patients we may assume that unlike psychotic patients, they are capable of distinguishing between that which exists objectively and that which exists as subjective phenomena. In other words they have not replaced external reality with a subjective reality as do psychotics. However, their reality testing is fragile since they are not sufficiently able to inhibit the pleasure/unpleasure mechanism as a protection against stimulation from within.

Thus we may conclude that the judgement functions of both the reality ego and the pleasure ego presuppose that experiences of satisfaction going right back to and constituting the very first separation between internal and external have been stable and continuous. Freud commented that the child learns to distinguish between internal and external through muscle activity. We must add that this relies on a basis of sufficiently satisfactory experiences, which constitute the foundation of the child's experience of being, or to express it in terms of classical theory, the creation of a sufficiently cathected ego.

This continued affirmation of being based on a sufficiently cathected ego is capable of binding the energy, which forms the foundation on which the gradually developed ego can make both affective and intellectual judgements. Federn (1977) called this phenomenon ego feeling in order to emphasize that this is not a mere matter of consciousness, but of something felt and experienced in a bodily as well as a psychic sense. He linked this imminent phenomenological experience of being to time, and believed that when ego feeling fails to reach the borders of the ego, it gives rise to what we call de-personalization. Karlsson (1998) expressed a similar thought, which appears capable of bridging the gap between Federn and Winnicott. He also perceives the affirmatory experience of existence as a temporal phenomenon and says: 'To affirm existence means paradoxically a binding together of presence and absence' (Karlsson 1998: p. 46).

As previously mentioned, Winnicott also suggested that this existential dimension is a prerequisite for all satisfaction. He also linked this experience to time and believed that the mother's capacity for being forms the basis of her ability to provide the child with such experiences of undisturbed being: 'This sense of being is something that antedates the idea of being-at-one-with, because there has not yet been anything else except identity' (Winnicott 1971: p. 80). He adds that this is perhaps what we are to understand by primary identification. Either the mother has a breast that is such that the child may experience being, or else she lacks this ability, obliging the child to develop without the ability to be, or with a crippled ability in this respect. At this level of affirming existence it is meaningless to speak of frustrating the child. The antithesis of being is not frustration but destruction, writes Winnicott.

Thus he heralds the theme which led to the concept of negative experience. To paraphrase Winnicott, something has taken place which has not found a psychic place. Foreclosure gains its vital significance precisely in the attempt to avoid such experiences. The price, however, as Freud writes, is that the ego, while trying to foreclose an idea, creates a splitting in its own function, which leaves the psyche with a mere negative contour of an idea. This is how I interpret Winnicott's statement: 'It seems that frustration belongs to satisfaction seeking. To the experience of being belongs something else, not frustration, but maiming' (Winnicott 1971: p. 81).

I shall conclude this attempt at a theoretical determination of the borderline concept by referring to my analysand Finn, who at one point told me of an experience that gave me access to one of these negatively outlined images within the psyche.

In one of our sessions (see Chapter 7) he provided me with a very vivid impression of how such an experience can leave a child with a feeling of emptiness as a frightening void of nothingness.

He had seen Michael Cunningham's film *The Hours* and told me of his reactions to a certain scene in the film: Mrs. Brown is preparing a cake for her husband's birthday with her son Richie, but inside she is preoccupied with planning her suicide. The boy follows her closely but is of course unable to reach her. Finn's experience is strong. The terrible, painful thing is that she says nothing. If she had screamed or shouted, the pain would not have been as great. In a flash he understands that this is why he himself has created 'noise' around and within himself throughout his entire life through his restlessness, inner agitation, rocking etc. These were meant to drown out the roar of silence caused by the piece of inner death he bore within him. I perceived the image of the dead princess as the outline of an experience that never became life-giving but represented the desire to suspend all these forms of agitation, where the pain does not exist either.

Notes

1 In recent research by Bateman and Fonagy (2004) we find the same kind of reasoning: 'Underpinning our approach is the assumption that

understanding borderline personality disorder (BPD) depends on an understanding of *normal human development*' (Bateman & Fonagy 2004: p. 55).

2 Laplanche (1999) suggested the terms 'intromission' and 'implantation' to denote two different ways in which these enigmatic signifiers inscribe themselves in the childish psyche. The first is a form of violence which prevents both repression and symbolization. See also Chapter 4 for more on trauma as an internal foreign body.

3 Notice that in his discussion of psychosis Freud uses the word *Verleugnung* (disavowal) and not *Verwerfung* (foreclosure), which was the term he used in the Wolf Man case. Freud started to use the term *Verleugnung* in his 1923 paper 'The Infantile Genital Organization'; in my opinion this shift represents an attempt to make a theoretical bridge from his theory of neurosis to that of psychosis.

4 In an unpublished thesis from the University of Copenhagen Allan Blaabjerg (2003) attempts to defend the theory that Freud's concept of foreclosure conceptually presupposes the concept of projection and that the decisive difference between foreclosure and repression is that while the latter presupposes primal repression, the foreclosure mechanisms of psychosis must be considered the result of lacking or incomplete primal repression.

5 It is thought-provoking that writers as early as Federn (1977 [1953]) have suggested understanding schizoid personality structures as a decathexis of the ego and thus as the opposite of narcissistic cathexis. Federn's *Ego Psychology and the Psychoses* (1977) precedes Hartmann's publication on ideas on the adaptive and autonomous functions of the ego by a decade (Hartmann 1964). However, where Hartmann was busy defining the ego independently of drives as a function in the psyche which adapts to reality, Federn forestalled Laplanche's (1976) reading of Freud's concept of the ego, since he presented it as a narcissistically cathected representation within the psyche.

Postscript

In the introduction I pointed out that from the very beginning the concept and phenomenon of borderline have rendered visible a quandary of borders not only in the patients themselves, but also in the various discourses that have delimited and explicated them. Historically speaking, first systems of justice and psychiatry were on a collision course on how to deal with these patients, while later psychiatry and psychoanalysis approached them from the angles of psychosis and neurosis. Although a level of consensus has been reached at the purely descriptive diagnostic level, there are still significant theoretical differences between clinicians and researchers in understanding borderline pathology.

These differences have not diminished since this book was first published in 2004. Rather, differences in understanding and treating these patients have been exacerbated even within a narrowly defined psychoanalytic understanding. This is a consequence of a widening gap between empirical and developmental research, and research that seeks to adapt psychoanalytic metapsychology to experiences arising in our work with these non-neurotic patients. This latter contradiction was what motivated me to add a postscript to my original work. In light of the analytic work carried out with this group of patients in recent years, an antithesis between different schools of psychoanalysis has become increasingly clear, to the extent that in my eyes it constitutes a paradigmatic break (Kuhn 1962) in the science of psychoanalysis.

On the one hand Peter Fonagy (Fonagy *et al.* 2002, Bateman & Fonagy 2004) and his colleagues are widely recognized for their understanding of borderline based on the theory of mentalization.

Recently this theory has engendered a treatment model for severely disturbed borderline patients which has been widely used (Bateman & Fonagy 2006). Just as Kernberg was the main bridge-builder between psychiatry and psychoanalysis, Fonagy and his colleagues are currently the harbingers of a success story for psychoanalysis at a time when classical psychoanalysis is in many ways in crisis as its scientific weakness is exposed in light of the currently dominant empiricist, positivist scientific paradigm.

On the other hand – and quite opposite to Fonagy's cognitively inspired theories and treatment – other psychoanalysts have proceeded along the track laid out by André Green (1997b, 1999) with his books *On Private Madness* and *The Work of the Negative*. Significant in this respect is the work of two French analysts, César and Sára Botella, who have been inspired by Green to make highly significant contributions to the understanding of borderline both clinically and theoretically. Unlike the cognitive tendency of the mentalization theory to reduce the classical psychoanalytic concepts of drive and the unconscious, the Botellas declare their starting point to be Freudian metapsychology, although naturally their goal is not to dogmatically reproduce classical terms. In accordance with French psychoanalytic tradition after Lacan they have set the concepts of classical theory to work in order to comprehend a pathology beyond neurosis – to use a term from Laplanche – and capture the moment of non-representation which they believe to be characteristic of borderline patients. In reading their 2005 book *The Work of Psychic Figurability*, I experienced that particular joy of recognition that accompanies an encounter with a text that permits one's own ideas to materialize and gain clarity. One particular theme has been clarified in my mind after reading these two French psychoanalysts, which I shall outline in order hopefully to stimulate renewed debate not only concerning delimited psychoanalytic themes but also fundamental problems in psychoanalytic science, not least its theory of the subject.

In brief the issue at stake is the relationship of the psyche to external reality – conceptualized in psychoanalysis as the tension between perception and representation – and the task at hand is to link these epistemological and psychodynamic approaches to our experiences of a defence beyond repression. The relationship between perception and representation constitutes a pivotal point in the ongoing debate on severely traumatized and disturbed patients presented by Botella and Botella. In the following I shall attempt to discuss this problematic in the light of my own experiences and theoretical considerations.

Non-representation and psychic figurability

Although representation is a key concept in psychoanalytic theory, it has proven insufficient to elucidate that form of pathology beyond neurosis. Working with borderline and other deeply traumatized patients has prompted the thought of the negative, which the Botellas have implemented in the concept of non-representation. In psychoanalytic theory, the idea of the negative, as we have seen, dates back to Freud who early in his career drew attention to the existence of a type of defence which – unlike repression – does not permit representation to resurface in the unconscious, but instead negates it. Thus where ideas should be there is nothingness, a void, which in itself constitutes precisely what these patients fear the most. In other words, they fear not so much loss and the absence of the object as the loss and absence of the representation of the object. 'Indeed, in our view, it is not the loss of the object but the danger of the loss of its representations and by extension, the risk of non-representation, which denotes distress' (Botella & Botella 2005: p. 30).

The Botellas' work has been driven by the desire to understand this non-represented area of the psyche and they have realized that this cannot take place through the processes we know from mental representation and symbolization. In other words the non-represented is not immediately accessible through language. It is ephemeral, generally avoiding our attempts at bringing it into words. Thus we must find a different way of approaching it.

The two French analysts have described this as formal regression equivalent to the processes with which we are familiar from dreams, and which result in the production of a visual image. The Botellas have introduced the term 'figurability' to denote what Freud termed '*Darstellung*' in his theory of dreams, a word that is not equivalent to the English term representation. On the contrary here we are dealing with a form of inner perception that makes it possible for the analyst to produce an image in the place marked as a void in order to create the first contours of something which can then subsequently be absorbed by the area of representation.

In other words the Botellas have once more taken up Freud's theory of dream work – particularly that process which permits the dream to appear visually within – and have linked this process to the classical theory of the child's hallucinatory satisfaction, which gains an entirely new and surprising significance in this context.

It is the dream process which must convince us that hallucinatory activity takes place on an axis connecting perception to representation. In analysis we have become accustomed to working with what might be termed the axis of representation. This is where the condensing and displacing processes of dreams take place, and where the analyst's evenly suspended attention attempts to draw forth meaning from the free associations of the patient. This purely representative axis, however, must be supplemented by an axis connecting perception and representation, and which crosses the other axis. The dream process is the best illustration of the back-and-forth movement between perception and representation, not least because it shows the movement from representation to perception. Freud says of the dream that it 'moves in a *backward* direction. Instead of being transmitted towards the *motor* end it moves toward the *sensory* end and finally reaches the perceptual system' (Freud 1900b: p. 542). The Botellas demonstrate that dreams are not the only phenomena to evince this movement from representation to perception, for under the right conditions waking consciousness has access to the hallucinatory activity of dreams. The latter is generally impeded by reality testing, but is available for the work of dreams and for that primordial process which they have termed 'the work of psychic figurability'. Phenomena like déjà vu and déjà raconté may serve to illustrate these occasional hallucinations which may occur in otherwise healthy people and which Freud (1936) has exemplified in his charming description of the memory disturbance that caught up with him during his visit to the Acropolis.

The two French analysts do not wish to limit this hallucinatory activity to dreams and these relatively rare disturbances of vision and memory. They believe that we preserve – in the form of secondary thinking – remains of the animist forms of thought characteristic of children and expressed so clearly in the regressive patterns we know, e.g. from obsessive neurotics. In analysis the analyst utilizes this capacity for formal regression in thought which loosens the secondary processes, thus opening up the possibility of the hallucinatory production of images as the final guard against the void of non-representation.

Psychiatry's long tradition of associating hallucination with psychosis has made it difficult to investigate normal hallucinatory phenomena, and has thus prevented us from acknowledging the difference between psychotic hallucination and the hallucinations of dreams. I shall go further into this later in discussing the Botellas' explanations of foreclosure and psychotic defence.

Representation

Modern infant research, attachment theories and object-relations theories all emphasize the intersubjective matrix as the aporia of mental development. They have thus made the earliest experiences of being with the primary object into the basis of what we understand as the internal world. We have learned to formulate this internal world in relational terms constituting more or less stable self and object representations. The Botellas would not necessarily disagree. They draw our attention, however, to the fact that the infant – prior to these experiences – lives through a loss which will forever leave a negative trace in its psyche, which means that the fear of non-representation exists as a possibility within the subject.

This loss is of a dual nature. We are dealing with both the loss of the primary object *and* of the first object of hallucinatory satisfaction. I previously mentioned that the Botellas have continued to work on Freud's theory of the hallucinatory satisfaction of the child and embedded it in the theory of hallucinatory activity briefly outlined above. This assumption of an original loss and the resulting 'primal trace of the lack' (Botella & Botella 2005: p 170) is significant to our understanding of the formation of what we term self and object representations. We must understand these representations as acquisitions the child is obliged to carry out over and over again. In fact we must assume that what we term psychic reality will always be coloured by this primal trace of the lack.

In order to illustrate this thinking concerning the child's acquisition of self and object representation, the Botellas refer to Freud's (1920) observation of the one-and-a-half-year-old child playing with a spool. This observation demonstrates the frailty of the child's early attempts at compensating the threat of loss, and the destabilizing effect this has on the child's representation of its own self.

When the child is jubilantly able to produce the missing spool in its perceptual system, it has in that same instant diminished the fear of a loss it is unable to control: the coming and going of the mother. However – as the Botellas point out – this is not all. They note that during this game the little boy is not in bed but outside it, and so one assumes he is throwing the spool into the bed and subsequently using the string to pull it out again. Thus the spool may not only represent the mother, as we are used to interpreting this story, but also the child itself: an assumption supported by the following additional observation reported by Freud.

The boy plays the same game of peek-a-boo in front of a large mirror by letting his own mirror image disappear and appear once again in the same place, over and over again. This effort to control loss by creating an internal representation of the object is intimately and frighteningly associated with the fear of loss of the representation of the self. In other words what we call object representation is not an internal reflection of an external object, but the result of a process of realization, where the reflecting absence of the subject is just as important as the real absence of the object. In this perspective self and object representation are understood as processes, both created by absence and underpinned by the fear of loss – not only of the object but of its representation. In his essay 'Negation' Freud writes 'that a precondition for the setting up of reality-testing is that objects shall have been lost which once brought real satisfaction' (Freud 1925a: p. 238). That does not mean, however, that this process can be understood as purely and simply cognitive. For it is not Cogito but Eros whose double motion holds both self and object. One movement leads towards the libidinously cathected object, while the other turns upon the subject's own self in an autoerotic movement. Unfortunately I am not here able to expand on the Botellas' concept of autoeroticism as one element of a theory claiming – in keeping with classical psychoanalysis – that sexuality is fundamentally significant for all psychic life (Zeuthen & Gammelgaard 2009). Here we are dealing with a discussion of the psychoanalytical concept of representation, which contains a paradox that must be explored rather than dissolved.

In its simplest form representation is linked to perception, while the actual psychoanalytical meaning of the word has always referred to the representation of drives within the psyche. This double meaning permits an acknowledgement that object representation is created as a movement from the perceived object to its internal representation *and* as representation cathected by drives. Although they may of course coincide, they are not by definition identical.

In psychoanalysis we accept that an object may be defined in two contradictory ways; one that allows our understanding of the world to be upheld, and one that operates internally from a notion which is antagonistic to this understanding. Freud's discussion of the mechanism of foreclosure in the story of the Wolf Man showed how the boy was internally able to maintain a conviction of gender relations which was in opposition to what he was obliged to observe.

In other words we are dealing with two logically oppositional statements concerning the same issue or – as emphasized by the Botellas – a duality in the represented object itself. They illustrate this duality – not only in thinking but in the represented object – with Freud's reference to a boy who on being confronted with his father's death was able to declare without any sense of contradiction: 'I know father's dead, but what I can't understand is why he doesn't come home for supper' (Freud 1900[a]: p. 254, quoted in Botella & Botella 2005: p. 23).

As we have seen, it was the observation of fetishism and negation that posed a serious challenge to the idea of a straightforward relationship between perception and representation. What is it the child sees when confronted with the reality of anatomical gender difference? In order to answer this simple question, whose implications are so complex, we must reconsider the concept of reality testing which has already been discussed several times in this book and which, referring to Freud (1895a), was defined as a primary inhibitory process. The Botellas have added important aspects to this inhibitory process that demonstrate the frailty of the recognition of external reality.

Only inside–also outside

As is no doubt evident by now the Botellas' book is rich in ideas as well as in conceptual and theoretical discussion. Like much French literature it can in places be a little difficult to follow, not least because discussions regarding concepts and theories are unfolded en route and with due consideration to the wealth of clinical material rather than being presented in a systematically collected form. On the other hand it opens up perspectives rarely discussed among psychoanalysts: this applies not least to the discussion of perception, a topic which has brought psychoanalysis in close contact with recent research in cognitive science. I refer not to attempts to revise the metapsychology of psychoanalysis to bring it into harmony with certain parts of cognitive research (Erdelyi 1985, Bucci 1997, for a critique see Gammelgaard 2007), but to authors such as Edelman (1992) and Cohen and Varela (2006), who have demonstrated the complexity of the process of perception. Naturally perception depends on our sensory receptors, but it cannot be limited to them alone. Perception is no simple process of information processing where external input reaches the brain via the sensory apparatus. It refers equally to the way in which the human brain 'forms from within' the opinions we deduce from the things outside ourselves, as the Botellas express it using a formulation from Varela.

I shall not go further into the discussion of perception, merely pointing out – prior to examining the idea of reality testing – that the Botellas believe that recent cognitive and brain research validates their hallucination theory, for example demonstrating that 'hallucinations activate the primary zones of perception, the very ones which process external sensory information' (Botella & Botella 2005: p. 160).

In their discussion of reality testing the Botellas take their cue from Freud's (1925a) short and concise definition of this concept in his essay on negation. Reality testing, writes Freud, is not about what is absorbed or not absorbed by the ego, but about whether something already existing within the ego may be refound as perceptions of reality. 'The first and immediate aim, therefore, of reality-testing is, not to *find* an object in real perception, which corresponds to the one presented, but to *refind* such an object, to convince oneself that it is still there' (Freud 1925a: pp. 237–238). He continues: 'What is unreal, merely a presentation and subjective is only internal; what is real is also there *outside*' (Freud 1925a: pp. 237–238).

These two statements encompass Freud's whole idea of how the child may reach a secure realization of reality and the ensuing distinction between the subjective and the objective. For as Freud writes, '[t]he antithesis between subjective and objective does not exist from the first' (Freud 1925a: p. 237).

The Botellas would add to the definition of reality testing as the refinding of the object in real perception that this takes place in spite of the negation we inflict on the object of perception. They interpret Freud's two statements as illustrating a complex process involving both negation of perception with a view towards cathecting the object in its hallucinatory form, and subsequently refinding what has been negated in perception. The Botellas refer to this process as a 'double contradictory conviction' (Botella & Botella 2005: p. 137). In other words the object is 'only inside–also outside' (Botella & Botella 2005: p. 90). This is a contradiction which also constitutes a continuity, or, in other words, establishes separation at the same time that it establishes a connection between what is outside and what is inside. The capacity for psychic representation is constituted through this oppositional 'only–also' contraction. Elsewhere the Botellas refer to this alliance between negation and conviction as anti-traumatic, thereby indicating that the child must of necessity negate the object of perception in order to cathect the idea of the object, thereby rendering itself secure in the face of relations over which it has no other control: the coming and going of the object in external reality.

Thus negation of the object of perception lies at the heart of reality testing – this is neither to be understood as foreclosure nor as negative hallucination, the Botellas claim – while the existence of the object is confirmed and becomes what we term a conviction at the internal level.

Freud's concept of reality testing is not without ambiguity. Therefore work like that of the Botellas has been necessary in order to develop Freud's outlines, delineate a concept in accordance with his thinking, and prevent the significance of the concept from being diluted and reduced. The latter is what we see illustrated in the widespread and oversimplified understanding of the concept which involves reality as a yardstick against which to measure whether or not the notions and fantasies of the subject can be termed realistic. Where, in other words, reality is elevated to the status of an authority by which to judge these subjective phenomena.

There appears to be evidence of clear – if undeclared – inspiration from Sartre's (1995) argument in *Being and Nothingness* and Winnicott's (1971: p. 89) idea of the destruction of the object (see page 98). This is evident in the Botellas' idea of the negation of the object of perception as a prerequisite for psychic representation. Such interpretations of reality testing may help clarify the following question: what does the child see when confronted with the reality of anatomic gender difference? When the child sees the absent penis as an expression of castration, this means that it has cathected this idea in its representation of gender difference. If the difference does not assume the nature of a conviction created by the child's theory of sexuality it will remain a mere and simple observation leaving the child at most with an anxiety-free experience of: 'Aha!' This representation of the idea of castration, however, is preceded by a form of thinking that the authors – with Freud – would term animistic. Animistic thought does not operate with a clear distinction between perception and representation. Under the influence of such thinking the child will typically solve the riddle of gender difference by convincing itself that the girl does have a penis, but that it is a tiny one that will grow as she herself grows. Such animistic solutions must be dissolved in the face of the reality principle, and this is where the negation of perception comes in. Meanwhile, the idea of castration becomes conviction in accordance with the child's fantasies as they appear at this time, i.e. as an internal conviction that the object would be able to do such a thing as, for example, effect castration. This leads us to the question of how the theory of negating defence as presented in this book appears within the framework presented by the Botellas.

The negative of the trauma

The discussion of the mechanism of foreclosure takes place as part of the work concerning the negative effect of trauma, a concept the Botellas have gleaned from Freud's (1939: pp.75–77) brief notice in *Moses and Monotheism*, but which they have imbued with a radically different meaning in light of their clinical work with severely traumatized children and adults, which provides the convincing backdrop for their theoretical discussions.

The Botellas are convinced that we are at this point in time obliged to put behind us not only the idea of traumatic neurosis but also the *Nachträglichkeit* model if we are to comprehend the nature of infantile trauma. The vertical axis between perception and representation is also useful in this context. The main point of their discussion of infantile trauma consists in it neither being understood as intensified perception nor based on the contents of the material represented but as resulting 'from the incapacity to transform, to give psychic quality to a state that, owing to this very incapacity becomes an excess of energy, an unbound perception' (Botella & Botella 2005: p. 116). The result is a gaping void in both perception and representation or, in other words: 'Neither inside – nor outside' (Botella & Botella 2005: p.116).

Here, to my mind, lies a significant therapeutic implication for working with traumatized patients. The fragments of memories that may appear – possibly accompanied by sensory flashbacks – should be understood not as a reproduction of historical facts but as a defensive strategy against the fear of non-representation. In other words such flashbacks are not actual memories with content. We are dealing not with the perception of traumatic content but with a '*non-binding . . . a total absence of intelligibility and*, a fortiori, *of content*' (Botella & Botella 2005: p. 116). In consequence the Botellas do not use positive terms to describe the traumatic experience, suggesting instead a rewriting of Winnicott's (1992b) formulation from the article 'Fear of Breakdown': 'Something fundamentally evident for the subject that should have happened did not happen' (Botella & Botella 2005: p. 116). When Winnicott speaks of something having taken place that could not be experienced, the Botellas would argue that this is because what took place is in fact negative. When my patient Hanne, as I described on page 81, told me that she had a clear image of the white car that her father – long dead – would collect her in outside my front door, this theory permitted an understanding of this phenomenon as a hallucinatory production serving to defend Hanne against the non-representation of a loss she has never been helped to live through.

The Botellas describe a little Vietnamese girl named Jasmine. Both her parents were killed during the Vietnam War and she was found at the age of two next to her mother's dead body. Treatment of this girl was marked by the fact that Jasmine 'was condemned to live in the immediate present' (Botella & Botella 2005: p. 100). In her attempt to uphold her identification with her white adoptive parents and avoid all memories of her early traumatic loss, Jasmine defended herself through massive disavowal of her past, her race, and her skin colour. Naturally, sensory traces were brought to life during treatment, but only as actual transferential experiences, just as Hanne was only transferentially able to produce a recollection in the form of a non-represented sense image produced as reality. The interesting thing in these cases is not so much the sensory content itself as the function of the memory. In both cases memory images surface not in the form of memories of the past but in the form of visualizations associated with the present. The Botellas conclude that this is a result of the work of figurability created by patient and analyst with the analyst functioning as the double of the analysand.

This brings us to Schreber and the Wolf Man. The Botellas believe that the negative effect of trauma can only be approximately described using the mechanism of foreclosure, which Freud hinted at in the case of Schreber: 'It was incorrect to say that the perception which was suppressed internally is projected outwards; the truth is rather, as we now see, that what was abolished internally returns from without' (Freud 1911a: p. 71).

But the negative of the trauma is not sufficiently described by Freud's internal abolition. According to the Botellas this is, rather, a case of lacking inscription, a lack of representation. Although there are similarities between Freud's description of psychotic foreclosure and the negative of the trauma, there is also a difference in that the road back cannot be the same. Psychotic hallucinations consist in actual distortion of reality testing so that representation is transformed into perception – into something 'only outside' – while the return of the negative of the infantile trauma does not contain an actual disturbance of reality testing. This peculiar 'neither inside–nor outside' status means that the trauma neither returns from the external since no abolition has taken place within, nor does it, so to speak, return from the inside, since no traces of memory have been repressed.

It is already clear that the Wolf Man is not Schreber. In other words, he is not psychotic. We may observe what this means for the mechanism of negation in this case if we follow the Botellas' argument. As I understand it, Schreber and the Wolf Man are distinguished by the same things that distinguish psychotic hallucinations from normal forms of hallucination. In other words, the moment he experiences the hallucinated finger, the little Wolf Man is able to retrogressively move along the axis from the representation of castration to its perception. At the time of his hallucination, the boy experiences one of those rare moments where we are able to activate our capacity for waking figurability, thus avoiding further regression towards a psychotic state. I must leave this interpretation open for further discussion and shall hereby conclude with my discussion of the Botellas' understanding of the negative.

Freud was torn between the neurosis model and experiences of the negative. In response to this the Botellas have introduced the axis of perception and representation and offer an understanding of psychosis and of the effect of infantile trauma. According to the Botellas, trauma results in a 'rupture of the fragile equilibrium of reality testing as a duality representation–perception instead of reducing the distortion of reality to the consequence of a defensive procedure of the ego alone' (Botella & Botella 2005: p.133).

In other words, the Botellas do not wish to ascribe the disturbances we see in borderline and traumatized patients to the ego and its defences. Instead they suggest that the disturbances we encounter in these patients should be understood as ruptures on the axis they have described as representation–perception.

Conclusion

There are many things in the work of these two French analysts that invite further discussion, not least their idea of hallucinatory activity, which they have taken over from Freud and developed as part of their theory on the connecting line between perception and representation. In their clinical work with severely disturbed and traumatized patients this theory has proved convincingly valuable. With their concept of psychic figurability they have made a significant contribution to our understanding of how we as analysts may approach that irrepresentable area which characterizes our meetings with severely disturbed patients. I wish to conclude, however, by using the concept of representation to open the field to a discussion between the two paradigms I initially outlined. Fonagy and his colleagues have already made their mark as significant contributors to the current debate on borderline and its treatment. Through their work the Botellas have opened up a discussion concerning an alternative approach to this clinically and theoretically challenging field of research. In this respect it is of course impossible to speak of any form of comprehensive account of the theory of mentalization in comparison with the work of the Botellas. Suffice it here to indicate a single theme which to my mind appears central in light of their previously outlined work. In order to stimulate discussion on this topic I shall – in full awareness of the risk of appearing reductivist – suggest that the decisive difference at the theoretical level consists of the interpretation of the Freudian concept of representation. However, this difference has implications for other significant concepts such as that of psychic reality, the question of aetiology, and finally for the treatment of borderline and other severely traumatized patients.

In brief, Fonagy and his colleagues work with a concept of representation which refers solely to relations to the external world, or to the axis that was previously termed the axis of perception and representation.

I would argue, however, that cognitive and learning-based theories of mentalization do not leave room for a concept of representation that upholds the notion of the displacement of drive towards the psychic. In other words, we are not dealing with an axis internally following the route of the drive towards psychic representation. The tendency to let representation be about relations to external reality has become increasingly evident as the theory of mentalization has developed from, for example, Fonagy and Target's (1996a, 1996b, 2000) interesting series of articles entitled 'Playing with Reality' to their cooperation with Jurist and Gergely (Fonagy *et al.* 2002) to, most recently, Bateman and Fonagy's work from 2004 and 2006. This tendency is clearly expressed through the replacement of the concept of representation by that of mentalization.

To answer the question of how the child reaches an understanding of internal and external reality Fonagy and Target assume a duality in the child's experience of what the authors understand by psychic reality.

> The child generally operates in 'psychic equivalence' mode, where ideas are not felt to be representations, but, rather, direct replicas of reality and consequently always true. At other times, however, the child uses "pretend mode" in which ideas are felt to be representational but their correspondence with reality is not examined.
>
> (Fonagy *et al.* 2002: p. 257–258)

The concepts of 'equivalent mode' and 'pretend mode' constitute highly apt terms for the child's gradual appropriation of the representational nature of the thoughts, emotions and fantasies of the internal world, while indicating that this conviction may fail, allowing the child to fall back into 'equivalent mode' or withdraw into an as-if world. This idea of the dual nature of the child's sense of psychic reality deserves far greater attention than I am able to provide here.[1] I shall content myself with indicating that although the theory of mentalization operates – in keeping with classical psychoanalytic theory – with the assumption that the capacity for mentalization is not given a priori, but is, rather, gradually acquired through optimal interaction with the surroundings, the theory provides no trace of the classical concept of the psychic representation of drive. Naturally this is mainly because the theory of mentalization does not seek to make a statement on the representation of drives, offering up instead a theory as to how the developing child understands the scope of what is simply represented and is able to distinguish this from its perception of external reality.

In a discussion of the concept of psychic equivalence, where Fonagy and Target (2000) wish to specify their concept in relation to Hanna Segal's concept of 'symbolic equation', the latter is emphasized as concerning the relationship between signifier and signified while the former concerns the relationship between the external and internal.

> We are concerned with the quality of states of mind and here the term *equivalence* does not denote an equation of the symbolic vehicle with the idea represented, but rather the assumption that what is sought about has to be actual.
>
> (Fonagy & Target 2000: p. 855)

I see this as an expression of the fact that the authors' understanding of the child's ability to distinguish the simply imagined from factual reality is not preoccupied with disturbances that may arise because the representations of the child can also constitute the psychic expression of drives in their capacity of 'symbolic vehicle' besides simply representing the external world.

An example may serve to clarify what I mean. The authors refer to a three-year-old boy who wanted a Batman outfit. His father had succeeded in locating one, but the costume was so realistic that the child was frightened when he saw himself in the mirror and refused to wear it again.

The point of this little example is of course about what the authors understand by the term 'realistic'. Would a psychoanalytic interpretation not consist in pointing out that the child's fantasies – created by unconscious drives – have thus materialized to meet the child as its own mirror image? With their latest theory of mentalization, however, Fonagy *et al.* (2002) leave out this part of the classical concept of representation, which may also be read in the concept of psychic reality.

Today the concept of psychic reality holds 'a variety of connotations' for which reason Fonagy and his colleagues have opted to use their own term, ' "psychic equivalence" to denote domination by psychic reality in Freud's sense' (Fonagy & Target 2000: p. 255). This refers to the neurotic tendency to react just as earnestly to thoughts as normal people react to reality. It is this very condition, that the neurotic treats psychic reality as though it were identical with physical reality, that underlies the authors' definition of the concept of psychic reality as psychic equivalence, and they use Laplanche and Pontalis' (1988) definition of psychic reality to express that same 'sense of equivalence'. In their *Language of Psychoanalysis* Laplanche and Pontalis use this comparison with physical materiality to emphasize the 'consistency' and 'resistance' that characterize psychic reality, which it should be noted is not – as suggested by Fonagy and his colleagues – *influenced* by the unconscious. That which Freud denotes using the term psychic reality *is* unconscious, as exemplified in his (1919) essay 'A Child is Being Beaten'.

In short the problem appears to lie in the term equivalence, which to Fonagy and his colleagues implies an overlap between the internal and external worlds. The subjective is experienced as objective and real. When Laplanche and Pontalis in their definition of psychic reality refer to material reality, however, they are referring to a comparison of different things which can only analogously speaking be said to have certain identical moments.

I do not want this to be misunderstood as a pedantic discussion of definitions, but rather as a sliding of the concept of psychic reality, which from being anchored in the theory of the unconscious is now tending towards being understood as that which has subjective – understood as phenomenologically accessible – significance. In the theory of mentalization we are no longer dealing with the route of drives into the psychic area, but with the ability to 'imagine different perspectives' as a 'crucial indicator of the child's assumptions about the status of his thoughts. How his psychic reality corresponds to the external world' (Fonagy *et al.* 2002: pp. 258–259).

No wonder, then, that the theory of the child's ability to balance the relationship between the external and the internal – as founded on an integration of the two modes of experience created through an optimal interaction with the surroundings – has led to a theory of borderline as lacking mentalization or as disintegration. This in turn has led to a model of treatment that helps borderline patients understand that thoughts and fantasies are separate from reality, and may therefore be managed or represented.

Juxtaposed with this theory we have the Botellas' theory of psychic representation as a fragile acquisition created through the duality that characterizes our thoughts and fantasies, and which claims that these are products not only of the route of drives to psychic representation but also of the internal perceptual depiction of the external world. This frailty is evident in the anxiety that characterizes borderline patients and which this theory understands as the fear of nothingness and non-representation that borderline patients are desperately attempting to avoid by their various destructive actings-out, memory fragments and hallucinatory phenomena.

Note

1 In this context I must refer to an as yet unpublished PhD thesis by Signe Holm Petersen, of the Department of Psychology at the University of Copenhagen, which deals with the concept of representation in the theory of mentalization.

References

Aarkrog, T. (1994). *Borderline Adolescents, 20 Years Later.* Copenhagen, Denmark: Bispebjerg Hospital.

Abraham, K. (1982). Ansätze zur Psychoanalytischen Erforschung und Behandlung des Manisch-Depressiven Irreseins und verwandter Zustände. In *Karl Abraham Gesammelte Schriften in Zwei Bänden*. Frankfurt am Main, Germany: Fischer Taschenbuch Verlag (Original work published 1912).

Adair, M. J. (1993). A Speculation on Perversion and Hallucination. *International Journal of Psycho-Analysis*, *74*(1), 81–92.

Adler, G. (1975). The Usefulness of the Borderline Concept in Psychotherapy. In J. E. Mack (Ed.), *Borderline States in Psychiatry*. New York: Grune and Stratton.

Adler, G., & Buie, D. H. (1979). Aloneness and Borderline Pyschopathology – The Possible Relevance of Child Development Issues. *International Journal of Psycho-Analysis*, *60*(1), 83–97.

Anzieu, D. (1989). *The Skin's Ego* (C. Turner, Trans.). New Haven and London: Yale University Press (Original work published 1985).

Atwood, G. E., & Stolorow, R. D. (1993). *Psychoanalytic Inquiry: Vol. 4. Structures of Subjectivity – Explorations in Psychoanalytic Phenomenology*. New York: The Analytic Press (Original work published 1984).

Aulagnier, P. (2001). *The New Library of Psychoanalysis: Vol. 41. The Violence of Interpretation: From Pictogram to Statement* (A. Sheridan, Trans.). East Sussex: Brunner-Routledge (Original work published 1975).

Balint, M. (1979). *The Basic Fault: Therapeutic Aspects of Regression* (Original work published 1968).

Bateman, A., & Fonagy, P. (2004). *Psychotherapy for Borderline Personality Disorder. Mentalization-Based Treatment*. Oxford: Oxford University Press.

Bateman, A., & Fonagy, P. (2006). *Mentalization-Based Treatmen for Borderline Personality Disorder. A Practical Guide*. Oxford: Oxford University Press.

Beck, S. J. (1959). Schizophrenia without Psychosis. *Archives of Neurology and Psychiatry, 81*(1), 85–96.

Bion, W. R. (1981). Notes on Memory and Desire. In R. Langs (Ed.), *Classics in Psychoanalytic Technique*. London: Jason Aronson (Original work published 1967).

Bion, W. R. (1984). *Attention and Interpretation*. London: Karnac Books (Original work published 1970).

Bion, W. R. (1988). *Learning from Experience*. London: Karnac Books (Original work published 1962).

Bion, W. R. (1990a). Attacks on Linking. In *Second Thoughts*. London: Karnac Books (Original work published 1959).

Bion, W. R. (1990b). Differentiation of the Psychotic from the Non-Psychotic Personalities. In *Second Thoughts*. London: Karnac Books (Original work published 1967).

Bion, W. R. (1992). *Cogitations*. London: Karnac Books (Original work published 1962).

Blaabjerg, A. (2003). *Hvad blev der af det ubevidste? Et psykoanalytisk studie i overføring og projektion i grænsefeltet mellem neurosen og psykosen*. Unpublished masters thesis, University of Copenhagen.

Bleger, J. (1967). Psycho-Analysis of the Psycho-Analytic Frame. *The International Journal of Psycho-Analysis, 48*, 511–519.

Bleuler, E. (1950). *Dementia Praecox or the Groups of Schizophrenias*. New York: International Universities Press (Original work published 1911).

Bollas, C. (1989). *Forces of Destiny: Psychoanalysis and Human Idiom*. London: Free Association Books.

Bollas, C. (1993). The Aesthetic Moment and the Search for Transformation. In P. Rudnytsky (Ed.), *Transitional Objects and Potential Spaces: Literary Uses of D.W. Winnicott*. New York: Columbia University Press (Original work published 1978).

Bollas, C. (2000). *Hysteria*. London: Routledge.

Bolognini, S. (1994). Transference: Erotised, Erotic, Loving, Affectionate. *International Journal of Psycho-Analysis, 75*(1), 73–86.

Botella, C., & Botella, S. (2005). *The New Library of Psychoanalysis: The Work of Psychic Figurability. Mental States without Representation* (D. Birkstead-Breen, Ed., A. Weller & M. Zerbib, Trans.). New York: Brunner-Routledge.

Bowlby, J. (1980). *Attachment and Loss: Vol. 3. Loss: Sadness and Depression*. London: The Hogarth Press and The Institute of Psycho-Analysis.

Britton, R. (1989). The Missing Link: Parental Sexuality and the Oedipus Complex. In R. Britton, E. O'Shaughnessy, M. Feldman & J. Steiner (Eds.), *The Oedipus Complex Today – Clinical Implications*. London: Karnac Books.

Britton, R. (1998). *Belief and Imagination: Explorations in Psychoanalysis*. London: Routledge.

Britton, R. (2003). *Sex, Death, and the Superego: Experiences in Psychoanalysis*. London: Karnac Books.

Bucci, W. (1997). *Psychoanalysis and Cognitive Science. A Multiple Code Theory*. New York: The Guilford Press.

Bychowski, G. (1953). The Problem of Latent Psychosis. *Journal of the American Psychoanalytic Association, 1*, 484–503.

Camus, A. (1984). *The Fall* [La chute] (J. O'Brien, Trans.). Vintage Books (Original work published 1956).

Christensen, I. (2000). *Hemmelighedstilstanden*. Copenhagen, Denmark: Gyldendal.

Cohen, A. E., & Varela, F. J. (2006). At tage besværet på sig. Subjektiviteten i neurovidenskabelig og psykoanalytisk erfaring [Taking the Trouble. Subjectivity in the Light of Neuroscientific and Psychoanalytic Experience]. In J.-C. Delay & E. Holst (Eds.), *En fandens bestilling – kan vi slippe for det ubevidste* [A devilish task – can we escape the unconscious]. Copenhagen, Denmark: Frydenlund.

Deutsch, H. (1986). Some Forms of Emotional Disturbance and their Relationship to Schizophrenia. In M. H. Stone (Ed.), *Essential Papers on Borderline Disorders: One Hundred Years at the Border*. New York: New York University Press (Original work published 1942).

Dunaif, S., & Hoch, P. H. (1955). Pseudopsychopathic Schizophrenia. In J. Zubin & P. H. Hoch (Eds.), *Psychiatry and the Law – The Proceedings of the 43rd. Annual Meeting of the American Psychopathological Association, held in New York City, June 1953*. New York: Grune & Stratton.

Edelman, G. M. (1992). *Bright Air, Brilliant Fire: On the Matter of the Mind*. New York: Basic Books.

Enckell, H. (2002). *Metaphor and the Psychodynamic Functions of the Mind*. Doctoral Dissertation. Kuopio, Finland: Kuopio University Publications, D. Medical Sciences, 265.

Erdelyi, M. H. (1985). *Psychoanalysis. Freud's Cognitive Psychology*. New York: W. H. Freeman.

Erikson, E. H. (1986). The Problem of Ego Identity. In M. H. Stone (Ed.), *Essential Papers on Borderline Disorders: One Hundred Years at the Border*. New York: New York University Press (Original work published 1956).

Fairbairn, W. R. D. (1994). *Psychoanalytic Studies of the Personality*. London: Routledge (Original work published 1952).

Falret, J. P. (1890). *Études Cliniques sur les Maladies Mentales et Nerveuses*. Paris, France: J. B. Baillière et Fils.

Federn, P. (1977). *Ego Psychology and the Psychoses.* London: Maresfield Reprints (Original work published 1953).

Ferenczi, S. (1982). Sprachverwirrungen zwischen den Erwachsenen und dem Kind. In *Schriften zur Psychoanalyse (Vol. 2).* Frankfurt am Main: Fischer (Original work published 1933).

Ferenczi, S. (1988). *The Clinical Diary of Sándor Ferenczi* (J. Dupont, Ed., M. Balint & N. Z. Jackson, Trans.). Cambridge, MA: Harvard University Press.

Fonagy, P., Gergely, G., Jurist, E. L., & Target, M. (2002). *Affect Regulation, Mentalization, and the Development of the Self.* New York: Other Press.

Fonagy, P., & Target, M. (1996a). Playing With Reality: I. Theory Of Mind And The Normal Development Of Psychic Reality. *International Journal of Psycho-Analysis,* 77(2), 217–233.

Fonagy, P., & Target, M. (1996b). Playing With Reality: II. The Development Of Psychic Reality From A Theoretical Perspective. *International Journal of Psycho-Analysis,* 77(3), 459–479.

Fonagy, P., & Target, M. (2000). Playing With Reality: III. The Persistence Of Dual Psychic Reality In Borderline Patients. *International Journal of Psycho-Analysis, 81*(5), 853–873.

Foucault, M. (1973). *Madness and Civilization* [Histoire de la folie à l'âge classique – Folie et déraison] (R. Howard, Trans.). New York: Random House (Original work published 1961).

Fraiberg, S. (1969). Libidinal Object Constancy and Mental Representation. *Psychoanalytic Study of the Child, 24,* 9–47.

Freud, A. (1992). *The Ego and the Mechanisms of Defence* (C. Baines, Trans.). Karnac Books (Original work published 1936).

Freud, S. (1894). The Neuro-Psychoses of Defence. In J. Strachey (Ed. & Trans.), *The Standard Edition of the Complete Psychological Works of Sigmund Freud: Vol. 3. Early Psychoanalytic Publications (1893–1899)* (pp. 45–62). London: The Hogarth Press.

Freud, S. (1895a). Project for a scientific psychology. In J. Strachey (Ed. & Trans.), *The Standard Edition of the Complete Psychological Works of Sigmund Freud: Vol. 1. Pre-Psycho-Analytic Publications and Unpublished Drafts (1886–1899)* (pp. 295–399). London: The Hogarth Press.

Freud, S. (1895b). Studies on Hysteria. In S. Freud & J. Breuer, *The Standard Edition of the Complete Psychological Works of Sigmund Freud: Vol. 2. Studies on Hysteria (1893–1895)* (J. Strachey, Ed. & Trans) (pp. 1–253). London: The Hogarth Press.

Freud, S. (1896). Further Remarks on the Neuro-Psychoses of Defence. In J. Strachey (Ed. & Trans.), *The Standard Edition of the Complete Psychological Works of Sigmund Freud: Vol. 3. Early Psychoanalytic Publications (1893–1899)* (pp. 162–189). London: The Hogarth Press.

Freud, S. (1900a). The Interpretation of Dreams. In J. Strachey (Ed. & Trans.), *The Standard Edition of the Complete Psychological Works of Sigmund Freud: Vol. 4. The Interpretation of Dreams (first part) (1900)*. London: The Hogarth Press.

Freud, S. (1900b). The Interpretation of Dreams. In J. Strachey (Ed. & Trans.), *The Standard Edition of the Complete Psychological Works of Sigmund Freud: Vol. 5. The Interpretation of Dreams (second part) and On Dreams (1900–1901)*. London: The Hogarth Press.

Freud, S. (1905). Three Essays on the Theory of Sexuality. In J. Strachey (Ed. & Trans.), *The Standard Edition of the Complete Psychological Works of Sigmund Freud: Vol. 1. A Case of Hysteria, Three Essays on Sexuality and Other Works (1901–1905)* (pp. 130–244). London: The Hogarth Press.

Freud, S. (1909). Notes upon a case of obsessional neurosis. In J. Strachey (Ed. & Trans.), *The Standard Edition of the Complete Psychological Works of Sigmund Freud: Vol. 10. Two Case Histories: 'Little Hans' and the 'Rat Man' (1909)* (pp. 155–251). London: The Hogarth Press.

Freud, S. (1911a). Psycho-analytic notes on an autobiographical account of a case of paranoia (dementia paranoides). In J. Strachey (Ed. & Trans.), *The Standard Edition of the Complete Psychological Works of Sigmund Freud: Vol. 12. Case History of Schreber, Papers on Technique and Other Works (1911–1913)* (pp. 9–85). London: The Hogarth Press (Original work published 1911).

Freud, S. (1911b). Formulations on the Two Principles of Mental Functioning. In J. Strachey (Ed. & Trans.), *The Standard Edition of the Complete Psychological Works of Sigmund Freud: Vol. 12. Case History of Schreber, Papers on Technique and Other Works (1911–1913)* (pp. 218–227). London: The Hogarth Press.

Freud, S. (1914). On Narcissism. In J. Strachey (Ed. & Trans.), *The Standard Edition of the Complete Psychological Works of Sigmund Freud: Vol. 14. On the History of the Psycho-Analytic Movement, Papers on Metapsychology and Other Works (1914–1916)* (pp. 67–102). London: The Hogarth Press.

Freud, S. (1915). The Unconscious. In J. Strachey (Ed. & Trans.), *The Standard Edition of the Complete Psychological Works of Sigmund Freud: Vol. 14. On the History of the Psycho-Analytic Movement, Papers on Metapsychology and Other Works (1914–1916)* (pp. 166–205). London: The Hogarth Press.

Freud, S. (1916). Mourning and Melancholia. In J. Strachey (Ed. & Trans.), *The Standard Edition of the Complete Psychological Works of Sigmund Freud: Vol. 14. On the History of the Psycho-Analytic Movement, Papers on Metapsychology and Other Works (1914–1916)* (pp. 239–259). London: The Hogarth Press.

Freud, S. (1918). From the History of an Infantile Neurosis. In J. Strachey (Ed. & Trans.), *The Standard Edition of the Complete Psychological Works of Sigmund Freud: Vol. 17. An Infantile Neurosis and Other Works (1917–1919)* (pp. 7–123). London: The Hogarth Press.

Freud, S. (1919). A child is being beaten: A contribution to the study of the origin of sexual perversions. In J. Strachey (Ed. & Trans.), *The Standard Edition of the Complete Psychological Works of Sigmund Freud: Vol. 17. An Infantile Neurosis and Other Works (1917–1919)* (pp. 179–205). London: The Hogarth Press.

Freud, S. (1920). Beyond the Pleasure Principle. In J. Strachey (Ed. & Trans.), *The Standard Edition of the Complete Psychological Works of Sigmund Freud: Vol. 18. Beyond the Pleasure Principle, Group Psychology, and Other Works (1920–1922)* (pp. 7–67). London: The Hogarth Press.

Freud, S. (1923a). The Ego and the Id. In J. Strachey (Ed. & Trans.), *The Standard Edition of the Complete Psychological Works of Sigmund Freud: Vol. 19. The Ego and the Id and Other Works (1923–1925)* (pp. 12–69). London: The Hogarth Press.

Freud, S. (1923b). The Infantile Genital Organization: An Interpolation into the Theory of Sexuality. In J. Strachey (Ed. & Trans.), *The Standard Edition of the Complete Psychological Works of Sigmund Freud: Vol. 19. The Ego and the Id and Other Works (1923–1925)* (pp. 141–149). London: The Hogarth Press.

Freud, S. (1924a). The Loss of Reality in Neurosis and Psychosis. In J. Strachey (Ed. & Trans.), *The Standard Edition of the Complete Psychological Works of Sigmund Freud: Vol. 19. The Ego and the Id and Other Works (1923–1925)* (pp. 183–191). London: The Hogarth Press.

Freud, S. (1924b). Neurosis and Psychosis. In J. Strachey (Ed. & Trans.), *The Standard Edition of the Complete Psychological Works of Sigmund Freud: Vol. 19. The Ego and the Id and Other Works (1923–1925)* (pp. 149–157). London: The Hogarth Press.

Freud, S. (1925a). Negation. In J. Strachey (Ed. & Trans.), *The Standard Edition of the Complete Psychological Works of Sigmund Freud: Vol. 19. The Ego and the Id and Other Works (1923–1925)* (pp. 235–243). London: The Hogarth Press.

Freud, S. (1925b). Some Psychical Consequences of the Anatomical Distinction Between the Sexes. In J. Strachey (Ed. & Trans.), *The Standard Edition of the Complete Psychological Works of Sigmund Freud: Vol. 19. The Ego and the Id and Other Works (1923–1925)* (pp. 248–261). London: The Hogarth Press.

Freud, S. (1925c). A Note upon the 'Mystic Writing-Pad'. In J. Strachey (Ed. & Trans.), *The Standard Edition of the Complete Psychological Works of Sigmund Freud: Vol. 19. The Ego and the Id and Other Works (1923–1925)* (pp. 227–235). London: The Hogarth Press.

Freud, S. (1926). Inhibitions, Symptoms and Anxiety. In J. Strachey (Ed. & Trans.), *The Standard Edition of the Complete Psychological Works of Sigmund Freud: Vol. 20. An Autobiographical Study, Inhibitions, Symptoms and Anxiety, Lay Analysis and Other Works (1925–1926)* (pp. 87–173). London: The Hogarth Press.

Freud, S. (1927a). Fetishism. In J. Strachey (Ed. & Trans.), *The Standard Edition of the Complete Psychological Works of Sigmund Freud: Vol. 21. The Future of an Illusion, Civilization and its Discontents and Other Works (1927–1931)* (pp. 152–159). London: The Hogarth Press.

Freud, S. (1927b). The Future of an Illusion. In J. Strachey (Ed. & Trans.), *The Standard Edition of the Complete Psychological Works of Sigmund Freud: Vol. 21. The Future of an Illusion, Civilization and its Discontents and Other Works (1927–1931)* (pp. 5–59). London: The Hogarth Press.

Freud, S. (1933). New Introductory Letters on Psycho-Analysis. In J. Strachey (Ed. & Trans.), *The Standard Edition of the Complete Psychological Works of Sigmund Freud: Vol. 22. New Introductory Lectures on Psycho-Analysis and Other Works (1933–1936)*. London: The Hogarth Press.

Freud, S. (1936). A Disturbance of Memory on the Acropolis. In J. Strachey (Ed. & Trans.), *The Standard Edition of the Complete Psychological Works of Sigmund Freud: Vol. 22. New Introductory Lectures on Psycho-Analysis and Other Works (1933–1936)* (pp. 239–251). London: The Hogarth Press.

Freud, S. (1937a). Analysis Terminable and Interminable. In J. Strachey (Ed. & Trans.), *The Standard Edition of the Complete Psychological Works of Sigmund Freud: Vol. 23. Moses and Monotheism, An Outline of Psycho-Analysis and Other Works (1937–1939)* (pp. 216–255). London: The Hogarth Press.

Freud, S. (1937b). Constructions in Analysis. In J. Strachey (Ed. & Trans.), *The Standard Edition of the Complete Psychological Works of Sigmund Freud: Vol. 23. Moses and Monotheism, An Outline of Psycho-Analysis and Other Works (1937–1939)* (pp. 255–271). London: The Hogarth Press.

Freud, S. (1938a). Splitting of the Ego in the Process of Defence. In J. Strachey (Ed. & Trans.), *The Standard Edition of the Complete Psychological Works of Sigmund Freud: Vol. 23. Moses and Monotheism, An Outline of Psycho-Analysis and Other Works (1937–1939)* (pp. 275–279). London: The Hogarth Press.

Freud, S. (1938b). An Outline of Psycho-Analysis. In J. Strachey (Ed. & Trans.), *The Standard Edition of the Complete Psychological Works of Sigmund Freud: Vol. 23. Moses and Monotheism, An Outline of Psycho-Analysis and Other Works (1937–1939)* (pp. 144–209). London: The Hogarth Press.

Freud, S. (1939). Moses and Monotheism: Three Essays. In J. Strachey (Ed. & Trans.), *The Standard Edition of the Complete Psychological Works of Sigmund Freud: Vol. 23. Moses and Monotheism, An Outline of Psycho-Analysis and Other Works (1937–1939)* (pp. 6–141). London: The Hogarth Press.

Freud, S. (1940). Some Elementary Lessons in Psycho-Analysis. In J. Strachey (Ed. & Trans.), *The Standard Edition of the Complete Psychological Works of Sigmund Freud: Vol. 23. Moses and Monotheism, An Outline of Psycho-Analysis and Other Works (1937–1939)* (pp. 279–287). London: The Hogarth Press.

Freud, S. (1954). *The Origins of Psycho-Analysis. Letters to Wilhelm Fliess, Drafts and Notes (1887–1902)* (M. Bonaparte, A. Freud, & E. Kris, Eds.; E. Mosbacher &

J. Strachey, Trans.). New York: Basic Books (Original work published 1887–1902).

Freud, S., & Ferenczi, S. (1993). *The Correspondence of Sigmund Freud and Sándor Ferenczi Vol. 1: 1908–1914* (E. Brabant, E. Falzeder, & P. Giampieri-Deutsch, Eds., P. Hoffer, Trans.). Cambridge, MA: The Belknap Press of Harvard University Press.

Frosch, J. (1990). The Psychotic Character: Clinical Psychiatric Considerations. In M. H. Stone (Ed.), *Essential Papers on Borderline Disorders: One Hundred Years at the Border*. New York: New York University Press (Original work published 1964).

Fyer, M. R., Frances, A. J., Sullivan, T., Hurt, S. W., & Clarkin, J. (1988). Comorbidity of Borderline Personality Disorder. *Archives of General Psychiatry, 45*, 348–352.

Gabbard, G. O. (2000). *Psychodynamic Psychiatry in Clinical Practice* (3rd ed.). Washington, D.C.: American Psychiatric Press (Original work published 1990).

Gabbard, G. O., & Wilkinson, S. M. (1994). *Management of Countertransference with Borderline Patients*. Washington, D.C.: American Psychiatric Press.

Gammelgaard, J. (1996). Brændt barn skyer ilden [Once burned, twice shy]. In T. R. Eriksen (Ed.), *Erfaringer: et humanistisk og sundhedsvidenskabeligt felt* (pp. 72–96). Copenhagen, Denmark: Munksgaard.

Gammelgaard, J. (2000). *Mellem Mennesker. Træk af Indfølingens Psykologi* [Between people. Traits of the psychology of empathy]. Copenhagen, Denmark: Gads Forlag.

Gammelgaard, J. (2001). The Oedipus Complex and the Third Position. In P. Hartocollis (Ed.), *Mankind's Oedipal Destiny: Libidinal and Aggressive Aspects of Sexuality*. Madison, CN.: International Universities Press.

Gammelgaard, J. (2003a). The Unconscious: A Re-reading of the Freudian Concept. *The Scandinavian Psychoanalytic Review, 26*(1), 11–21.

Gammelgaard, J. (2003b). Ego, Self and Otherness. *The Scandinavian Psychoanalytic Review, 26*(2), 96–108.

Gammelgaard, J. (2007). Den psykoanalytiske behandlingsmetode [The psychoanalytic method of treatment]. In B. Katzenelson & B. Karpatschof (Eds.), *Klassiske og Moderne Psykologiske Teorier*. Copenhagen, Denmark: Hans Reitzels Forlag.

Gantheret, F. (1983). L'Impensable Maternel et les Fondements Maternals du Penser [The maternal unthinkable and the maternal foundations of thinking]. *Liens. Nouvelle Revue de Psychanalyse* [Ties. New Review of Psychoanalysis], *28, Autumn*, 7–27.

Glover, E. (1956). *Selected Papers on Psycho-Analysis: Vol. 1. On the Early Development of Mind*. New York: International Universities Press.

Green, A. (1995). Has Sexuality Anything to do with Psychoanalysis? *International Journal of Psycho-Analysis, 76*(5), 871–885.
Green, A. (1997a). The Intuition of the Negative in 'Playing And Reality'. *International Journal of Psycho-Analysis, 78*(6), 1071–1084.
Green, A. (1997b). *On Private Madness*. London: Rebus Press (Original work published 1972).
Green, A. (1998). The Primordial Mind and the Work of the Negative. *International Journal of Psycho-Analysis, 79*(4), 649–665.
Green, A. (1999). *The Work of the Negative* [Le travail du négatif] (A. Weller, Trans.). London: Free Association Books (Original work published 1988).
Green, A. (2000a). *André Green at the Squiggle Foundation* (J. Abram, Ed.). London: Karnac Books.
Green, A. (2000b). *Chains of Eros: The Sexual in Psychoanalysis* [Les chaînes d'Eros] (L. Thurston, Trans.). London: Rebus Books (Original work published 1997).
Green, A. (2000c). The Intrapsychic and Intersubjective in Psychoanalysis. *Psychoanalytic Quarterly, 69*(1), 1–39.
Green, A. (2000d). The Central Phobic Position: A New Formulation Of The Free Association Method. *International Journal of Psycho-Analysis, 81*(3), 429–451.
Green, A. (2005). *Play and Reflection in Donald Winnicott's Writings. The Donald Winnicott Memorial Lecture*. London: Karnac.
Green, A., & Stern, D. (2000). *Psychoanalytic Monographs, 5: Clinical and Observational Psychoanalytic Research: Roots of a Controversy* (J. Sandler, A.-M. Sandler & R. Davies, Eds.). London: Karnac Books.
Greenacre, P. (1941). The Predisposition to Anxiety – Part II. *Psychoanalytic Quarterly, 10*, 610–638.
Grinker, R. R., Werble, B., & Drye, R. C. (1968). *The Borderline Syndrome: A Behavioral Study of Ego Functions*. New York: Basic Books.
Gunderson, J. G., & Singer, M. T. (1986). Defining Borderline Patients. In M. H. Stone (Ed.), *Essential Papers on Borderline Disorders: One Hundred Years at the Border*. New York: New York University Press (Original work published 1975).
Guntrip, H. (1983). *Schizoid Phenomena, Object-relations and the Self*. London: The Hogarth Press (Original work published 1968).
Hartmann, H. (1964). *Essays on Ego Psychology*. New York: International Universities Press.
Heidegger, M. (2001). *Sein und Zeit*. Tübingen: Max Niemeyer Verlag (Original work published 1927).
Herman, J. L. (1992). *Trauma and Recovery*. New York: Basic Books.
Herman, J. L., Perry, J. C., & van der Kolk, B. A. (1989). Childhood Trauma in Borderline Personality Disorder. *American Journal of Psychiatry, 146*, 490–495.

Hoch, P., & Polatin, P. (1949). Pseudoneurotic Forms of Schizophrenia. *Psychiatric Quarterly*, *23*, 248–276.

Høeg, P. (1994). *Borderliners. A Novel* (B. Haveland, Trans.). New York: Farrar, Straus and Giroux (Original work published 1993).

Hughes, C. H. (1986). Moral Affective Insanity: Psychosensory Insanity. In M. H. Stone (Ed.), *Essential Papers on Borderline Disorders: One Hundred Years at the Border*. New York: New York University Press (Original work published 1884).

Janet, P. (1898). *Névroses et idées fixes*. Paris: Alcan.

Jensen, K. D. (2001). *Det bliver sagt*. Copenhagen, Denmark: Gyldendal.

Johnson, J. G., Cohen, P., Brown, J., Smailes, E. M., & Bernstein, D. P. (1999). Childhood Maltreatment Increases Risk for Personality Disorders During Early Adulthood. *Archives of General Psychiatry*, *56*, 600–606.

Joseph, B. (1994). The Patient Who Is Difficult to Reach. In M. Feldman & E. B. Spillius (Eds.), *Psychic Equilibrium and Psychic Change*. London: Routledge (Original work published 1975).

Kafka, F. (1994). *The Trial* (I. Parry, Trans.). London: Penguin Classics (Original work published 1925).

Kapadia, S. (1998). On Borderline Phenomena. *International Journal of Psycho-Analysis*, *79*(3), 513–528.

Karlsson, G. (1998). Beyond the Pleasure Principle: The Affirmation of Existence. *Scandinavian Psychoanalytic Review*, *21*(1), 37–52.

Keats, J. (1952). *Letters* (H. B. Forman, Ed.). London: Oxford University Press (Original work published 1895).

Kernberg, O. (1966). Structural Derivatives of Object Relationships. *International Journal of Psycho-Analysis*, *47*, 236–252.

Kernberg, O. (1972). Early Ego Integration and Object Relations. *Annals of the New York Academy of Sciences*, *193*, 233–247.

Kernberg, O. (1982). Self, Ego, Affects, and Drives. *Journal of the American Psychoanalytic Association*, *30*(1), 893–917.

Kernberg, O. (1985). *Borderline Conditions and Pathological Narcissism*. New Jersey: Jason Aronson (Original work published 1975).

Kernberg, O. (1986). Borderline Personality Organization. In M. H. Stone (Ed.), *Essential Papers on Borderline Disorders: One Hundred Years at the Border*. New York: New York University Press (Original work published 1967).

Kernberg, O. (1993). *Aggression in Personality Disorder and Perversions*. New York: Jason Aronson.

Khan, M. R. (1989). Beyond the Dream Experience. In *Hidden Selves: Between Theory and Practice in Psychoanalysis*. London: Karnac Books.

Khan, M. R. (1996a). The Concept of Cumulative Trauma. In *The Privacy of the Self*. London: Karnac Books (Original work published 1963).

Khan, M. R. (1996b). Dream Psychology and the Evolution of the Psychoanalytic Situation. In *The Privacy of the Self.* London: Karnac Books (Original work published 1962).

Khan, M. R. (1996c). The Role of Illusion in the Analytic Space and Process. In *The Privacy of the Self.* London: Karnac Books (Original work published 1971).

Khan, M. R. (1996d). The Use and the Abuse of Dream in Psychic Experience. In *The Privacy of the Self.* London: Karnac Books (Original work published 1972).

Khan, M. R. (1996e). Vicissitudes of Being, Knowing and Experiencing in the Therapeutic Situation. In *The Privacy of the Self.* London: Karnac Books (Original work published 1969).

Killingmo, B. (1989). Conflict and Deficit: Implications for Technique. *International Journal of Psycho-Analysis, 70,* 65–79.

Killingmo, B. (1995). Affirmation in Psychoanalysis. *International Journal of Psycho-Analysis, 76,* 503–518.

Klauber, J. (1987). *Illusion and Spontaneity in Psychoanalysis.* London: Free Association Books.

Klein, M. (1986). *The Psycho-Analysis of Children: Vol. 2. The Writings of Melanie Klein.* London: The Hogarth Press (Original work published 1932).

Klein, M. (1987a). Envy and Gratitude. In *Envy and Gratitude and Other Works 1946–1963: Vol. 3. The Writings of Melanie Klein.* London: The Hogarth Press (Original work published 1957).

Klein, M. (1987b). Notes on Some Schizoid Mechanisms. In *Envy and Gratitude and Other Works 1946–1963: Vol. 3. The Writings of Melanie Klein.* London: The Hogarth Press (Original work published 1946).

Klein, M. (1992). A Contribution to the Psychogenesis of Manic-Depressive States. In *Love, Guilt and Reparation and Other Works: Vol. 1. The Writings of Melanie Klein.* London: Karnac Books (Original work published 1935).

Knight, R. P. (1986). Borderline States in Psychoanalytic Psychiatry and Psychology. In M. H. Stone (Ed.), *Essential Papers on Borderline Disorders: One Hundred Years at the Border.* New York: New York University Press (Original work published 1953).

Kohut, H. (1971). *The Psychoanalytic Study of the Child: Vol. 4. The Analysis of the Self: A Systematic Approach to the Psychoanalytic Treatment of Narcissistic Personality Disorders.* New York: International Universities Press.

Kohut, H. (1977). *The Restoration of the Self.* Chicago, IL: University of Chicago Press.

Kohut, H. (1984). *How Does Analysis Cure?* Chicago, IL: University of Chicago Press.

Kraepelin, E. (1986). Psychiatrie. In M. H. Stone (Ed.), *Essential Papers on Borderline Disorders: One Hundred Years at the Border*. New York: New York University Press (Original work published 1905).

Kuhn, T. S. (1962). *The Structure of Scientific Revolutions*. Chicago, IL: University of Chicago Press.

Lacan, J. (1988). Introduction and Reply to Jean Hyppolite's Presentation of Freud's Verneinung. In A. Miller (Ed.), J. Forrester (Trans.), *The Seminar of Jacques Lacan Book 1: Freud's Papers on Technique 1953–1954*. Cambridge: Cambridge University Press (Original work published 1954).

Lacan, J. (2002). On a Question Preliminary to any Possible Treatment of Psychosis. In A. Sheridan (Trans.), *Écrits: A Selection*. London: Routledge (Original work published 1977).

Laing, R. D. (1990). *The Divided Self: An Existential Study in Sanity and Madness*. London: Routledge (Original work published 1960).

Laplanche, J. (1976). *Life and Death in Psychoanalysis* [Vie et mort en psychanalyse] (J. Mehlman, Trans.). Baltimore, MD: The Johns Hopkins University Press (Original work published 1970).

Laplanche, J. (1989). *New Foundations for Psychoanalysis* [Nouveaux fondements pour la psychanalyse: la séduction originaire] (D. Macey, Trans.). Cambridge: Wiley Blackwell (Original work published 1987).

Laplanche, J. (1997). The Theory of Seduction and the Problem of the Other. *International Journal of Psycho-Analysis*, *78*(4), 653–666.

Laplanche, J. (1999). *Essays on Otherness* (J. Fletcher, Ed.). London: Routledge.

Laplanche, J., & Pontalis, J. B. (1988). *The Language of Psycho-analysis* [Vocabulaire de la psychoanalyse] (D. N. Smith, Trans.). London: Karnac Books (Original work published 1973).

Lecours, S., & Bouchard, M. (1997). Dimensions of Mentalization: Outlining Levels of Psychic Transformation. *International Journal of Psycho-Analysis*, *78*(5), 855–875.

Lehtonen, J. (1997). On the Origins of the Body Ego and its Implications for Psychotic Vulnerability. In V. D. Volkan & S. Akhtar (Eds.), *The Seed of Madness: Constitution, Environment, and Fantasy in the Organization of the Psychotic Core*. Madison, WI: International Universities Press.

Lewin, B. (1946). Sleep, the Mouth, and the Dream Screen. *Psychoanalytic Quarterly*, *15*, 419–434.

McDougall, J. (1992). *Plea for a Measure of Abnormality* [Plaidoyer pour une certaine anormalité]. London: Free Association Books (Original work published 1978).

McDougall, J. (1995). *The Many Faces of Eros: A Psychoanalytic Exploration of Human Sexuality*. London: Free Association Books.

Mahler, M. S. (1971). A Study of the Separation–Individuation Process – And

Its Possible Application to Borderline Phenomena in the Psychoanalytic Situation. *Psychoanalytic Study of the Child, 26*, 403–424.

Mahler, M. S., & Kaplan, L. J. (1977). Developmental Aspects in the Assessment of Narcissistic and So-Called Borderline Personalities. In P. Hartocollis (Ed.), *Borderline Personality Disorders: The Concept, the Syndrome, the Patient.* New York: International Universities Press.

Masterson, J. F. (1972). *Treatment of the Borderline Adolescent: A Developmental Approach.* New York: Wiley-Interscience.

Masterson, J. F. (1973). The Borderline Adolescent. In S. C. Feinstein & P. L. Giovacchini (Eds.), *Adolescent Psychiatry, Vol. 2: Developmental and Clinical Studies.* New York: Basic Books.

Masterson, J. F. (1990). *The Search for the Real Self: Unmasking the Personality Disorders of Our Age.* New York: Free Press (Original work published 1988).

Masterson, J. F. (2000). *The Personality Disorders: A New Look at the Developmental Self and Object Relations Approach – Theory, Diagnosis, Treatment.* Arizona: Zeig, Tucker.

Masterson, J. F., & Rinsley, D. B. (1975). The Borderline Syndrome: The Role of the Mother in the Genesis and Psychic Structure of the Borderline Personality. *International Journal of Psycho-Analysis, 56*(2), 163–177.

Meissner, W. W. (1984). *The Borderline Spectrum: Differential Diagnosis and Developmental Issues.* New York: Jason Aronson.

Meissner, W. W. (1988). *Treatment of Patients in the Borderline Spectrum.* New York: Jason Aronson.

Merleau-Ponty, M. (2002). *The Phenomenology of Perception* [Phénomènologie de la perception]. London: Routledge (Original work published 1945).

Milne, A. A. (1954). *Winnie-the-Pooh.* New York: Yearling Books (Original work published 1926).

Milner, M. (1950). *On Not Being Able to Paint.* Madison, CT: International Universities Press.

Milner, M. (1969). *The Hands of the Living God: An Account of a Psycho-Analytic Treatment.* London: The Hogarth Press.

Milner, M. (1996). The Role of Illusion in Symbol Formation. In *The Suppressed Madness of Sane Men: Forty-Four Years of Exploring Psychoanalysis.* London: Routledge (Original work published 1952).

Morris, H. (1993). Narrative Representation, Narrative Enactment, and the Psychoanalytic Construction of History. *International Journal of Psycho-Analysis, 74*(1), 33–54.

Muller, J. P. (1996). *Beyond the Psychoanalytic Dyad: Developmental Semiotics in Freud, Peirce, and Lacan.* New York: Routledge.

Nasio, J.-D. (2001). *Enseignement de 7 concepts cruciaux de la psychanalyse.* Paris: Éditions Payot & Rivages (Original work published 1988).

Ogden, T. (1994a). *Subjects of Analysis*. London: Karnac Books.
Ogden, T. (1994b). The Analytic Third: Working with Intersubjective Clinical Facts. *International Journal of Psycho-Analysis*, *75*(1), 3–19.
Ogden, T. (1997). Reverie and Metaphor: Some Thoughts on How I Work as a Psychoanalyst. *International Journal of Psycho-Analysis*, *78*, 719–732.
Ogden, T. (1999). Analysing Forms of Aliveness and Deadness of the Transference–Countertransference. In G. Kohon (Ed.), *The Dead Mother: The Work of André Green*. London: Routledge.
Pontalis, J.-B. (1981). *Frontiers in Psychoanalysis: Between the Dream and Psychic Pain* [Entre le rêve et la douleur] (C. Cullen & P. Cullen, Trans.). London: The Hogarth Press (Original work published 1977).
Prichard, J. C. (1986). A Treatise on Insanity. In M. H. Stone (Ed.), *Essential Papers on Borderline Disorders: One Hundred Years at the Border*. New York: New York University Press (Original work published 1835).
Proust, M. (1982). *Remembrance of Things Past* (C. K. Moncrieff & T. Kilmartin, Trans., Vol. 1). New York: Random House (Original work published 1913–27).
Reitan, R. (1994). *At arve Freud. Lystprincip og urfortrængning. Metapsykologiske forelæsninger* [Inheriting Freud. Pleasure principle and primal repression. Metapsychological lectures]. Aarhus, Denmark: Klim.
Renik, O. (1998). The Analyst's Subjectivity and the Analyst's Objectivity. *International Journal of Psycho-Analysis*, *79*(3), 487–497.
Rey, H. (1994). *Universals of Psychoanalysis in the Treatment of Psychotic and Borderline States* (J. Magagna, Ed.). London: Free Association Books.
Rinsley, D. B. (1977). An Object-Relations View of Borderline Personality Disorders. In *Borderline Personality Disorders: The Concept, the Syndrome, the Patient*. New York: International Universities Press (Original work published 1976).
Rosenfeld, H. (1990). *Impasse and Interpretation: Therapeutic and Anti-Therapeutic Factors in the Psycho-Analytic Treatment of Psychotic, Borderline, and Neurotic Patients*. London: Routledge (Original work published 1987).
Rosse, I. (1986). Clinical Evidences of Borderline Insanity. In M. H. Stone (Ed.), *Essential Papers on Borderline Disorders: One Hundred Years at the Border*. New York: New York University Press (Original work published 1890).
Rycroft, C. (1968). On Idealization, Illusion and Catastrophic Disillusion. In *Imagination and Reality*. London: Maresfield Library.
Ryle, G. (1990). *The Concept of Mind*. London: Penguin Books (Original work published 1949).
Salonen, S. (1979). On the Metapsychology of Schizophrenia. *International Journal of Psycho-Analysis*, *60*, 73–81.
Salonen, S. (1989). The Restitution of Primary Identification in Psychoanalysis. *Scandinavian Psychoanalytic Review*, *12*, 102–115.

Sartre, J.-P. (1962). *Sketch for a Theory of the Emotions* [Esquisse d'une théorie des émotions]. London: Methuen (Original work published 1939).

Sartre, J.-P. (1995). *Being and Nothingness* [L'Être et le néant]. London: Routledge (Original work published 1943).

Scarfone, D. (2002). Sexual and Actual. In D. Widlöscher (Ed.), S. Fairfield (Trans.), *Infantile Sexuality and Attachment* (pp. 97–111). London: Karnac.

Scarfone, D. (2002–2003). It was not my Mother: From Seduction to Negative. *New Foundations, 48*, 69–77.

Schmideberg, M. (1986). The Treatment of Psychopaths and Borderline Patients. In M. H. Stone (Ed.), *Essential Papers on Borderline Disorders: One Hundred Years at the Border*. New York: New York University Press (Original work published 1947).

Searles, H. (1979). *Countertransference*. New York: International Universities Press.

Segal, H. (1992). *Dream, Phantasy and Art*. London: Routledge (Original work published 1991).

Spence, D. P. (1982). *Narrative Truth and Historical Truth: Meaning and Interpretation in Psychoanalysis*. New York: W. W. Norton.

Steiner, J. (1993). *Psychic Retreats: Pathological Organizations in Psychotic, Neurotic, and Borderline Patients*. London: Routledge.

Stern, A. (1986). Psychoanalytic Investigation of and Therapy in the Borderline Group of Neuroses. In M. H. Stone (Ed.), *Essential Papers on Borderline Disorders: One Hundred Years at the Border*. New York: New York University Press (Original work published 1938).

Stern, D. (1995). *The Motherhood Constellation. A Unified View of Parent-Infant Psychotherapy*. New York: Basic Books.

Stern, D. (2004). *The Present Moment in Psychotherapy and Everyday Life*. New York: W. W. Norton.

Stern, D. (2006). *The Interpersonal World of the Infant: A View from Psychoanalysis and Developmental Psychology*. London: Karnac (Original work published 1985).

Stone, L. (1986). The Widening Scope of Indications for Psychoanalysis. In M. H. Stone (Ed.), *Essential Papers on Borderline Disorders: One Hundred Years at the Border*. New York: New York University Press (Original work published 1954).

Stone, M. H. (Ed.) (1986). *Essential Papers on Borderline Disorders: One Hundred Years at the Border*. New York: New York University Press.

Turner, J. (1993). Wordsworth and Winnicott in the Area of Play. In P. L. Rudnytsky (Ed.), *Transitional Objects and Potential Spaces: Literary Uses of D. W. Winnicott*. New York: Columbia University Press.

Turner, J. F. (2002). A Brief History of Illusion: Milner, Winnicott and Rycroft. *International Journal of Psycho-Analysis, 83*(5), 1063–1082.

Ulman, R. B., & Brothers, D. (1988). *The Shattered Self: A Psychoanalytic Study of Trauma.* New York: Analytic Press.

Vanggaard, T. (1979). *Borderlands of Sanity.* Copenhagen, Denmark: Munksgaard.

Winnicott, D. W. (1971). *Playing and Reality.* London: Tavistock Publications.

Winnicott, D. W. (1975a). The Observations of Infants in a Set Situation. In *Through Paediatrics to Psycho-Analysis.* New York: Basic Books (Original work published 1941).

Winnicott, D. W. (1975b). Primary Maternal Preoccupation. In *Through Paediatrics to Psycho-Analysis.* New York: Basic Books (Original work published 1956).

Winnicott, D. W. (1975c). Primitive Emotional Development. In *Through Paediatrics to Psycho-Analysis.* New York: Basic Books (Original work published 1945).

Winnicott, D. W. (1975d). Psychoses and Child Care. In *Through Paediatrics to Psycho-Analysis.* New York: Basic Books (Original work published 1952).

Winnicott, D. W. (1975e). Transitional Objects and Transitional Phenomena. In *Through Paediatrics to Psycho-Analysis.* New York: Basic Books (Original work published 1951).

Winnicott, D. W. (1990a). The Capacity to be Alone. In *The Maturational Processes and the Facilitating Environment.* London: Karnac Books (Original work published 1958).

Winnicott, D. W. (1990b). Communicating and Not Communicating Leading to a Study of Certain Opposites. In *The Maturational Processes and the Facilitating Environment.* London: Karnac Books (Original work published 1963).

Winnicott, D. W. (1990c). Ego Distortion in Terms of True and False Self. In *The Maturational Processes and the Facilitating Environment.* London: Karnac Books (Original work published 1960).

Winnicott, D. W. (1990d). A Personal View of the Kleinian Contribution. In *The Maturational Processes and the Facilitating Environment.* London: Karnac Books (Original work published 1962).

Winnicott, D. W. (1990e). Psychotherapy of Character Disorders. In *The Maturational Processes and the Facilitating Environment.* London: Karnac Books (Original work published 1963).

Winnicott, D. W. (1990f). The Theory of the Parent–Infant Relationship. In *The Maturational Processes and the Facilitating Environment.* London: Karnac Books (Original work published 1960).

Winnicott, D. W. (1992a). Critical Notice of 'On Not Being Able to Paint'. In C. Winnicott, R. Sheperd & M. Davis (Eds.), *Psycho-analytic Explorations.* Cambridge, MA: Harvard University Press (Original work published 1951).

Winnicott, D. W. (1992b). Fear of Breakdown. In C. Winnicott, R. Sheperd &

M. Davis (Eds.), *Psycho-analytic Explorations*. Cambridge, MA: Harvard University Press (Original work published 1963).

Yeomans, F. E., Clarkin, J. F., & Kernberg, O. F. (2002). *A Primer on Transference-Focused Psychotherapy for the Borderline Patient*. New Jersey: Jason Aronson.

Zanarini, M. C., & Frankenburg, F. R. (1997). Pathways to the Development of Borderline Personality Disorder. *Journal of Personality Disorders, 11*(1), 93–104.

Zanarini, M. C., Gunderson, J. G., Frankenburg, F. R., & Chauncey, D. L. (1990). Discriminating Borderline Personality Disorder from Other Axis II Disorders. *American Journal of Psychiatry, 147*(2), 161–167.

Zeuthen, K. (2002). *Fantasien i virkeligheden: Om psykisk realitet, infantil seksualitet og forførelse*. Unpublished masters thesis, University of Copenhagen, Denmark.

Zeuthen, K., & Gammelgaard, J. (2009). *Confusion of Tongues. On the Question of the Origin and Character of Infantile Sexuality*. Unpublished paper presented at Perspectives on Child Psychoanalysis Today, arranged by the University of London and the Anna Freud Centre, July 2009.

Zillboorg, G. (1957). Further Observations on Ambulatory Schizophrenia. *American Journal of Orthopsychiatry, 27*, 677–682.

Index

For Product Safety Concerns and Information please contact our EU
representative GPSR@taylorandfrancis.com
Taylor & Francis Verlag GmbH, Kaufingerstraße 24, 80331 München, Germany

www.ingramcontent.com/pod-product-compliance
Ingram Content Group UK Ltd.
Pitfield, Milton Keynes, MK11 3LW, UK
UKHW022223190926
475702UK00003B/476

* 9 7 8 0 4 1 5 5 4 3 8 9 7 *